AN
ALMANAC FOR
MODERNS

Donald Culross Peattie

AN
ALMANAC FOR
MODERNS

Afterword by Lewis Thomas, M.D.
and wood engravings by Charles H. Joslin

A NONPAREIL BOOK

David R. Godine · Publisher · Boston

This is a NONPAREIL BOOK published in 1980 by

David R. Godine, Publisher, Inc.
306 Dartmouth Street
Boston, Massachusetts 02116

LIBRARY OF CONGRESS CATALOGING
IN PUBLICATION DATA

Peattie, Donald Culross, 1898-1969.
  An almanac for moderns.
    1. Natural history – Outdoor books. 2. Natural
history – Addresses, essays, lectures. I. Title.
QH81.P4 1980 574 79-90410
ISBN 0-87923-356-7
ISBN 0-87923-314-1 (pbk.)

NONPAREIL
BOOKS

PRINTED IN THE UNITED STATES OF AMERICA

"He who sees things grow from the beginning will have the best view of them."

—ARISTOTLE

A R I E S

MARCH 21 — APRIL 19

MARCH TWENTY-FIRST

On THIS chill uncertain spring day, toward twilight, I have heard the first frog quaver from the marsh. That is a sound that Pharaoh listened to as it rose from the Nile, and it blended, I suppose, with his discontents and longings, as it does with ours. There is something lonely in that first shaken and uplifted trilling croak. And more than lonely, for I hear a warning in it, as Pharaoh heard the sound of plague. It speaks of the return of life, animal life, to the earth. It tells of all that is most unutterable in evolution—the terrible continuity and fluidity of protoplasm, the irrepressible forces of reproduction—not mystical human love, but the cold batrachian jelly by which we vertebrates are linked to the things that creep and writhe and are blind yet breed and have being. More than half it seems to threaten that when mankind has quite thoroughly shattered and eaten and debauched himself with his own follies, that voice may still be ringing out in the marshes of the Nile and the Thames and the Potomac, unconscious that Pharaoh wept for his son.

It always seems to me that no sooner do I hear the first frog trill than I find the first cloud of frog's eggs in a wayside pool, so swiftly does the emergent creature pour out the libation of its cool fertility. There is life where before there was none. It is as repulsive as it is beautiful, as silvery-black as it is slimy. Life, in short, raw and exciting, life almost in primordial form, irreducible element.

MARCH TWENTY-SECOND

FOR the ancients the world was a little place, bounded between Ind and Thule. The sky bent very low over Olympus, and astronomers had not yet taken the friendliness out of the stars. The shepherd kings of the desert called them by the names Job knew, Al-Debaran, Fomalhaut, Mizar, Al-Goth, Al-Tair, Deneb and Achernar. For the Greeks the glittering constellations made pictures of their heroes and heroines, and of beasts and birds. The heavenly truth of their Arcadian mythology blazed nightly in the skies for the simplest clod to read.

Through all this celestial splendor the sun plowed yearly in a broad track that they called the zodiac. As it entered each constellation a new month with fresh significances and consequences was marked down by a symbol. Lo, in the months when the rains descended, when the Nile and the Tigris and Yangtse rose, the sun entered the constellations that were like Fishes, and like Water Carriers! In the hot dry months it was in the constellation that is unmistakably a scorpion, bane of the desert. Who could say that the stars in their orderly procession did not sway a man's destiny?

Best of all, the year began with spring, with the vernal equinox. It was a natural, a pastoral, a homely sort of year, which a man could take to his heart and remember; he could tell the date by the feeling in his bones. It is the year which green things, and the beasts and birds in their migrations, all obey, a year like man's life, from his birth cry to the snows upon the philosopher's head.

4

MARCH TWENTY-THIRD

THE old almanacs have told off their years, and are dead with them. The weather-wisdom and the simple faith that cropped up through them as naturally as grass in an orchard, are withered now, and their flowers of homely philosophy and seasonable prediction and reflection are dry, and only faintly, quaintly fragrant. The significance of the Bull and the Crab and the Lion are not more dead, for the modern mind, than the Nature philosophy of a generation ago. This age has seen the trees blasted to skeletons by the great guns, and the birds feeding on men's eyes. Pippa has passed.

It is not that man alone is vile. Man is a part of Nature. So is the atomic disassociation called high explosive. So are violent death, rape, agony, and rotting. They were all here, and quite natural, before our day, in the sweet sky and the blowing fields.

There is no philosophy with a shadow of realism about it, save a philosophy based upon Nature. It turns a smiling face, a surface easily conquered by the gun, the bridge, the dynamite stick. Yet there is no obedience but to its laws. Hammurabi spoke and Rameses commanded, and the rat gnawed and the sun shone and the hive followed its multiplex and golden order. Flowers pushed up their child faces in the spring, and the bacteria slowly took apart the stuff of life. Today the Kremlin commands, the Vatican speaks. And tomorrow the rat will still be fattening, the sun be a little older, and the bacteria remain lords of creation, whose subtraction would topple the rest of life.

Now how can a man base his way of thought on Nature and wear so happy a face? How can he take comfort from withering grass where he lays his head, from a dying sun to which he turns his face, from a mortal woman's head pressed on his shoulder? To say how that might be, well might he talk the year around.

5

MARCH TWENTY-FOURTH

PERHAPS in Tempe the wild lawns are thick with crocuses, and narcissus blows around Paestum, but here on this eastern shore of a western world, spring is a season of what the embittered call realism, by which they mean the spoiling of joy. Joy will come, as the joy of a child's birth comes—after the pains. So dry cold winds still walk abroad, under gray skies.

It is not that nothing blooms or flies; the honey bees were out for an hour, the one hour of sunlight, and above the pools where the salamander's eggs drift in inky swirls, the early midges danced. Down the runs and rills I can hear the calling of a red-bird entreating me to come and find him, come and find him! There is a black storm of grackles in the tree limbs where the naked maple flowers are bursting out in scarlet tips from their bud scales, and a song-sparrow sits on an alder that dangles out its little gold tails.

We are so used to flowers wrapped up in the pretty envelopes of their corollas and calyces, so softened in our taste for the lovely in Nature, that we scarcely rate an alder catkin as a flower at all. Yet it is nothing else—nothing but the male anthers, sowing the wind with their freight of fertilizing pollen. The small, compact female flowers, like tiny cones, wait in the chill wild air for the golden cargo.

So does our spring begin, in a slow flowering on the leafless wood of the bough of hazel and alder and poplar and willow, a hardy business, a spawning upon the air, like the spawning in the ponds, a flowering so primitive that it carries us back to ancient geologic times, when trees that are now fossils sowed the wind like these, their descendants —an epoch when the world, too, was in its naked springtime.

6

MARCH TWENTY-FIFTH

THE beginnings of spring, the true beginnings, are quite unlike the springtides of which poets and musicians sing. The artists become conscious of spring in late April, or May, when it is not too much to say that the village idiot would observe that birds are singing and nesting, that fields bear up their freight of flowering and ants return to their proverbial industry.

But the first vernal days are younger. Spring steals in shyly, a tall, naked child in her pale gold hair, amidst us the un-innocent, skeptics in wool mufflers, prudes in gum-shoes and Grundies with head-colds. Very secretly the old field cedars sow the wind with the freight of their ancient pollen. A grackle in the willow croaks and sings in the uncertain, ragged voice of a boy. The marshes brim, and walking is a muddy business. Oaks still are barren and secretive. On the lilac tree only the twin buds suggest her coming maturity and flowering. But there in the pond float the inky masses of those frog's eggs, visibly life in all its rawness, its elemental shape and purpose. Now is the moment when the secret of life could be discovered, yet no one finds it.

MARCH TWENTY-SIXTH

Out of the stoa, two thousand years ago, strode a giant to lay hold on life and explain it. He went down to the "primordial slime" of the seashore to look for its origin. There if anywhere he would find it, he thought, where the salt water and the earth were met, and the mud quivered like a living thing, and from it emerged strange shapeless primitive beings, themselves scarce more than animate bits of ooze. To Aristotle it seemed plain enough that out of the dead and the inanimate is made the living, and back to death are turned the bodies of all things that have lived, to be used over again. So nothing was wasted; all moved in a perpetual cycle. Out of vinegar, he felt certain, came vinegar eels, out of dung came blow-flies, out of decaying fruit bees were born, and out of the rain pool frogs spawned.

But the eye of even Aristotle was purblind in its nakedness. Of the spore and the sperm he never dreamed; he guessed nothing of bacteria. Now man can peer down through the microscope, up at the revealed stars. And behold, the lens has only multiplied the facts and deepened the mystery.

For now we know that spontaneous generation never takes place. Life comes only from life. Was not the ancient Hindu symbol for it a serpent with a tail in its mouth? Intuitive old fellows, those Aryan brothers of ours, wise in their superstitions, like old women. Life, we discover, is a closed, nay, a charmed circle. Wherever you pick it up, it has already begun; yet as soon as you try to follow it, it is already dying.

8

MARCH TWENTY-SEVENTH

FIRST to grasp biology as a science, Aristotle thought that he had also captured the secret of life itself. From the vast and original body of his observation, he deduced a cosmology like a pure Greek temple, symmetrical and satisfying. For two millenniums it housed the serene intelligence of the race.

Here was an absolute philosophy; nothing need be added to it; detraction was heretical. It traced the ascent of life from the tidal ooze up to man, the plants placed below the animals, the animals ranged in order of increasing intelligence. Beyond man nothing could be imagined but God, the supreme intelligence. God was all spirit; the lifeless rock was all matter. Living beings on this earth were spirit infusing matter.

Still this conception provides the favorite text of poet or pastor, praising the earth and the fullness thereof. It fits so well with the grandeur of the heavens, the beauty of the flowers at our feet, the rapture of the birds! The Nature lover of today would ask nothing better than that it should be true.

Aristotle was sure of it. He points to marble in a quarry. It is only matter; then the sculptor attacks it with his chisel, with a shape in his mind. With form, soul enters into the marble. So all living things are filled with soul, some with more, some with less. But even a jellyfish is infused with that which the rock possesses not. Thus existence has its origin in supreme intelligence, and everything has an intelligent cause and serves its useful purpose. That purpose is the development of higher planes of existence. Science, thought its Adam, had but to put the pieces of the puzzle together, to expose for praise the cosmic design, all beautiful.

MARCH TWENTY-EIGHTH

THE hook-nosed Averroës, the Spanish Arab born in Cordova in 1126, and one time cadi of Seville, shook a slow dissenting head. He did not like this simile of Aristotle's, of the marble brought to life and form by the sculptor. The simile, he keenly perceived, would be applicable at best if the outlines of the statue were already preformed in the marble as it lay in the quarry. For that is precisely how we find life. The tree is preformed in the seed; the future animal already exists in the embryo. Wherever we look we find form, structure, adaptation, already present. Never has it been vouchsafed to us to see pure creation out of the lifeless.

And Galileo, also, ventured to shake the pillars of the Schoolmen's Aristotelian temple. Such a confirmed old scrutinizer was not to be drawn toward inscrutable will. The stars, nearest of all to Aristotle's God, should have moved with godlike precision, and Galileo, peering, found them erring strangely all across heaven. He shrugged, but was content. Nature itself was the miracle, Nature with all its imperfections. Futile for science to try to discover what the forces of Nature are; it can only discover how they operate.

MARCH TWENTY-NINTH

COMFORTING, sustaining, like the teat to the nursling, is Aristotle's beautiful idea that everything serves a useful purpose and is part of the great design. Ask, for instance, of what use is grass. Grass, the pietist assures us, was made in order to nourish cows. Cows are here on earth to nourish men. So all flesh is grass, and grass was put here for man.

But of what use, pray, is man? Would anybody, besides his dog, miss him if he were gone? Would the sun cease to shed its light because there were no human beings here to sing the praises of sunlight? Would there be sorrow among the little hiding creatures of the underwood, or loneliness in the hearts of the proud and noble beasts? Would the other simians feel that their king was gone? Would God, Jehovah, Zeus, Allah, miss the sound of hymns and psalms, the odor of frankincense and flattery?

There is no certainty vouchsafed us in the vast testimony of Nature that the universe was designed for man, nor yet for any purpose, even the bleak purpose of symmetry. The courageous thinker must look the inimical aspects of his environment in the face, and accept the stern fact that the universe is hostile and deathy to him save for a very narrow zone where it permits him, for a few eons, to exist.

ARCHAIC and obsolete sounds the wisdom of the great old Greek. Life, his pronouncement ran, is soul pervading matter. What, soul in a jellyfish, an oyster, a burdock? Then by soul he could not have meant that moral quality which Paul of Tarsus or Augustine of Hippo were to call soul. Aristotle is talking rather about that undefined but essential and precious something that just divides the lowliest microörganism from the dust; that makes the ugly thousand-legged creature flee from death; that makes the bird pour out its heart in morning rapture; that makes the love of man for woman a holy thing sacred to the carrying on of the race.

But what is this but life itself? In every instance Aristotle but affirms that living beings are matter pervaded by a noble, a palpitant and thrilling thing called life. This is the mystery, and his neat cosmology solves nothing of it. But it is not Aristotle's fault that he did not give us the true picture of things. It is Nature herself, as we grow in comprehension of her, who weans us from our early faith.

MARCH THIRTY-FIRST

ARISTOTLE'S rooms in the little temple of the Lyceum were the first laboratory, where dissection laid bare the sinews and bones of life. The Lyceum was a world closer to the marine biological station at Wood's Hole, Massachusetts, than it was to its neighbor the Parthenon. Its master did for marine biology what Euclid did for geometry; his work on the embryology of the chick still stands as a nearly perfect monograph of biological investigation. The originality, the scope of his works, the magnificence of his dream for biology as an independent science, have probably never been surpassed by any one who has lived since.

Unlike many of the more timid or less gifted investigators of today, Aristotle could not help coming to conclusions about it all. For his cosmology it should be said that it was the best, perhaps the only possible, philosophy of the origin and nature of life which the times permitted. We can all feel in our bones how agreeable it were to accept the notion of design, symmetry, purpose, an evolution toward a spiritual godhead such as Aristotle assures us exists.

But as it was Aristotle himself who taught us to observe, investigate, deduce what facts compel us to deduce, so we must concede that it is Nature herself, century after century—day after day, indeed, in the whirlwind progress of science—that propels us farther and farther away from Aristotelian beliefs. At every point she fails to confirm the grand old man's cherished picture of things. There are persons so endowed by temperament that they will assert that if Nature has no "soul," purpose, nor symmetry, we needs must put them in the picture, lest the resulting composition be scandalous, intolerable, and maddening. To such the scientist can only say, "Believe as you please."

APRIL FIRST

I s A y that it touches a man that his blood is sea water and his tears are salt, that the seed of his loins is scarcely different from the same cells in a seaweed, and that of stuff like his bones are coral made. I say that physical and biologic law lies down with him, and wakes when a child stirs in the womb, and that the sap in a tree, uprushing in the spring, and the smell of the loam, where the bacteria bestir themselves in darkness, and the path of the sun in the heaven, these are facts of first importance to his mental conclusions, and that a man who goes in no consciousness of them is a drifter and a dreamer, without a home or any contact with reality.

APRIL SECOND

EACH year, and above all, each spring, raises up for Nature a new generation of lovers—and this quite irrespective of the age of the new votary. As I write this a boy is going out to the marshes to watch with field glasses the mating of the red-winged blackbirds, rising up in airy swirls and clouds. Or perhaps he carries some manual to the field, and sits him down on an old log, to trace his way through Latin names, that seem at first so barbarous and stiff. There is no explaining why the boy has suddenly forsaken the ball and bat, or finds a kite less interesting in the spring skies than a bird. For a few weeks, or a few seasons, or perhaps for a lifetime, he will follow this bent with passion.

And at the same time there will be a man who all his life has put away this call, or never heard it before, who has come to the easier, latter end of life, when leisure is his own. And he goes out in the woods to collect his first botanical specimen and to learn that he has much to learn for all his years.

They are never to be forgotten—that first bird pursued through thicket and over field with serious intent, not to kill but to know it, or that first plant lifted reverently and excitedly from the earth. No spring returns but that I wish I might live again through the moment when I went out in the woods and sat down with a book in my hands, to learn not only the name, but the ways and the range and the charm of the windflower, *Anemone quinquefolia.*

APRIL THIRD

IT WAS on this day in 1837 that there was born in the Catskill country the sage of "Slabsides," John Burroughs. Friend, in his youth, to Whitman, with whom he made hospital rounds in Washington in the Civil War, he was linked in our minds in his latter days with Edison and Henry Ford and John Muir as one of the grand old men. To the doors of "Slabsides" and "Riverby" and "Woodchuck Lodge" trooped interviewers, fellow loafers, naturalists young and old to see the raiser of bees, the husbandman of grapes. He was anything but the hermit that Thoreau had been.

The recluse of Walden, of course, was one of John's models, at least in his early years—along with Emerson and Audubon and Wordsworth. One of his first essays submitted to the *Atlantic Monthly* sent William Dean Howells to running through Emerson's works to see if it were not plagiarized. Burroughs modeled himself throughout upon the lines of genius and succeeded in giving a good imitation of it. If he was only partially rated as a naturalist in scientific circles, that is simply because he discovered little new—except as it was new to him.

But John was honest; he never pretended even to himself that he was a scientist. He was an appreciator, and in a wide sense, a poet of science, but a poet who would take no license. With Roosevelt he made war upon nature fakers; more than any other writer he forced Darwin, and the idea of evolution, upon a sentimental and still fundamentalist America—an America that would never have accepted such heresies from one who looked and spake less like Elijah.

APRIL FOURTH

THE life of John Burroughs cannot be told alone in its outward events. Its greatest significance lies in the changes that went on inside the man himself, for they reflect the changes of an age which began with such stirring, idealistic democrats as Lincoln and Gladstone, Whitman and Emerson, underwent the racking controversy between religion and science, submitted to the triumph of the German mechanists, saw the vanishing of the American wilderness, the waning popularity of the essay, of contemplation and simplicity, and ended in the fiery hells of the World War.

It was as a penman, a loafer, a buoyant talker that John began his career. A delightful humanizer, a popularizer accepted on face value from the start, Burroughs was at first a slipshod observer. He had a positive distaste for exactitude. But he was always sensitive to bigger men about him. Darwin's painstaking work on the movements of plants, and the observations of Fabre—"the Sherlock Holmes of insects" as Burroughs aptly called him—brought him in middle life to serious study. He dropped Wordsworth and Tennyson from his shelves and gave place to Carlyle and Fiske and Bergson. He grew steadily more muscular.

A little more, and Burroughs might have become a scientist. But the World War was too crushing a blow for the man who had once stood in the crowd to hear Lincoln's Second Inaugural speech. In his hatred of Germany and the soul-less thought which she embodied for him, he became, as he declared, "a savage old man." Never a thorough convert to methodic science, he recanted in horror, only to find that he could no longer read the gentle poets.

APRIL FIFTH

E VERYWHERE spring unfurls her slim green standards—
here a freshening of the dun grass and there a rush of vivid
life to the twigs of the sassafras saplings that line the
country roads. The onion grass is shooting up, spindling
and strong-scented in the woods. Sulphurous hellebore
leaves, inviting but poisonous, expand in the cress beds
around the springs and little rills. The crumpled rank leaf
of skunk cabbage opens out, a sultry color one might expect
to see rather in a tropical rain forest.

In the stagnant ponds and the cross country ditches
through the low meadows by the river the green scum has
appeared. It is algae, of different sorts, each with its shade
of the new dominant color. A brilliant primal green is
spirogyra, so exquisite under the microscope; there is an
unwholesome blue-green of a more primitive, slimier alga,
and a yellow-green one I cannot name at all. These are
the colors of the first green things that ever grew upon an
uninhabited earth, for from the fresh water algae all plant
life must be descended.

And on the tree trunks algae of deep moss-green and soft
grass-green are freshening after the rains. So everywhere
the color of life returns to the earth, returns to gladden the
eye that was hungry for it. Not all of these greens are
pretty or quite *nice*, as the tender golden green haze of
leaves in the tulip trees is lovely in the landscape now.
But all of life is not nice—perhaps the most of it and
even the best of it is not.

APRIL SIXTH

THE last fling of winter is over, save for tingling nights and dawns rimed with a silver frost. Everywhere I hear the metallic clinking of the cricket frogs, the trilling of the toads, the gabble of the grackles. Today the first dragonflies have emerged to dart about in an afternoon sunshine that in the leafless thickets seemed as intense as a summer day, and over the swell of the fields, still high with their brown and yellow stands of grass and weeds, the heat waves shimmer. The earth, the soil itself, has a dreaming quality about it. It is warm now to the touch; it has come alive; it hides secrets that in a moment, in a little while, it will tell. Some of them are bursting out already—the first leaves of windflowers uncurling, the spears of mottled adder's tongue leaves and the furled up flags of bloodroot. Old earth is great with her children, the bulb and the grub, and the sleepy mammal and the seed.

APRIL SEVENTH

I T was the way of seers of old to read in the flight of birds and the entrails of a ram, destiny's intentions. Prophets there are today—economists, social theorists, iconoclasts and makers of new ikons for old—who read the doom of this and predict the rise of that, in the configuration of events as they fly overhead, or in the investigation of the past's cold carcass.

Man's ultimate fate is not written in the works of Spengler or Veblen or Marx, but in the nucleus of his own cells; his end, if it be predestined, is in the death of a star, or in a rising of the bacteria. He will do well to have a heed to the nature of life, for of life there is but one kind. Man shares it with the corn and the crow, the oak and the mayfly. Therefore in such natural things may he well search for auguries.

On any clear-skied day of the year I may be found engrossed in nothing weightier than watching an anthill or gathering inedible fungi, to all appearance strayed from the argument of my philosophy. But in truth it is philosophy that has a weakness toward straying; the facts upon which it is builded rest firm, and impel the philosopher to seek them, even aside, down the bypaths, under the bracken, in the small, anonymous places. Even here, escaped from all but a bright bird eye, all sound of traffic but the brook's over its stones, man is not rid of his crying inner query. And the smiling woodland silence falls knowledgeably upon his ears.

APRIL EIGHTH

THERE is something classic about the study of the little world that is made up by our first spring flowers—all those which bloom not later than April. They are delightfully easy to learn, in case you do not already know them, for there are so few of them that any local manual of the spring flowers will swiftly make you friends for life with them. Happy are those who this year, for the first time, go wood wandering to find them, who first crack open the new manual, smelling of fresh ink, and rejoice in the little new pocket lens. And many, many are the feet that have trod that way before, the boy Linnæus, the young Asa Gray, the child prodigies like Rafinesque and Haller, the wearied great scholars seeking rest and distraction, like Jacob Grimm and John Stuart Mill.

So great names lend their luster to this innocent delight. But the classicism of the earliest wildflowers derives also from the fact that they fall into a few families, the lily, pink, buttercup, crucifer, rose, violet, umbellifer, heath and composite families, whose unmistakable ear-marks are as decisive as the national traits of Greeks, Persians, Hindus, Englishmen and Norsemen. Characteristic of the northern hemisphere, these give us blossoms that turn up to us the dainty face upon the delicate stalk. They mean to us all that is brave and fresh and frail in the name of spring. Summer flowers distract us with well upon a hundred families, with a strong tropical element; autumnal flowers are confined almost wholly to the tall rank composites. But something in the spring flora, perfect in its simplicity and unity, carries us back to Arcady.

APRIL NINTH

WHENEVER I walk in the marshy ground I find the spikes of Equisetum thrusting up in a pale, almost a fleshy turret, soft and moist to the touch, and hollow like a pipe. Like the cinnamon fern, this fern-ally throws up a strange spore-bearing frond almost devoid of coloring matter, quite unlike the purely vegetative green shoot that rises beside it.

Somewhere in the now scattered fragments of the great evolutionary line of the ferns, through Equisetum to the clubmosses and Selaginella, the lost trace of the flowering plants must have branched away, through stages that we shall never know, through families whose unreal fossils take us step by step toward the cycads and the pines. The odd thing is that these emergent groups should be gone from the world, never again to know the grip of the earth between their roots, the warmth of sunlight on their fronds.

But each spring little, ancient Equisetum pushes up again, to enjoy the old, old sunshine and bare its spores to the wind. It is like some wizened ancient race of men whose stature is cretin, whose language is cryptic, that has been driven down into the marshes, isolated, decimated, and spared at last because time has simply forgotten to finish it off.

APRIL TENTH

AFTER the long spell of bad weather the birds, who were banked up, I fancy, somewhere in the Carolinas, are coming through in a torrent. There are so many that I can keep but the most delirious count of them. My records are carried away in fluttering confusion, like a wind gauge in a hurricane. Every time I approach the marsh I hear the warning cries of the herons, like the drop of an old chain on its own coils, and from beyond the cat-tail lances the snaky neck and archaic head of the bittern is turned to look at me, with the astonished and disapproving gaze that archæopteryx might have turned on an anachronistic human.

In the wet maple woods, where the skunk cabbage leaf is expanding in its unabashed ugliness, the grackles are already quieting, and in their place I hear, morning and evening, the first sounds of mourning doves. Along the runs and rills kingfishers are setting up their riparian claims with loud cries, like the whirling of a boy's wooden rattle. I have simply lost all account of the order of arrival of the sparrow tribe, of the swallows, vireos and warblers and wrens. There is no order; they all seemed to come on the same day, and continue to arrive in increasing numbers every day.

Now is the moment when the novice at bird-gazing needs a friend. Flowers are best identified, if one is a neophyte, by one's self. The mere exercise of tracking them to their names will fix them in the memory. But with the birds, a guide, a friend by the side, to point out what you ought to have seen, to pass you the binoculars and whisper eagerly in your ear, is worth a shelf of books.

S O M E call them fiddle heads, those first elvish green coils of fern that are pushing up in the woods, breaking a wet and sullen sod as mushrooms do. Compare them if you like to the scrolled head of a fiddle, or call them bishop's staves. But as soon as the coil is half expanded, then from the cunningly involuted roll begin to shoot the tendrily side branches of the frond, the pinnæ that may again be divided into pinnules. Now they are called lady's fingers, from their dainty charm, but as they grope upwards as if they were reaching for the pale sunlight, their name is dead men's hands. Truly, out of the darkness, where forever the stems of our little northern ferns are hid, the frond reaches up an eager hand for the blessed sunlight.

In the tropics there are ferns, tree ferns, with true stems, but a moment's thoughtful glance will show any one that the apparent stem of a fern is but a leaf stalk. Most of the plant lives a mole's existence in this harsher clime. Only a leaf or two, a spore-bearing frond, is ever thrown up to the light and air.

All that concerns the fern has filled the human mind with thoughts of mystery and dread. Martagon and lunary, moonwort and rattlesnake fern, male fern and lady fern, these names suggest the mingled confusion and superstition which they roused in the antique mind. Witches allegedly gathered fern seed to work their spells. It is safe to suppose that none but supernatural folk could do so, since ferns have no seeds. In this, perhaps, lay their quality of evil for the medieval mind.

> "Fern, that vile, unuseful weed
> That grows equivocally without seed."

APRIL TWELFTH

THERE came a moment in this chill, palely green afternoon, as all the world was watery with running ponds, and the river boiling high and yellow, when I stood among the uncoiling fronds of the cinnamon ferns and listened to the first piping of the tree frog. I used not to distinguish him from the pond frogs, but my ear at last is attuned to the difference. A pond frog is a coarse and booming creature compared with the eery, contented and yet lonely little tree frog thrilling the light airs with its song.

It is strange how a note that must assuredly bespeak contentment, almost in this case a hymn of domestic felicity, can so trouble the heart of the listener. For the song rises over the creak-crack of the swamp frogs with an unearthly soaring wail, a note of keening that the country folk will say foretells a coming rain. And they are right in this. The tree frog never cries but a soft, oppressive dampness hangs upon the air, and spring thunder speaks in the western sky. Just so, in summer, do the cicadas, early in the morning, foretell a blazing day, and crickets in the autumn grass predict their deaths of frost.

APRIL THIRTEENTH

FIRST, a frog's egg is encircled vertically by a single groove —the future right and left of the animal. Then another longitudinal line cuts it at right angles, and by the third day if not sooner, there always appears that horizontal slice, a girdle round the egg not at its equator but above it— half way to the egg's north pole. Significant inequality that divides the body from the head! Splendid injustice that we may thank for all the brains that we possess!

Now the original grant of life is broken up by an intricate inheritance into cells increasingly fine, increasingly significant. Small matter if you no longer follow all the events in strict detail, for the division proceeds internally, with dazzling swiftness. On the fourth day the low-power microscope is needed, and a few days later the high-power lens, with which one may see the first rush of blood along the veins.

But still the naked eye can distinguish externally the ridge of the nerve cord, that so swiftly vanishes in the shroud of flesh. Then the gills rush out, only themselves to be buried. The awkward head takes shape, the tail, like the legs of a man in a sack, struggles to expand itself, and so at last, with a sort of horror and delight, we watch the animal shouldering potently about in the prison of its larval state as it prepares to emerge upon the year with all its hungers, its needs and its cries.

APRIL FOURTEENTH

THE tadpoles in the quiet bay of the brook are now far past the stage of inky black little wrigglers attached by their two little sticky pads to any stick or leaf, merely breathing through their gills, and lashing with their hair-fine cilia. A dark brown skin—really gold spots mottling the black— now proclaims the leopard frogs they will become. Now the hunger of the open mouths is insatiable; a tadpole, when not resting in sheer exhaustion, will not (and I suppose could not safely) cease for one moment to eat. They all scrape the slime from the sticks and stones; they nibble the water weeds; they are launched upon life with all its appetites and delights and perils.

And what perils! The water is now alive with treacherous, fiercely biting back-swimmers and their cousins the giant water bugs with ugly sucking mouths. The dragonfly nymphs emerge as if perfectly timed to live upon a banquet of frog larvæ prepared for them, tigers of the ponds with legs that snatch, and jaws that devour. Fish, turtles, and water birds might all well die in early spring but for the monstrous fertility of the female leopard frog. She must spawn enough children to pay tribute to hundreds of merciless ogre overlords and still more, so that by good fortune June shall hear the marshes rattling with her children's hymns.

So already the contest is begun, not, in reality the battle between death and life, but life locked naked with life, in a sort of terrible mating of substances, dissolving and fusing from one species into another, one instant palpitant batrachian jelly and the next the wry croak of a stilted shorebird.

APRIL FIFTEENTH

THERE is one spot in my neighborhood where I can literally wade into the very medium of life itself, and that is the marsh and the pond. With a net—or with nothing better than my hands, if need be, I can scoop up the teeming stuff of it—the decaying twigs bearing fresh-water sponges, the shard of a crayfish that went to make a meal for a bittern, the strands of the first algæ, a handful of mud out of which small nameless things come kicking and twisting. Here is the world of the fairy shrimp, of the thin tubifex worms poised for retreat into their mud chimneys, the caddis-fly larvæ, like centaurs with their dragging cases hampering half their bodies, of the transparent Leptodora, the phantom snatcher of that netherworld.

All about me rise the cries of the redwings, sweet gurgling watery whistles, and the angry *peent, peent* when I come too near their nesting places. The waters lap the tiny shores of this impermanent sea; the ancient sunlight warms me, and dances on the ripples. The feel of life, the joy of it, the thrill and the warmth of it are in my bones, and the same sensations penetrate, I know, to the very bottom of the pond.

APRIL SIXTEENTH

UPON the bottom of any pond in spring are pastured its tiny grazing animals, its pollywogs and snails, its microscopic flagellates, each one of which will produce a thousand descendants in a month, its rotifers of which each, seventy hours after hatching from the egg, becomes itself a spawning factory. Just above them wait and prowl the small creatures of prey, the crayfish and the tigerish dragonfly nymphs, the nymphs of the mayflies, agile as minnows. Voracity awaits these too; they are destined to vanish down greater jaws and bills and gullets. Life in the casual pond, like life in the sea or the jungle, is like a pyramid with the multiplex and miniform for the broad base.

A bucketful of water may support ten thousand copepods; but a water snake may require a marsh to himself, as a whale needs league upon league of sea, or a bear the half of a mountainside. It is a question if there be any biologic advantage in mastering your environment when you need such a quantity of it to support you. Necessity presses just as sternly on the great beasts as on the small. The problem of population and food is the same, and the increased consciousness of the so-called higher forms is harshly compensated for by their increased capacity for suffering. True, it were pleasanter to eat than be eaten, but in the end even kings must come to dust.

APRIL SEVENTEENTH

YOU can never tell what they will be teaching next, but when I was a student they taught that plant life began in the fresh-water ponds, and not in the sea, as many people suppose. For the fresh-water algæ, the little green and blue-green pond scums, are not only, upon the face of it, the simplest green plants alive today, but their fossil record is buried in the ancient rocks. From the fresh water the algæ invaded the sea, and so the seaweeds came into being. The story of evolution runs from the fresh water to the sea, and from the sea to the land, and, oddly enough, one part of the tale runs from the land back into the pond.

The pond, of course, contains animals and plants that have been aquatic since the beginning of their time on earth, but the great majority of its inhabitants have re-entered the water from the land. The insects in these April waters must be considered as erstwhile air-breathing, flying creatures of the upper world, that have had to learn through ages of evolution to swim, to breathe through gills or carry their air supply with them. They are under the water only by virtue of a tremendous amount of adaptation to the liquid airless medium. The turtle on the log, the muskrat with his home in the bank, these too have chosen water life and display adaptation to it—the streamline form, the lifted snout and eye so perfectly adapted to swimming just at the surface, the feet fit either for burrowing or a flipper-like swimming. And creatures who go back to life's earlier, watery home return equipped with all the advantages that the harshly competitive life on land or in the air brought out in them.

APRIL EIGHTEENTH

T H E ancient forms from which today's world evolved have not become impotent with age. From the old stumps new shoots spring up. Primitive as they are, those clouds of diatoms that fill the ponds in the first days of spring are new; these modern algæ are adapted to the cold seas and the frozen ponds of our barely post-glacial era, little hard infrangible atoms carven as it were out of silicon crystals. Those bacteria that prey exclusively upon men and the higher animals cannot be anything but recent developments. Everywhere is flow and flux.

So far from being a steady progress in our exalted direction, evolution for the most is tending quite otherwheres. It may troop joyfully backwards (or it looks backward from our view point) toward simplification, toward a successful laziness. Parasitism, for example, is a highly lucrative mode of life that has probably never been more abundant than in the present.

In short, evolution is not so much progress as it is simply change. It does not leave all its primitive forms behind. It carries them over from age to age, well knowing that they are the precious base of the pyramid on which the more fantastic and costly experiments must be carried.

APRIL NINETEENTH

IF progress is an increasing power to master and mold environment, then there is a strong current of progress in evolution. A one-celled flagellate certainly has but the dullest awareness of its environment as it bumps aimlessly about, but the redwinged blackbird hanging its nest on the cattails and the muskrat digging crafty passages into and out of his home—these highly sentient, motile, instinctive and often intelligent creatures are a world and many ages beyond the blind and stupid flagellate. And last, in his majesty comes man, who if he does not like the marsh, will dig ditches and drain it off. In a year he will be turning a furrow there, sowing his domesticated crop, the obedient grain; he will drive out every animal and plant that does not bow down to him.

Man—man has the world in the hollow of his hand. He is a standing refutation of an old superstition like predestination—or a new one like determinism. His chances seem all but boundless, and boundless might be his optimism if he had not already thrown away so many of his opportunities. That very marsh was the home of waterfowl as valuable as they were beautiful. Now they must die, because in this world all breeding grounds are already crammed full. When he slays the birds, he lets loose their prey, and his worst enemy, the insects. He wastes his forests faster than he replaces them, and slaughters the mink and the beaver and the seal. He devours his limited coal supply ever faster; he fouls the rivers, invents poison gases and turns his destruction even on his own kind. And in the end he may present the spectacle of some Brobdingnagian spoiled baby, gulping down his cake and howling for it too.

T A U R U S

APRIL 20 — MAY 19

APRIL TWENTIETH

SOME ONE is forever telling us that one swallow does not make a summer. But what is the good of the first swallow, skimming on his side through the April afternoon, if it cannot raise a vaunted hope or encourage us to defy the gloomy and the unco circumspect! If they are right, those folk who are forever deriding the first man to try a thing, forever predicting disaster and living cautiously for a perfectly hypothetical old age, then let me, pray, be wrong. May I still, when I can count my hairs, be given grace and fortitude in the chill spring weather to say when first I see the wild spiral of the swallow that winter is over and done.

APRIL TWENTY-FIRST

Upon this day was born John Muir in Glasgow, Scotland, but for us he will ever be the boy of the Wisconsin farm, the youth of the Thousand Mile Walk to the Gulf, John of the Big Trees and the Yosemite, John of Alaska and of Australia. The very last of the roving naturalists was Muir. Above all, he is linked in the mind with California, the state that he loved best, where he was host over his campfire to Asa Gray and Emerson and Sir Joseph Dalton Hooker and Burroughs. No other man knew the Big Trees or the alpine flora of the Sierras and the forests of the coast ranges as Muir. But he was a catholic Nature lover. The tropics, the desert, the tundra, the glaciers and the prairies all found a place in his heart.

As Burroughs was the people's poet of birds, so Muir took his delight in every continent's green mantle of vegetation. John Burroughs in the east, John Muir in the west, birdman and plantsman, they are a pair that the mind inevitably links. Burroughs was the philosopher (if a bewildered one) and the bearded sage whom all conditions of people sought. Far more than Muir was he lionized, and successful with his pen. But Muir was the genuine explorer, humble of heart, iron of frame. He was immeasurably closer to the Nature that both of them loved, and to the scientific frame of mind which does not humanize or sweeten what it must report.

APRIL TWENTY-SECOND

THE time to hear bird music is between four and six in the morning. Seven o'clock is not too late, but by eight the fine rapture is over, due, I suspect, to the contentment of the inner man that comes with breakfast; a poet should always be hungry or have a lost love. When the day is well launched with its train of little business, the chorus revives a bit. But not overwell. The cardinal still cheers and the song-sparrow titters, and the bluebird sings, but there is something a bit humdrum about a bird's mid-morning, as there is in ours.

There is an admirable class of ornithologists who rise at three and by four are out with the songsters under the trees. They say the ten o'clock scholar might just as well not attend the feathered school. But he who rises so early misses an exciting sport—the game of birding in bed. Anybody, I submit, can identify a bird when he can see it through binoculars. But can you name the birds from your pillow? Can you pick out a single voice in all that blab-school of the early chorus, and trace the thread of its melody back to some familiar corner of the memory? I maintain that this is a great deal more strenuous and taxing to one's science than all this officious matutinal ornithologizing.

APRIL TWENTY-THIRD

SUDDENLY on the drowsy airs that have been almost naked of insects, the big, fuzzy golden bumble bee, *Bombus pennsylvanicus,* is abroad—a bit late this year and seeming to bustle like people who are tardy and wish to appear to make up for it by surpassing industry. The mother bee is visiting the spring flowers in the garden, and if she does any pollinating it is inadvertently, for in fact she is only intent upon collecting all the pollen she can to carry off to her burrow in the ground—usually some deserted field mouse's home. Of the pollen she makes a pile in her nest which she hastily lines with wisps of old dead grass, and then moistens the pollen with honey. Next she will make a waxen pot and place it near the doorway and fill it with mellifluence.

Now the queen, who has been fertile since the marriage flight last autumn, begins to lay her eggs upon the pollen mass, and in cold weather she herself will incubate them, eating from the honey pot until the weather clears. When at last the larvæ hatch, they feed upon the pollen hoardings, and from time to time the mother chews up some of this and mixes it with honey in order to give them a special pabulum. Within ten days or two weeks the larvæ spin a thin papery cocoon and when they emerge from this the patient queen mother will have her reward at last in a brood of maiden daughters, golden amazons, slaves who will keep her in royal state.

APRIL TWENTY-FOURTH

THE little winter birds are now definitely taking their departures. Gray and brown creatures, they leave us without our thanks for the pleasure of their esteemed company, so intent are we upon the gorgeous tropical fellows that are arriving as fast as thistledown in September. Only the patient thoroughness of a professional ornithologist, perhaps, would suffice to keep accurate count of the flitting away of the winter wren, the brown creeper, the sapsucker, the golden-crowned kinglet. Yet they too are feeling the great impulse to migration. The juncos and Lapland longspurs and larks take wing, and the white-throat sparrow is already singing, in revery of the rapture to come.

There is something especially brave and adventurous about these little fellows, who will seek out the frozen tundras of the north for their courting, and will build their nests in the wild fastness, amidst the swiftly-sprung, wide-eyed arctic wildflowers. When they return to us next winter, driven south by shortening days and snow and blast, they will treat our region as a land of exile enforced, a shelter to be endured till they can return to the chill, lost wildness of Ungava.

APRIL TWENTY-FIFTH

I BELIEVE it was Alexander Wilson, the early American ornithologist, who began the custom of keeping a record, through a chain of correspondents, of what Emerson called "the trusty almanac of the birds' first coming back." He described himself as happily so situated that not a titmouse or a wren would wing its way northward but he should know of it. But Wilson's correspondents were surely not two dozen in number. Today the Audubon Societies and the American Ornithological Union combine to keep a great census of bird migration.

What is needed is information about the bulk arrival and departure, the great waves of migration. The careless remark only upon the year's first robin, and take no further census. All through commonplace observation of Nature runs an infatuation with the rare that is the mark of limited understanding. Its amateurish emphasis stamps most collecting. The prideful and personal amassing of objects of some one sort, with self-congratulation upon having items that others do not possess, is antithetical to the aim or morality of science. It is better turned loose upon antique furniture or postage stamps than upon the material of the natural world. The really scientific mind cares little for a personal collection, and the veteran student knows that rarity is chiefly one of the illusions of the provincial point of view.

Not that a boy has no right to the marvelous miscellany he assembles in his pockets. His inquisitiveness is of the very essence of research. Those untidy birds' nests adorning his walls, the stones or shells he is hoarding, may be the crude beginning to a lifetime's happy labor.

APRIL TWENTY-SIXTH

O N this day in 1785 was born Jean Jacques Audubon, in Santo Domingo, natural son of a French captain of Nantes, who was brought up in France by the captain's forgiving wife, spoiled, petted, raised as a little fop—this man who was to give himself to the American wilderness. When first he came to Philadelphia, a young foreigner, a dilettante, a country gentleman, we see him out shooting in the woods in satin breeches, wig and pumps. We see him encounter there his English neighbor, Bakewell, who takes him home to meet a blue-eyed daughter, rising tall among the dogs by the fire—Lucy Bakewell, his wife to be.

But Nature has her eye upon the man in the elegant clothes. First she must teach him that you cannot well dream out of a window in a counting house, you cannot play the indigo market without knowledge, nor mail a thousand dollars in an open envelope, nor manage a mill while you are out hunting vireos and wrens, painting warblers and cardinals. Then, when she had broken him with misfortunes, she sent him out into the Kentucky wilderness, singing to it with his Cremona violin at his shoulder, and to his young bride.

There amidst the beeches, the passenger pigeons and the wild deer, John James Audubon let his gold hair grow long to his shoulders, learned to handle a fire and a woman and a gun. There, unknown to all the world, he painted birds, watched them, lived with them, knew them as he knew his children or his Lucy. In the cane brakes, on the Mississippi, in the Texas bayous, the palmetto islands of Florida, the sea-girt bird rocks of the Gaspé, this child of Nature, untaught in science, saw what he saw and knew what he knew.

NEVER was there a naturalist who got himself into higher circles or more unseemly scrapes than the daring Audubon. Forever losing money, Audubon in times of stress could lift himself out of poverty by teaching dancing, or by drawing the frontier belles' portraits. Now he would be penniless, and then he would be the guest of Washington Irving; his graceful manners would win him the friendship of the ornithologist Lucien Bonaparte, and carry him to the drawing-rooms of the Baron Rothschild.

But he was flawed with impish faults. He hoaxed poor Rafinesque, that mad genius and eccentric, into solemn belief in the "red-headed swallow," concocted for his benefit, and even got him to accept drawings of imaginary fishes and publish them as new species. When Alexander Wilson, rival ornithologist, arrived at Audubon's store in Louisville, Kentucky, Audubon praised Wilson's drawings, but, perhaps out of jealousy, drew back from subscribing. The sour little Wilson records of Louisville that he met there not one friend or man of cultivation. But Audubon maintains that he entertained him and loaned him a drawing, which Wilson stole and published as his own. An examination of the two drawings shows only a faint resemblance.

After Wilson's death his angry friends charged, and we fear with justice, that one of Audubon's plates is really Wilson's, printed backwards. The puckish Audubon could make mischief when he chose, but it is so easy to love him, so hard to care for the bitter, humorless little Wilson, in that still reëchoing combat of an elf and a Scottish dominie!

APRIL TWENTY-EIGHTH

UNDER Audubon's brush, birds live as they live in the wild—forever in motion, now teetering on a bough, now flinging themselves upon the blue sea of air, now diving like the kingfisher or osprey, now snapping up an insect or standing almost on their feathered heads to reach a pendent cherry. They come right off the page; they fly and swing, they scream and sing and fight, they eat, court, preen, flutter, hunt lice under their wings, or hide their little cold heads against the storm.

Nor are they merely bits of emotional impressionism, these bird paintings; when Audubon was not pressed for time he rendered the finest details of plumage, bent, it would seem, on not slurring one barb on one pinion. His drawings thus became actually more valuable to the scientist, who would not give a farthing for a bird by an impressionist, than even museum specimens. For it was Audubon's way to paint from creatures which had been dead only an hour or two; he maintained that the luster of the living plumage flies before sundown. He invented a unique method, too, of so wiring the little dead body that it caught again the attributes of life.

And more. He painted the birds in their habitats. In the foregrounds he would place the vegetation of his subject's haunt, and he never fails to give us the food it eats, be it berry, insect or fish. And like an Italian master of old, he delights in completing the environmental study by little landscapes as background, perfect little glimpses of the wilderness he knew. He gives us the dark cypress swamp, the dreamy live-oaks hung with Spanish moss, the shining wood-ringed lakes and the slow vast rivers. No greater technical demands were ever made upon draughtsmanship than to represent these exquisite landscapes in the background while keeping the proportion of microscopic attention to detail in the bird of the foreground.

APRIL TWENTY-NINTH

AND while the brilliant Audubon flew from continent to continent, became the darling eccentric of the worldly great, was busied weightily with publishers, or roamed the wilds—all the time, biding at home, was Lucy. She was the faithful little gray mate who built the nest, who sat the eggs and fed the fledglings, while the gorgeous plumaged male swept through the skies, singing and vaunting his triumphs, and bringing down tumultuous applause.

Delicate child of an English immigrant, child of wealth as it went in those days, she chose to wed a lad who was forever in a scrape, forever doing and saying the things so annoying to in-laws. John James lost her money; John James left her for his birds for months at a time. John James went to jail, and John James wanted to print the most costly ornithological work America had ever heard of —wherein everything that flew should be figured life size, be it an eagle.

Lucy never wavered. She rejoiced when he rejoiced, was cheerful in his mercurial desponds. Lucy earned money when John James could not, and never for one moment ceased being either a brave warm woman or a perfect lady. Nature asks no better of a mate than that!

APRIL THIRTIETH

O N this day in 1834 was born in London Sir John Lubbock, first baron Avebury, one of the most delightful souls
who ever ornamented science. He came out of the class out
of which naturalists beyond the purely amateur and personal sort are least to be expected—the English gentleman
who is trained at Eton and makes his way in the City, the
banker, peer, chairman of committees on coinage, mone-
tary reform, shop hour regulations, open spaces, public
libraries and bank holidays.

It is not surprising that such a man should be the author
of *The Pleasures of Life, The Uses of Life, The Beauties of
Nature*. But his *Ants, Bees and Wasps,* which seems to be
no more than a notebook kept while observing these social
insects in the artificial observation nest that he invented,
is, in reality, the very stuff of science. It is built up page
by page of the intensive watching, often minute by minute,
the ingenious and controlled experimentation by which
alone true knowledge may progress. We see him experi-
menting on the color sensitivity of bees; we find him in an
Italian railway carriage with a tame, educated wasp! And it
in no way detracts from the charm of his book to have him
break off sometimes with a notation that he was called to
London at this point, and we imagine him journeying to
some philanthropic public undertaking.

Lubbock was also an excellent botanist, with an instinct
for picking up the pieces that purely systematic and formal
botanists often neglect, such as seeds and seedlings, and
making first class biology out of them. But it is his book
on ants that I read repeatedly, and each time with an in-
increasing fondness for the kindly old man behind it all.

MAY FIRST

Spring in any land has its special sweetnesses. Tulips and hyacinths, crocuses and narcissus that are wild flowers of the Mediterranean spring, are more familiar to the city dweller in the New World than the shy, frail spring flowers of his own country side. An English spring with the innocent faces of primroses looking up from their pale leaves, with celandine braving the winds of March, and bluebells in the woods when cuckoos call and nightingales return, is ours by right of poesy.

In this our western world, Thoreau has made New England springs immortal, and a host of lesser writers have followed him; indeed, most of the popular wildflower books emanate from the northeastern states where a rather bleak flora has been better loved, sung, and made decipherable than that of the richer lands to the south.

South of the Potomac spring comes on with balm and sweetness, with a peculiarly Appalachian fragrance, commingled of forests and mountains. It comes without treachery, without taking one step back, like the Sabine women, for every two steps forward. It sweeps up from Florida, past the sea islands of Georgia, through Hall and Habersham, through Charleston where the tea olive sheds its intense sweetness on the air, over the Carolinas, wakening the wild jasmine in the woods, filling the Blue Ridge with azalea and many kinds of trillium and the strange, earth-loving wild ginger, till it opens the bird-foot violet, and the redbud and dogwood of the two Virginias.

MAY SECOND

VERY fair grow the bird-foot violets in the high woods on the hill across the valley. The two upper petals are a deep pansy purple, the three large, lower petals pale lavender, and the leaves beside the flowering stalks are quaintly cleft like the claw of a bird. The little black children gather them in their dark hands for sale.

Unlike most of our violets, the bird-foot breeds true from the seeds in its fat little pods. All the others—nineteen of them hereabout—reproduce in a mass of hybrids, crosses untrue to their species.

How do any violets keep true to type when the customs of the clan permit all this miscegenation? You must dig down under the ground around the pretty blue and white Canada violet, the lovely yellow violet, the common blue, or the frail white marsh violet, to have your answer. There, on little runners from the stem, are minute, wizened, root-colored swellings that look like what they are—unopened, subterranean buds of flowers.

Here under ground, safe from the alien pollen borne by visiting insects, these gnomish, colorless flowers fertilize themselves and set pure seed. So far from suffering loss of strength through this perpetual inbreeding, the violets are all the better for it. Above, in the vagrant airs, their sister blossoms mingle as the caprice of the bees dictates.

MAY THIRD

ALMOST as inscrutable as the physical causes of the ascent of sap in trees are the psychical reasons for the return of birds in spring. There would seem to be no particular reason why the birds should not remain in the tropics. Indeed, many, perhaps most, never leave them.

Our birds, you may say, return because they wish to raise their young in the north. They reason that they can enjoy a food supply here where there is less competition than in the crowded tropics. This might argue well, if birds reasoned, but they don't.

Nor has anybody answered the pertinent question why some birds leave the tropics and some remain. What has determined this division of instincts, and converted some to various persuasions? The longer one ponders, the less ready is one's answer. All we can say is that in spite of winter and rough weather, the first migrants punctually arrived and now the great migratory wave is toppling to its crest.

The instinct of birds is so far from innately sagacious that every year there is a great mortality amongst them, from flying straight into storms or returning with such rash impetuosity that winter is overtaken by their wings. Here we have proof how far it is instinct and not reason which actuates them. Instinct, intended for the good of the race, turns out to be an automaton that walks into death in blind obedience.

MAY FOURTH

O N this fine May morning, at about six o'clock, I took up my station in a convenient tree, where I could make my long limbs comfortable, and lifted my binoculars. At my first coming I created the usual exodus and silence that a human being's presence always brings in the wood. After a time I ceased to be noticed—after far shorter an interval than would have been possible at any other season. But the birds were so intent upon their hurried affairs, every tree in the glade was so occupied, and the fresh arrivals were so many, that there simply was not time to give me more than a glance.

Catbirds and brown thrashers and thrushes and mourning doves and robins and wrens seemed to pour through like rain blowing horizontally. They came, they teetered, they ate if they could find anything, and sped on. Everywhere about me the chorus arose—the whistling, the alarm calls, the anger calls, the rapture and the loud demand for mates, mates! Of these I saw as yet but very few. As a general thing the males arrive before the females, no doubt to stake their local claims and drive off rivals.

No one who has not lived in the subtropics can imagine what the effect of the spring migration is there. To us here it brings returning joy, a sense that the world is full of brilliant and cheerful friends. But in the South it means the falling of a silence, a long sad monotony. I recall, like a cæsura in melody, those days by the Mediterranean, in July, when the nightingale had ceased to sing, the little European robin with his bright red vest was flown away, and gone were the chaffinch and the blackbird. Even the gulls deserted the harbor, where the fishing town lay burning beside the stagnant sea.

J o b wrote of the hawk that stretches out its wings for the South. Anacreon sang of the returning swallows, and the old Greek legend of the pigmies and the storks shows a knowledge that in winter the storks flew off to Africa. Dear to the wistful human heart is the return of the birds, that is like a renewal of our hopes. It is not nearly so prolonged, so sweeping as the autumnal flight, nor does it involve nearly the same numbers, since in autumn all the newborn are on the wing, while in spring many may never come back or they are seeking fresh homes. But the autumn migration is more difficult for the amateur to observe; it lacks the music and the plumage with which the army of the birds swings onto the stage in spring.

All the birds breed in the coldest part of their range, and the place where the nesting occurs is considered by most authorities to be the birds' true homes; the tropics or the antipodes thus become their exile. If we can suppose that the birds themselves feel any such distinction—and there is no reason why not; the homing instinct is almighty with them—then we can understand perfectly whatever of psychology enters into their northward flight.

But probably the whole matter is not psychological at all. It is instinctive, or it may be conditioned by physical factors, not only the environment pressing upon the bird, but physical or even chemical factors operating within the bird itself.

MAY SIXTH

WHAT can it be, this homing instinct, that brings the birds back to us every year? That brings the wrens and the swallows to the very same nests around the house and barn? That leads the carrier pigeon home across a hundred, five hundred miles?

The trainer of pigeons has something significant to tell about this. He cannot release his birds for the first time in Moscow and expect them to fly home to Paris. He must first take them not a mile from home, and when they have learned all landmarks thoroughly, he may take them thirty or forty miles away. Each pigeon must be educated in its route. Birds, then, in their migrations would seem to have a memory for landmarks, and flying very high as they do, they see so much country in one little eyeful that the memory need not be burdened with a crushing weight of detail.

But the slippery question of the ways of birds upon their majestic travels will not rest at this. If it be true that the young of the season, who have never made the flight before, often travel in little jaunty bands of adolescents, as they appear to, without the oldsters accompanying them, then memory for landmarks cannot be all the story. Something else draws on their restless wings across the sea and the unbroken forest, some feeling in their light, air-filled bones, that sweeps them north in a grand phalanx in spring, and surges south with them in autumn.

MAY SEVENTH

BIRDS are not the only animals which move in a mass in time with the seasons, but they are chiefest of the creatures which can properly be said to migrate. The best authorities I can discover confine the meaning of this fascinating word to rhythmic movements of the whole race from a breeding ground to another terrain, which need not be far away but must represent quite another sort of abode where somewhat different habits or stages of life history are experienced. The impulse must be hereditary, and there must be a return journey, if not by the same individual then by its offspring.

Such a definition will set us clear of other mass movements, such as the northward swarming of the great armies of fishes in the spring. These are simply following their food which is the plankton or minute plants and animals that appear in northern waters, as flowers appear on the earth, in a successive emergence as the warmth steals into the northern ocean. The swarming of locusts is really only a dispersal since there is no return journey, and the same is true of the seaward rush of the lemmings, who drown themselves in the North Sea. Some of the wild grazing animals of the steppes "follow the grass" like nomads, but quite without any special reference to bodily changes in themselves, or the sexual life. The fascinating movements of the pine processionary caterpillars, one of the most obstinate and stupid performances I ever witnessed, are mere flights from regions where food is scarce. So all these shifts and pilgrimages, interesting in themselves, teach us nothing concerning problems of migration.

MAY EIGHTH

T H E R E are a few groups of animals besides the birds, that, when the spring gets in their bones, make true migratory movements. The caribou in autumn leaves the wild uplands of Labrador for the warmer seacoast, traveling as a race, chiefly by day and at a brisk walking trot, the does, fawns, the young stags in the advance, the old bucks bringing up the rear. At this season they will be returning, more gradually, the does great with young and picking a sedate way, eating as they go. Very plainly they are reversing the bird's order of migration; they do their breeding in the south in winter and their vegetating in the north in summer.

The salmon, which leaps the falls of the great rivers hundreds of miles in the interior, are quite certainly migrants between salt water and fresh. Their journey answers every requirement of the word migration. Many even return to their native streams and creeks. The Alaskan fur seal is a genuine migrant; so too are some turtles; the march—or rather, hop—of the toads to water in spring and back again, is a migration within a small compass; the wood frogs make an autumnal trek to water and a vernal hegira. Bats, too, migrate—the few species that do not hibernate.

But when we have assembled all the migrants of our latitude, and some from without it, they make but a scattered array of pilgrims beside the great winged throngs of the Aves. In these the mystery must be sought and solved.

MAY NINTH

MAYFLIES emerge at that lush moment in the year when life brims over. Flowers are so many now that one has lost all count of the number of kinds. Birds arrive hourly each fine morning in such crowds that I have given up the resolve not to let an unidentified wing or song drift by. Ponds brim over their edges. Marshes send forth the multitudinous cacophony of song and croak and trill and call and scream. At this psychological moment the mayflies choose to emerge and pose the brief riddle of their whence and why. At times I really think of them as one organism too many.

The fact about mayflies that allures the philosopher is the shortness of their existence. The larval state is passed in water and at such a time one might mistake it for some sort of worm. Then the pre-adult emerges into aërial life. The air first rushes into its breathing pores. In a few minutes or at most twenty-four hours, the skin of the pre-adult is sloughed off and the wings burst forth and for the first time are lifted in flight. There will be a few days of fluttering—then death. Indeed, some species emerge in the morning, have mated before evening, and the next morning the female has laid the eggs in their glutinous covering. There being no further use for these parents, Nature allows them to die.

MAY TENTH

WAS it worth while for a mayfly to have been born, to have been a worm for weeks and a bride or a bridegroom for one day, only to perish? Such is not a question to which Nature will give the human mind an answer. She thrusts us all into life, and with her hand propels us like children through the rôle she has allotted us. You may weep about it or you may smile; that matters only to yourself. The trees that live five hundred years, or five thousand, see us human mayflies grow and mate and die while they are adding a foot to their girth. Well might they ask themselves if it be not a slavish and ephemeral soft thing to be born a man.

MAY ELEVENTH

A DAY of silver rain, pouring down straight and tumultuously on the roofs, on the trees; silver rain like a flight of javelins blown down from all over the sky. And the white-throat singing, perhaps for the last time before this little winter resident takes flight. Some say he sings of "Sweet Canada, Can-a-da, Can-a-da!" where he goes to mate, but to me he seems to cry "Oh, long ago, long ago, long ago!"

Compared to him the vaunting skylark of the poets does no more than twitter. The meadowlark is like the eery happy whistle of the wind through the grass in the time when Queen Anne's lace bobs in the fields of blue June, and the thrush is the voice of serenity, of green twilights in very lonely hushed woods, a singer who makes a cathedral wherever he lifts his voice.

But the white-throat's touching chromatic pierces the heart; it blends sadness and happiness in a way to catch the listener in either mood, and the only other bird song to which it can be compared is that of the nightingale. Their songs are physically alike in the delicate chromatic of the notes, the purity of the tone, and the way that they let their voices swell upon a note until the tears start in the eyes of the listener. The white-throat, too, has a song like a cry, a song that speaks of the antiquity of time, the briefness of life.

MAY TWELFTH

O N this day I am pleased to mark down the most un-expected name upon the green calendar of naturalists. For it is the anniversary of the birth in 1812 of Edward Lear, whose nonsense and limericks are household words. No more puckish spirit ever lived, but few are the nature lovers today who remember that at twenty he had made himself celebrated by his painting of the Psittacidæ, the parrots. Artistic skill combined with extreme fidelity to nature in these paintings drew from Swainson the remark that Audubon could not have done better. The parrots drew the attention of the thirteenth Earl of Derby, who became practically his patron, and it was for the child Edward Stanley, later fifteenth earl, that the *Book of Nonsense* was composed. His nonsense botany, with its inimitable drawings, is one of the unappreciated items on the rare book list. Only a botanist with a sense of humor would understand how funny it is. And these are even rarer than the copies of that slim volume.

To many people a warbler is simply a bird that warbles. They will not split hairs, or feathers, in order to distinguish between the species. But technical folk love the warblers, in part because every ornithologist is a Micawber, waiting for something to turn up, and if it is anything new, the chances are that it will be amongst the little known Mniotiltidæ. For many are on the hypothetical list, or have not been seen for years. The differences between them are subtle, and amateurs let them slip through on their migrations without much reluctance.

But some of the most mysteriously exciting moments of my life were spent in a mountain forest in the Blue Ridge, trying in vain to find the wandering sprite who let fall from the tops of the tulip trees his song of *beechy, beechy, beech-y, beeee!* that dropped with a sound like the waterfall beside which it rang.

The singing of the resident warblers is now reaching its height. Every copse and twig is lively with their outpourings. But I never hear my lost bird. I hear the myrtle warbler, who seems to be thinking of something else as he sings, and the clear-voiced yellow warbler, and the Maryland yellow-throat, proclaiming witchery, and the ovenbird, who ought really to be called the schoolboy bird, for he continually begs "teacher, teacher!" But never my bird in the wilderness, never the voice that sang above the rushing of the fall, where the fine spray drummed on the great rhombic leaves of the mountain trillium.

MAY FOURTEENTH

I LOVE a brook far better than a river. If ever I buy a country tract it is going to have a brook on it. Indeed, I'm not sure that it will not be mostly brook—two long strips of land on each side of the watercourse. After all, Egypt was just such a shape. Or I shall buy two brooks where they run together—a Mesopotamia—and between them pitch the invisible Babylon of my heart. No house; no garden; not even a path. It shall be nothing but my domain, where I can, alone, explore the little wild strands, and mine my country for its smooth quartz stone and its fool's gold in the sands, and learn to know my subjects, the red triton, the wood frog, the water wren, and the caddis flies, water striders and Dytiscus beetles.

MAY FIFTEENTH

THE most abundant butterfly on the wing just now is the little yellow clover; the males are especially numerous and this kind can be recognized at once by the medium-sized roundish and black-bordered wings, the forewings bearing each a small beauty spot of black. The ladies are yellow and white. Everywhere they are swarming around the rain puddles, males only, and the explanation of this phenomenon seems to be that there is an over-production of the war-like sex. What we must take to be the rejected suitors leave the overpopulated centers, cluster about a water hole and lead a sort of clubman's existence, entirely amicable when there are no womenfolk to set them at odds.

But what most amused me today was the sight of a single female of the orange clover who passed across the puddle club, and set up a quiver of excitement. I do not know if any miscegenation occurs but not only are the yellow males attentive to the orange females, but the smaller, weaker, and apparently less moral of the orange males will frequently take an interest in the little yellow females, who are not averse to flirting with them. The orange clover, a Rocky Mountain insect, was not seen here before 1888, but it has increased steadily, and the big pugnacious males attack the smaller yellow males on sight.

It seems likely, indeed, that it may drive out the harmless yellow species, as the European cabbage butterfly has forced our checkered white to retire. Unfortunately the caterpillars or alfalfa worms of the handsome orange are serious pests, and their increase in the last few years is alarming.

The milder yellow lover often carries his wife around on his back, but I am not sure that this is only gallantry. He would be justified in not wishing to let her far out of his sight.

MAY SIXTEENTH

I ENCOUNTERED in the steep rich woods above the river today the small yellow lady's slipper—my first orchid of the year. I was so late, and so loaded down with natural curiosities for the amusement of my children, that I could not carry it. Besides, there were some rites to be performed upon the flower soon, I hoped, that I wanted to see over again, to observe in the light of new thoughts. So I marked the spot and left the little plant where it was.

A popular belief has got abroad that orchids are unhealthy—besides much more fictional balderdash. It is true that they live with fungi growing in and around their roots, and cannot exist save when in this "diseased" condition, but men cannot exist either, without a large bacterial flora in the alimentary canal; beans and peas and other legumes live always with bacterial colonies on the roots, and so do heaths and other plants.

Such an intimate relation of two different organisms, often with what seem to be mutual adaptations, is a symbiosis. The physical contact is often as close and intense as in a case of parasitism, but in a symbiosis the benefits are mutual, not one-sided. The fungi living in the orchid root purvey to the plant above, which has no rootlets, and hence cannot eat or drink, the predigested elements of the soil. Without its particular fungus, each kind of orchid cannot live. Its seed will not, in some cases, even begin to germinate till a strand of the fungus bores into it and stimulates the embryo.

But at the other end of the orchid, where the blossom lifts to the sun, is to be seen another and more astonishing form of symbiosis.

MAY SEVENTEENTH

I RETURNED today to find my lady's slipper, and spent an hour of waiting, and five exciting minutes of watching. A bee, a small, metallic blue carpenter bee, followed her senses to the flower; she entered the slipper or sack-shaped lip by an opening at the top, and could be distinctly heard and roughly observed as she buzzed about collecting nectar drops from the internal hairs. I could judge when she endeavored to escape by the way she entered, and deduced her annoyance from her roar as she discovered that she was in a trap which opened one way but not the other.

What should be the orchid's third stamen is modified into a stiff, palate-like organ that blocks the way and cannot be forced up. Mistress bee crawls out at last under the stigma or receptive surface of the female organs, dusting off any pollen she may have brought with her and, just as she discovers an easy opening at the side of the lip, she receives a heavy charge of pollen on the shoulder. When thus conscripted to the flower's uses, she is allowed to escape by a small side door.

In the lady's slippers, with their two anthers, the pollen is coarse and granular, like that of most plants. But there are more elaborate devices among others of our orchids. In many of them the entire store of pollen is made up into two waxy pellets connected by a slender springy band, as two ear-phones are. This the bee, in her struggles, finds clapped on each side of her head as she escapes. When she enters the next flower, a neat little device upon the stigma hooks the pellets off, as an express train hooks the mail bag from a crane of a wayside station. Could anything be neater?

MAY EIGHTEENTH

T H E number, variety and intricacy of the adaptation of bees to orchids is simply dazzling. There are bees with tongues which, when unrolled, are twice as long as the length of the whole animal; tropical bees exist that could tap a nectary if it were buried nearly a foot deep in the most complicated orchid. There are bees with special pouches for carrying pollen in their legs, and others with pollen-brushes on their feet, on their heads, on their abdomens, depending whether they seem intended by Nature for deep flowers, irregular two-lipped flowers, one-lipped flowers, composite flowers, or simple open flowers. The bees have invented more types of brushes with special uses than the eminent Mr. Fuller.

There are orchids that can only be fertilized by one particular type of bee, like the fit of a Yale lock to its particular key, and possibly there are bees that could satisfy their ethereal lust for nectar at only one orchid, I cannot say. But nothing would surprise me after reading Darwin and Müller and Kerner. Tropical bats also enter into nicely adjusted symbioses with white, night-blooming orchids that reserve their perfume until twilight falls.

The specializations in what must be regarded as the age of orchids are possibly reaching a stage so extreme that they will defeat their own ends. A very slight change in the climate or insect fauna—no more difference than would easily exterminate over-specialized man—might suffice to dethrone the orchid family, with its ten thousand species, from its leadership, just as the dinosaurs grew too great for the world and evolved to self-destruction.

MAY NINETEENTH

S o the bee and orchid adaptation, that seems at first glance pat evidence of plan in Nature, turns out a witness for the other side of the argument. The extravagant and precarious exaggerations of this symbiosis do not assort with the ancient's simple scheme of a divine plan. And as soon as one ceases to regard only that which fits in with a theory, all the facts which do not conform besiege the attention.

As startling as the aptness of flower and insect symbiosis are their unsuccesses and futilities. Such are bees that get caught in the pollinating mechanism of the milkweed, and hang there miserably until they die. Orchids that, it turns out, do not need the bee at all, but can be made to set seed even without any male pollen ever reaching them, simply by tapping the stigma with a pencil! Fungi that eat up their orchid partners, and so deprive themselves of a home. Orchids that overtax the fungi that keep them alive, and so bring about their own destruction. These are but a few of the failures or exceptions in adaptation.

Intellectually honest men in the past nevertheless stopped their ears to these disharmonies in Nature, because they had been piously brought up to presuppose a symmetrical plan for creation, a purposive adjustment in life. This is the trap of teleology, an error so wide and attractive that every one at some time falls into it. But grant but a single teleological explanation in biology, and you have left the path of scientific thinking. Plan there may be, but only a working plan, a vast experimentation still in course.

GEMINI

MAY 20 – JUNE 20

MAY TWENTIETH

THE first night life of the year has begun for my brother animals. A few fireflies are to be seen, and the night moth, *Amphion nessus,* is abroad. And, as I strolled in this day's twilight, a night hawk swooped around my head as silently, and with as much boldness, as one of the bats which are now on the wing. His cousin the whippoorwill has already lifted his voice, just a few mysterious cries out of the depth of the wood.

In early spring, the dark hours are barren of life; each night is a little death, a return to winter. Now that the warm weather is assured, the woods and fields and even my garden are quite alive with nocturnal venturers. Small animal shapes move freely in the safety of the shadows. Sometimes I hear their faint footfalls on the leaves, sometimes I hear nothing, only know instinctively that some creature has passed by me, intent upon his private business in the kindly enveloping dark. Now against the screens the big May beetles bang, setting up an angry roaring with their harsh wings, and through the opened window breathes the perfume of night-flowering honeysuckle, the first of the year.

MAY TWENTY-FIRST

THIS is the month of aroids. Except for the skunk cabbage, which blooms in February, every one of our members of the calla family is now in flower—the beautiful golden-club rising from the mud, the stately arum just out of reach in the deeper water, beyond the pickerel weed and arrow-head, and the sweet-flag, with its sword-like leaves springing from the fresh green bank. In the woods Jack-in-the-pulpit is still at his preaching.

There is a special fascination in this family, as there must be about any which is sharply defined from all others. These families always have race, distinction, peculiarity, personality. Just such discrete, compact and strongly racial groups are the orchids, the palms, the conifers, the air-plants, the pipe-vines, the sedges—in which the strange or the harsh is blended with the attractive into family traits as distinct as those of the Hapsburgs.

No family more positive than the aroids exists. The calla lily is the queen of the lot; I must confess she has disreputable brothers—great, fleshy, tropical, inflorescences with impudic spadices, spathes like decaying meat and odors of skatol. Everything about them disgusts and repels us; but the carrion flies which frequent them do the work of pollinating them as effectively as the fairest sphinx moth sipping at the sweet nectary of any fragrant night flower.

Nature has gusto for everything. And bit by bit a man may arrive at the same liberated, and, his neighbors will say, inhuman view of things, where beauty for him is not limited to the sweet and pretty, no, nor even to the instructive and uplifting. An aroid, for such a catholic taste, will satisfy because it is an aroid, a thing with a look, and a touch, and a feel of its own.

YOU have to go looking for the green-dragon, with your mind intent on it and nothing else, or you will scarcely find one in twenty miles, even when it blooms. For this odd little relative of Jack-in-the-pulpit is not only our rarest aroid hereabout, but the flower is green. A queer, elvish, secretive green, thrusting out a little reptilian tongue.

I have called it a flower, but it is in reality but a spathe, an enveloping, especially modified floral leaf. We see the same sort of floral bract, but of a dry papery sort, at the base of the flower stalk in the dainty narcissus, the vulgar onion, the gorgeous amaryllis.

Peeling back the spathe of dragon's head I find within, the tongue— (in the case of Jack-in-the-pulpit, it is "Jack" himself). And this, of course, is the *spadix* of botanists, the spike or axis on which are clustered the innumerable tiny flowers themselves.

A flower, by definition, need be no more than a single reproductive organ, male or female or combined. All petals, sepals, spathes and bracts are mere embellishments. It is the fashion in which life's fundamental business is thus adorned or cloaked, that means to us a rose, a daisy, or an impudic, elfin aroid.

On this day in 1707, in southern Sweden, was born the man we know as Linnæus, Carolus, Linnæus or Karl von Linné. His father had literally enjoyed no surname; he was Nils, the son of Bengt, for in old Sweden there were only patronymics. But he took a name unto himself from *Lin*, the linden. For two hundred years, in a corner of Jonsboda Parish, there had stood a mighty linden, sacred in family tradition, and from this totem Nils made himself a learned-sounding Latin name.

At Upsala, Linnaeus passed the first year in dire want, putting paper in the soles of his worn shoes. The old botanical gardens, started by Rudbeck, had been allowed to fall into ruins, and the science of botany itself was then like a sleeping, dusty, dead-seeming garden in March, half full of lifeless brushwood—but for the rest secretly quick and budded and only awaiting a warming breath.

The only friend of Linnaeus at this time was Artedi, who would have become the Linnæus of zoölogy but for falling into a canal and drowning. This lad was so poor that Linnaeus and he loaned each other money, as only the destitute could do. These boys exchanged the usual wild ideas of young students—in this case nothing less than the principles of classification that ultimately brought order into the hopelessly muddled work of the herbalists struggling to find the plants of northern Europe in their Pliny and Theophrastus.

So like two winter birds, living on weed seeds, and sleeping in the lee of a tree trunk, the ragged hungry lads lived on till spring, when Dean Celsius, himself a naturalist, came to their aid with money, food, shelter, appointments, and gave them grace to think, without danger of turning into fasting visionaries.

MAY TWENTY-FOURTH

In May, 1732 there rode out of the gates of gray old Upsala a thin young man in a light coat of West Gothland linsey without folds, lined with red shalloon, having small cuffs and a collar of shag; he wore leather breeches, and a round wig topped by a green leather cap, his feet in a pair of half-boots. On his saddle he carried a small leather bag containing two pairs of false sleeves, two half-shirts and one whole one, an inkstand, pencase, microscope, a gauze cap to protect him from gnats, a comb, drying papers for plants, and a few books. A fowling-piece hung at his side, and a graduated stick for measuring. In his pocket was a passport for Lapland from the governor of Upsala.

Linnæus was going into the field. In a sense that journey was the first of its kind ever made. It was the morning, the springtide of science, after the dark winter of the book-ridden Middle Ages, when men wrangled over Aristotle and quoted Pliny's authority. Linnæus was the first naturalist to whom it occurred to take a great trip to Nature itself. No wonder that as he rode north, the very larks burst into song.

"*Ecce suum* tirile, tirile, *suum* tirile *tractat!*" they sang, or so he records it with his quaint blend of Latin and fantasy. "The sky was clear and warm, while the west wind refreshed one with delicious breath," he wrote. "The winter rye stood six inches high, and the barley was newly come into leaf. The birch was beginning to shoot and all the trees leafing except the elm and aspen. Though only a few spring flowers were in bloom it was obvious that the whole land was smiling with the coming of spring."

MAY TWENTY-FIFTH

WHEN Linnæus published his great Lapland report, it was swiftly translated into the languages of Europe. A door had been burst open, and all men beheld that, outside, the fields were burning with flowers, the sky ringing with bird song. Very disturbing, all that, to the medieval-minded schoolmen, the obscurantists who would have kept their science to themselves, like alchemists.

Dillenius of Oxford, looking out of his window at the young Swede walking about in the botanical garden, cried: "There goes a man who is bringing all botany into confusion!" He locked up the herbarium, would not give Linnæus the books he wanted. But in the end, Linnæus, patient and tactful, persuaded him to look at his great system of classification. Converted, the delighted Dillenius begged him to stay forever and share his salary with him. Philip Miller, last of the herbalists, went over enthusiastically to him. The rich Clifford became his patron. Gronovius published him at his own expense.

To understand Linnæus's "Sexual System" as he called it, we have to cast an eye at the medieval confusion of the past, when a plant not found in Theophrastus's two-thousand year old description of the Greek flora might be thrown away as heretical. Classification was so superficial that all prickly plants, for instance, were lumped together —cacti and roses and thistles and even some poppies. What Linnæus did was to classify by the number of stamens and pistils, every plant as a species and assign it to a genus or clan of related species, and give it two descriptive names in the universal language of Latin. Today all this is a commonplace, the sure footing on which we rest—thanks to the boy who would not become a tailor's apprentice.

MAY TWENTY-SIXTH

WHEN once the new system of Linnæus had swept aside resistance, all Europe was ready to acknowledge him. The King of Spain offered him a princely salary and complete liberty. Clifford wanted never to part with him, and Boerhaave, the rich Dutch scholar, offered him travel in Africa and America.

But Linnæus was a young man, and a human one, and at heart a bit of a peasant. Sara Morœa was waiting for him, and like a bird that does its mating in the north, he flew back to his Sara and made her his wife. For a man of the world it was a great mistake, for the thrifty, cleanly, strapping Sara was no great lady. She thrashed her daughters, spoiled her son, urged her husband toward a lucrative practice as a physician at the cost of science, and told magnificent Gustavus Third to treat his servants better.

And there are other errors of Linnæus's judgment. To his weak boy he willed his collections and high position at Upsala, so that the vain young man attained to honors he had not earned and responsibilities he was not fitted for.

It must be admitted, too, that Linnæus's work was hasty; he was never quite a success as a zoölogist, and, owing partly to the state of knowledge at that time, he did not quite know what he was doing amongst the lower plants, the fungi, algæ, and ferns. His attempt to classify genera and species of metals is entirely untenable, and he was not the equal of Jussieu in grouping genera into natural families. But without his haste, without his lusty courage to undertake an outline of everything—hang the details!—science would have been delayed for decades. Even the faults of his character were human, natural and lovable.

MAY TWENTY-SEVENTH

At this season it used to be the custom, and I hope it still may be, for botanists everywhere to do honor to Linnæus by meeting together for a light-hearted trip afield in search of plants, in the good old style. Formidable has grown that once gentle science of botany—a thing of laboratories and test tubes, of the complex mathematics of the geneticist. For such is the way of a science. It begins in medieval wonder and magic; then a door opens to the fields, it goes forth to its Lapland, to delight and describe and classify. Next come the lens, the laboratory, the investigation of structure, the experiment with function, and at last the mechanical control of the life processes themselves. Sometimes the youngsters of today look back upon the descriptive era as dry, dilettante, unworthy of the name of science.

But more seasoned men, conscious of the history of their science, still hold the name of Linnæus in reverence. They remember that he did not foist Latin binomials on plants and animals, but pared the latinity down from some twenty words to two! To them the time of Linnæus is an age of innocence and the true beginnings of modernism. Who would not, if he could, go back today and join Linnæus and his pupils—so many of whom were to die for him at the ends of the earth—and march afield today to push the moss apart and find the little twin-flowers that he loved above all others, *Linnæa borealis?* Who would not be glad to come back with them, to the fluttering of banners and the piping of hautboys, and unslinging his heavy case of plants, stand with Thunberg and Peter Kalm and Fabricius and give the rousing *"Vivat Scientia! Vivat Linnæus!"*

MAY TWENTY-EIGHTH

TWILIGHT by the marsh, and the full throated roaring of the bull frogs, very different from the first quavering of the little tree frogs in earliest spring. A bittern somewhere, pumping, as it is usually said; to me the sound is more like a cart rattling over an old corduroy road. A sense of the passing away of spring; of the lengthening of the days to a point where the heart aches, surfeited with too much light. A feeling that all about one trees are rushing out their leaves to full maturity, the last spring flowers are bursting everywhere from spathe and scale and bud and bough, too numerous now to remember—not so sweet, so frail, so few as those first classic little blooms, bluet and harbinger-of-spring, and purple cardamine. Wild flags elegant in deep water. Little stridulations, pluckings on chitinous strings from the orthopteran insects, that remind one of summer, nay, of autumn itself. And in the trees tanagers, and black-billed cuckoos calling "scurrilous, scurrilous," in that sultry way of theirs.

Already the room of life is too full for us to sort out its occupants. Before we learned anything about them the spring beauties have vanished; I stand where I picked them in March, and cannot find them. The bloodroot lifts its little seed pods up, above its leaf now grown great and thick and waxy. Tomorrow I may not find it. Everywhere, blooming and leafing, mating and spawning; already crying and death.

MAY TWENTY-NINTH

HERE is May, gone by, and with it will go something fresh and joyful that, I suppose, will not pass this way again in all the year. Of all months it is the floweriest. Never again, in this twelvemonth, will there be so many bird voices ringing out. There is little worth while, in any month, of which May does not have at least a little share, unless you are one of those robustious souls made of objectionably more solid stuff who prefer your trees naked, your flowers snow-covered and your birds sparrowish and cheepy.

Myself, I am all for the joyful, the colored and carnival. May coaxes even the reluctant oaks to leaf, and brings back to us the very last warbler and tanager and oriole and cuckoo. It combines the first and best of the summer splendor with the innocence of the flora of April.

Now is the moment when the woods begin to fill up with golden sundrops, and the banks are winey with the odor of wild grape and honeysuckle. The country lanes are a bower of flowering brambles, arching out on their prickly canes, spilling whiteness. Now all familiar spirits give voice in the downpouring of sunlight, the song-sparrow and the goldfinch and bluebird and all such small and merry choristers.

MAY THIRTIETH

THE fireflies are now grown numerous, drifting down the still garden paths, and they go glimmering amongst the lilies that gleam softly through the night by the fencerow. Fireflies in a garden are a sight at once tranquil and merry.

But I was lost once when nightfall overtook me—lost in a tract of deep swampy woods. Little by little the birds fell silent, first the black-billed cuckoo and then even the thrush, singing to the twilight. I had lost the sound of a distant highway on which I was relying to guide me, and from thinking that I was only temporarily off the path I came very soon to realize that I had missed it completely. Then the fireflies rose from the grass and drifted about in that eery way of theirs. Their little green lights did not comfort me. They only served to make me feel that the woods had a life of their own that was indifferent to me. The little Lampyrid beetles were at home there in contrast to my homelessness. They found their way upon the trackless air, moving at leisure, gliding an instant in darkness, then easily lighting their way once more. In the enveloping night I floundered, my plant box banging at my side, a mortal thing among these elvish little people. But I caught one in my hand, and by his light I read my watch. It was not really late, only somber in the forest. Heartened, I pressed on to a clearing and escaped.

Why does the firefly have a light? I capture one in my hands and touch its little luminous stern with my finger. There is no sensation of heat; on the contrary the nerves of my fingers tell me that the little creature is cool, almost damp. It can scarcely be electric; it is rather the soft glow of radium light. Is it phosphorus? Or is it sheer magic, as it seems to be?

MAY THIRTY-FIRST

EACH evening, when the young crickets are tuning up and the thirsty grass is longing for the dew, I walk out to watch the little linkmen of the field and garden come out and dance a soundless farandole just above the earth. When the firefly's wings are closed for an instant he appears to glide in darkness, this Puck of the air, but let him turn his back and lift his wings and his tiny greenish lamp is lit.

Does he light his own way? Does he affright his foes, or spy his enemies with his lantern? Or does he signal to the women-folk of his kind? This last is the general impression which has been held—that the light enables the sexes to find each other. This were a device so handy and pleasant that it is a pity that all nocturnal animals should not possess it.

But the latest researches indicate that our native fireflies harbor certain luminous bacteria. In this case the fireflies' light is by way of being an accident almost like the flush of fever that bacteria will cause in a human being. The comparison stops there, for the fireflies are not ailing. Beetle and bacteria may well sustain a symbiotic relationship, or if it is not actually beneficial to both parties, it does the firefly no harm. The luminosity might serve to guide the sexes to each other, but we can only guess this may be so. We cannot prove it. The firefly's cold green light, then, is no genuine product of the organism itself. It is not comparable to the odors of butterflies by which the sexes orient and allure each other, but rather to the luminous fungi which happen sometimes to grow upon a tree.

JUNE FIRST

N o w this is the best of life, that a man should have children who promise fair, and a loving wife, and that he should know what his work is, and own a sense of Nature. This sense is nothing less than a feeling for reality. I do not mean the reality intended by cantankerous and disagreeable people, who are so fond of calling upon *others* to face the unpleasant. They enjoy referring to the sores and cuts of life, to the power of evil, to their own disappointments and failures and the abysmal depths to which human nature can sink.

But all these things—war and money and cruelty—are passing illusions. These are the unquenchable realities—the power of the expanding seed to break a stone, the strength that sustains men to die for others, the shortness of life that makes it so precious, all futurity hungering in us, that makes woman taste so sweet.

JUNE SECOND

A MAN need not know how to name all the oaks or the moths, or be able to recognize a synclinal fault, or tell time by the stars, in order to possess Nature. He may have his mind solely on growing larkspurs, or he may love a boat and a sail and a blue-eyed day at sea. He may have a bent for making paths or banding birds, or he may be only an inveterate and curious walker.

But I contend that such a fellow has the best out of life —he and the naturalists. You are ignorant of life if you do not love it or some portion of it, just as it is, a shaft of light from a nearby star, a flash of the blue salt water that curls around the five upthrust rocks of the continents, a net of green leaves spread to catch the light and use it, and you, walking under the trees. You, a handful of supple earth and long white stones, with seawater running in your veins.

JUNE THIRD

N o w the slow-breathing land lies listening to the summer hum, that steady outpouring of sound that is like the drone of bagpipes from over the hill. Whoever has stopped to listen carefully to the field in full sunlight, will have noticed how many very fine sounds there are, and trained ears have sorted them out for us. With a few exceptions all the sounds are produced by cicadas and the great class of insects called Orthoptera—the katydids and grasshoppers and locusts and crickets. The little mole cricket emits a soft *g-r-u* about two octaves above middle C, and has been timed up to as many as one hundred and fifty notes a minute. The fork-tailed katydid, with his soft *zeep-zeep* is usually heard only on cloudy days, while the big, common Carolina locust stridulates on bright days, emitting his steady, booming *z-z-z-z*. In contrast with such a bold sound there are lisping noises so fine that my ear can barely detect them, as it cannot detect the swift faint ticking of my own watch more than an inch or two from the ear. Some of our tiniest grasshoppers emit this music. Yet taken all together such sounds make the volume of the summer hum, and to all this is added the harsh rattle of the Orthopteran wings that snap open and shut like a fan.

JUNE FOURTH

I WAITED for them at the bottom of the hill, listening to the sounds in the hot night that had no intention of trying to sleep before the stroke of midnight. There was the distant hum and outcry of machines on the highway, which is now become, by a modern paradox, the most human of all sounds. Beneath it ran the thirsty chanting of the insects in the dried grass. And listening, I heard more birds' voices than one would suppose. There were sleepy outcries from birds I could not guess—robins and catbirds, I think—and the calling of the whippoorwill somewhere three hills and dales away. Sometimes the song sparrow or the field sparrow spoke out suddenly from sleep, as if a dream had half awakened him. Then a voice arose—not drowsily or in petulance or fear—but in a genuine song, repeated at intervals, the canticle of some bird who was accustomed to sing vespers, and was at his best then, as the thrush sings best in twilight or the nightingale by moonlight.

Presently my friends came along. I heard their laughter and it fell like broken glass on the solid darkness. The bird fell silent, and I went along with them, regretting the singer, and the moment I knew I should never forget, when I stood in the darkness by the spring, listening for the first time to some bird that was new to me.

JUNE FIFTH

I KNOW him now, my singer in the dark—the vesper spar-row. He continued his singing tonight, not only in the twilight, as the books have it, but well on toward midnight, after which, as is the way with the whippoorwill and the nightingale, he falls silent, renewing his song again along about dawn. It falls upon my ear as a something most varied, but when I listen from my bed attentively I find that it consists in a simple trill of two or three notes, yet this canticle is most flexible and has the pure sweetness of all the best singers of the sparrow family. The whole per-formance consists simply in shifting the accent and rhythm —the length that the singer holds a note, or the speed with which he trills. He further varies this by diminu-endo and crescendo, and finally, he puts different expres-sions into one phrase. The first notes are pensive, the mid-dle notes bold, the end of the musical sentence pathetic like the white-throat's closing notes.

I do not mean to overpraise the song of the vesper sparrow. It is less fine than that of the white-throat, the song-sparrow, or the field sparrow, but considering that it does not alter pitch it is a marvelous performance. And issuing as it does in darkness, it turns the wood lot into an enchanted forest.

JUNE SIXTH

THEY came very secretly, in the night, perhaps; or it may have been that for several days they had been assembling, emerging like bad, buried deeds, out of the earth. I realize now that for several days I had been seeing strange, transparent shards of insects upon the pavement, and on the steps down through the grass. But only today when the children came in, bright-eyed with excitement, and interrupting each other with a tale of enormous bugs everywhere, did I suspect of what they spoke.

I found that the cicadas were thick even upon the steps of the porch, huge, greenish and ruddy-brown heavy-bodied things with beautiful great wings, two very long forewings and a shorter hind pair, through which I could see the grass beneath as plainly as through a thin sheet of mica. I only needed to reach down and pick one up to capture him; he was so sluggish that he seemed like some sleeper awakened, dazed, after having been lost to the world for many years.

Even then, so sluggish was I myself, I did not instantly understand what an exciting discovery I had hit upon. The creature looked familiar, and yet I knew I had never seen him before. I thought of the common dog-day locust with his loud crackling sizzling song, but it was weeks before he would be due. No sound came from the creature in my hand, and I went to explore the grounds for more.

I bagged a dozen, and went into the city with them. Delightful old Dr. Howard was at his desk when I burst in. He opened the box and one of my captives crawled out upon his hand. "Why, man," he cried, "it's the seventeen-year cicada!" He seemed surprisingly pleased. "An old entomologist can never tell," he explained, "whether he will live to hear them again."

JUNE SEVENTH

D r. H o w a r d spoke of hearing the cicadas again, but up to the present not one has lifted his voice. Every account tells of the frightful uproar which they make, a din so loud that one cannot make one's self heard amongst them save by shouting. This sounds like the notorious exaggeration of old tales about the wonders of nature, and I am still waiting to be shown. Since yesterday the number of cicadas has increased to an amount beyond my power to calculate. I can now discover the insects emerging from little mud craters in the soil, almost like a crayfish's chimney. Yesterday the earth was smooth; today it is pitted with these burrows, yet I never see the burrow in process of excavation. It is always already made, and in most cases already vacated by the emerging pupa. I find them in every stage of emergence—numb pupæ, adults struggling out of their translucent amber skins, rearing up with a clawing of the legs, falling backward out of the shard, then fully emerged, and creeping about. Others show various stages of their wing growth, and today a few are essaying a feeble flight.

JUNE EIGHTH

I HEARD this day the first cry of the new cicadas, akin to the song of the common summer species, but more penetrating and heavy, and infinitely more sad and menacing. *Tshe-eee-E-E-E-E-ah-ou.* The sound is nothing like any intonation of the human voice, but more like the sound of a knife laid, at first lightly, on a grindstone, then pressed down hard while unyielding steel and flying stone are ground together—a cry that dies away suddenly to a dismal wail. As the day wore on the sounds became more frequent. Mathilda, the shiny black cook, says "Dey's Bible locus's! You kin hear dem sayin' 'Pha-rrrr-a-oh, Pha-rrr-a-oh!'"

The females must now be emerging, since the males have begun to wail, but as yet there is certainly no great din, and the children are clamorous to hear the story of Pharaoh and the locusts, heedless of my pedantic insistence that technically this is not a locust but a cicada.

JUNE NINTH

M Y neighbors have never considered my opinion on any practical subject so worth while as their own, but today the telephone has been ringing constantly concerning the cicadas, including even a communication from the editor of a metropolitan paper for which I write upon such inconsequential matters as glow-worms and stars, and I have received two delegations from the local peasantry desiring to know what harm the "locusts" will do. The conviction is general that the insects migrated here from somewhere else, as the true locusts do, and that they will not leave a stalk of corn or a leaf on a bush. Mothers have even asked if it is safe to put their babies out of doors to sleep.

There is no danger save to orchards in the neighborhood of the woods. Unfortunately we have many such—half neglected apple and cherry groves on which the forest is encroaching—and there the punctures of the females when they lay their eggs may do great harm. There is very little redress one can take against the cicadas, owing to their immense numbers, and I can only solace with the promise that the plague will vanish in a few days. I do not tell them that the real damage will take place after the flight and the singing stop. Finally I cut all interviews short, because one of the children is suddenly tucked into bed with a flaming fever.

JUNE TENTH

THE singing of the cicadas began at dawn today and continued until sundown. It seemed to frighten the little boy so sick, so terrifyingly sick in bed; he talked of them through his fever in a confused way, and to the two of us, beside the bed, the cry of "Pharaoh" rang out with a wail of fatality. There was a din across the ravine that rose even above the yells of the insects, and looking out from our promontory I could see the negroes milling about as excitedly as ants making a sortie.

I walked over to them to ask them to be quiet for the child's sake. I could hear their voices, the women's shrill and excited, and the men's deep and booming, as I climbed up through the laurel and pines to them, and when I emerged on their plateau I found them banging on pans the way they do when they want to drown the voice of a queen bee during a swarming. In their superstitious terror of the cicadas they were worked up to a pitch of emotion with which I could not cope.

The insects are flying actively now and it is harder to catch them, but with a swoop of my hat I bagged one of the males. Investigation shows how the music is made. There are two ear-like drums on each side of the abdomen. These tense, dry, wrinkled membranes are shaken by the powerful muscles at the will of the male, producing a sound that, individually, is like the snapping in and out of a pie tin, but in full grand chorus is like the roar of a machine shop.

When I reported to Mathilda the failure of my expedition to the negroes, she indignantly plumped out of the house. I don't know what she did to her people, but presently the unnecessary din was stopped. But the child still tosses restlessly in his bed.

88

JUNE ELEVENTH

I SHALL never forget this day as long as I live. The tiny boy is safe, they say tonight. But all during the day the battle stood in the balance, and my heart was clutched till it was a small stone that weighed like steel. My tongue is still curled up tensely, though the nurse has drawn a red downward line of victory on the fever chart under the lamp just outside the baby's room.

The cicadas have ceased their singing with sundown, though tonight they woke up, once, like a renewal of my terrors, and wailed that their power was not yet broken. But even in the night silence the terrible sound of ten thousand knives shearing across ten thousand grindstones still rings in my head. I feel as though I would hear it forever, and forever remember when I stood by the window, waiting to hear what the thermometer would tell, certain that all joy is an elf gift and hope a treachery.

JUNE TWELFTH

N oth in g has done me more good than to hear that the cicadas have all got a plague. The newspapers are carrying stories about it. A blue-green mold which is always more or less present on the summer cicada has attacked the seventeen-year variety with terrific vehemence, and mycolo-gists and entomologists alike are excited about it. Apparently the fungus does not kill more than a fraction of the dog-day cicadas, who have probably built up a certain resistance to it. The periodical cicadas, emerging in tremendous numbers, comparable to overcrowding in our city slums, are seized upon by the disease and their vitals swiftly eaten out. Spores for spreading the malady push out from the corpses and sow the air with death to others.

So, though the cicadas emerge by the billions of billions in fourteen different states, a check upon them is always waiting. I have found several cicadas being carried off by predatory wasps, and the woods about the house are suddenly alive with woodpeckers, chewinks, orioles, flickers, sparrows, grackles and robins, fattening on the winged harvest.

JUNE THIRTEENTH

THERE is no diminution yet in the uproar, but my lightened heart gives me grace to take some interest in the biology of the creatures. The period of seventeen years is varied, in the southern states, to thirteen years, and the recurrence of the adults is further made irregular by the fact that there are more than a score of broods in different parts of the country, each having its own years for the rhythmic emergence, or, as we might say, starting off on a different beat, though all keeping the same rhythm. In some areas several broods overlap, so that the cicada years occur oftener than every seventeen years. Some of the broods occupy immense areas, but others are more restricted and feeble.

No other insect in the world has such a long life as this, nor a life history so disproportionate. To be sure, the summer cicada spends a year underground and another of life above it, but as there are two broods, we always have the common cicada with us. But the periodical cicada spends seventeen years as grub, and sometimes no better than seventeen days as a free creature of the sunlight and air.

The fate of the insect seems miserable enough to us, but in fact the strange life history is distinctly advantageous to the creature itself. Its seventeen years underground do not represent prison to the cicada, but comfort and safety, such as a mole or an earthworm knows. It is only when this animal, which we must regard as a naturally subterranean species, takes the dangerous step of emerging into the air that it has any reason to sorrow. For, as so often happens, the moment of sexual maturity is also the moment of predestined death. Nature flings the sexes at each other and then, having no more use for them, she draws her sword and slays them.

JUNE FOURTEENTH

THERE is no breeze today except the wind of rumor that perpetually blows through the cottonwoods, and it would be a mystery where they find it in this heavy atmosphere unless one examined their leaf-stalks with an attentive eye. For these are flattened and where the heart-shaped blade joins to the petiole it is as free, almost, to swing as if suspended on a pivot. The merest whisper of a breeze suffices to set the leaves twirling, to rustling and talking.

The wise of the earth assure us that all poplars, like the willows, are trivial trees, short of life, weak of stem, prey to more ills than mortal man. These things are so, and we are bidden only to admire the oak and pine, that outlive the centuries, that grow in surety and have the sterner virtues. But is there no room in the forest for the poplar, with its restless, talkative foliage? The strong and silent folk of earth—I would rather praise them than live with them. I have never grumbled at a chatterbox, providing that her tongue was kind.

JUNE FIFTEENTH

THERE was a noticeable diminution in the cicada chorus today. The couples have almost all done with their great, crass, mass mating, (and anything more incredible and flat than the way they go about it cannot be imagined,) and Nature is now prepared to let the males all go to the devil, and die by bird and wasp and mold. In any case they would probably starve to death, for only the females seem to partake of any food. The males did all the singing, but aside from that they were the most arrant drones. Nature still has a bit of use for the women folk and will not kill them till they have fulfilled their gross maternity.

How multiplex, how inhuman in its last detail, is the world of the insect! Fabre found my beloved Orthopterans, the locusts and grasshoppers, and crickets, particularly horrifying, but to me the Hemiptera, to which the cicadas belong, are the monsters of the insect world.

JUNE SIXTEENTH

O UT S I D E my window for many days now there has been a warbler that I haven't identified, who sings a little refrain that it is difficult to put into words. Perhaps he says: *Swiss sweets! Yes, see the sweets, sir. Sweet tibee!* Sometimes he speaks in Latin. He lisps: *Sui, sui, tibi, tibi.* And again he gives the unkind, Solomonic advice to: *Switch Mary! Yes sir-ree sir, switch sweet missie.*

These songs, like those of so many warblers, are not melodies, but the lisping of leaves, the whistle of a little wind through the meadow grass, the sibilant expression of a June day, and nothing less elusive.

I am not perfectly certain that I want to be able to identify all the warblers. There is a charm sometimes in not knowing what or who the singer is. Just so, when a mysterious bell rings softly through the airs, on irregular days, I am always afraid that some one will tell me that the sound comes from the Dunkers' Chapel at Higgins's Corners. As long as I do not know, my bell may be the *cloche* that tolls at the bottom of the Lake of Annecy, and my bird may be a bulbul.

JUNE SEVENTEENTH

THE moon rose tonight at the full, and from its half of all the skies it scatters away the stars; only the stabbing shafts of blue Vega pierce through the fields of lunar radiance. The fainter stars are all put out and heaven for once looks like the pictures in the star maps, with the constellations bared to the bone. It would be a moment for learning them as they are supposed to (and do not) look. But one peek at the moon even through the cheapest of lenses, is worth twenty Lions and Virgins and Scorpions. That tombstone world! Those snowless alps and frozen lava seas! The sense of its actual bulk, its spherical ponderability, when I first saw them through a telescope, were revolutionary to my feeling for all objects in heaven, and though I could not see it move, I felt the swing of it in my bones, as of a great cold ball hurled round upon an invisible leash by the earth's giant arm.

Not long ago the light from the moon was focused in a lens of a special telescope at Staradale University in Czechoslovakia and transferred to a photo-electric cell. Translated into sound, these waves were broadcast to London, and by report the noise was as the tolling of great bells deprived of resonance! Perfect symbol for a world that is dead. When Vega was heard, it was as the high pitched shouting of an angry crowd, but very far away; Vega, one hundred times the size of our sun, Vega, that incandescent blue giant, only twenty-six light years away, spoke to us with the voice of mass menace.

So after all there is music in the spheres, and though it is true that only light translated into sound may be heard, the sounds given out by an explosion or a nightingale are also but energy converted into waves that reach us through the ear.

JUNE EIGHTEENTH

EVEN more suddenly than it came, the din of the cicadas has ceased. And what is stranger still, I cannot find even the dead males, who ought to be lying about like paynims and Franks on the field of Roncesvalles. The females are still here, but it took an hour of looking to find one, who was trying to oviposit in a chink of cement! According to the best authorities the female makes a series of punctures, generally on the under side of a twig, about half an inch in length, and in them she lays down a row of eggs. Without moving, she then makes another row of punctures, and then moves up toward the tip of the twig, making another double row. Every sort of plant, except conifers, may be called on to suffer these stabs. Now is when the insect does its damage to forest trees and orchards. Even so the incredible story is not over, but, unseen by most people, the eggs hatch out, when mites do not devour them, and the larvæ crawl down and burrow deep in the ground. There, at last, they are free from their enemies, and they enter upon the seventeen-year torpor that is their real and normal life, that existence in a state of nothingness for which all that hubbub and horror and coupling was intended.

It was all a great entomological experience, and Fabre would have been transported with excitement had he been here. But, if it please, I hope I shall never again have to hear the periodical cicada, who exulted while my child battled with death, and will forever remind me how little the earth is made for me, and how terrible is life, terrible as an army with banners.

JUNE NINETEENTH

Now in the burning sunny fields, white with yarrow and bending Queen Anne's lace, the little field sparrow spills out his song—the most tumbled, ecstatic rapture of the year. Beginning slowly and with intent to deceive you into believing that he has nothing much to say, he surprises you with the piercing brilliance of his powers. *Weet...weet... weet, wat, wt, wt, wt, trrrrrrreeeeeeee!*—it sounds like a thin pure brook filling up a small jug, first the fat little belly of it, and then the tapered neck, until suddenly the whole sparkling, joyful, irrepressible liquid is overflowing with a laugh.

JUNE TWENTIETH

LISTENING in the woods at twilight to the twirling notes of the wood thrush, I was happy in the thought that as long as he sings at sunset the deadest season of summer is not yet upon the airs. Something of spring will linger while he comes forth in the cool of the day to spin a bit of magic for the weary. Cool, cool, and tranquil, he drops his notes into the evening, distilling peace.

One can never hear the thrush without feeling an intense sense of solitude. Whitman has made this feeling immortal; but it comes to us all, long before we are old enough to read Whitman. I once, in my childhood, knew genuine solitude when I dwelt alone with my mother on a mountain top for seven months. I had nothing to read but *Alice in Wonderland* and Keats, no one to play with except a tongue-tied girl who walked a barefoot two miles to join me, and knew no games save hunting in the brook for quartz, and building houses of pine cones.

When the burning day was over, we walked out together, carrying long sticks, with only the still, still woods and the rushing of the many brooks for company. Then it was that the thrush spoke to us out of the depths of the woods, a song inimitable by human syllables, but with the ring in it of old silver lightly dropped. Day after day he called, his song so clear that it carried for a mile, and no matter how distant, it always seemed near to us, intentionally delivered for our delight. And, solitary singer that he was, his very song reminded how still was all else in Nature, how intensely he and we were alone together.

JUNE 21 — JULY 21

JUNE TWENTY-FIRST

ON this day, on which I have such good reason to be grateful to my mother, I may perhaps be permitted to put down the profession of one naturalist's faith. Whatever rudiments of religion are innate in me are what ordinarily pass as pantheism, though I am not really prepared to worship everything. I could take oaks as seriously as a druid, but I draw the line at any Hindu idolatry of animals, so that I am not exactly an animist. On this, the summer solstice, I would enjoy lighting bonfires to the sun; I have ever loved the morning best. I could easily find it in me to worship some madonna or any symbol of woman and child, but I do not like symbols as well as I like the thing itself.

A man's real religion is that about which he becomes excited, the object or the cause he will defend, the point at which, spontaneously, he cries out in joy over a victory, or groans aloud from an injury. In France I once startled my wife by bursting into the house with a loud cry of joy. She hastened downstairs to learn what good fortune had befallen us in our old farmhouse above the Lake of Annecy. It was only that fresh snow had fallen on the Alps and sheeted their heads in pure glittering hoods. They looked to me like gods, standing just behind our house. If they were not gods to her, that is because her religion is several degrees less icy and remote. That morning happened to be memorable in the history of science because it was the day on which the discovery of a new planet was announced. This too wrung a cheer from me, and to the joy of my little son and with the tender indulgence of my wife, I declared a holiday, with a trip by steamer around the turquoise lake.

JUNE TWENTY-SECOND

A W A Y to make order, and the assurance order brings, in the natural world, is to get the trick of thinking in terms of families. No great experience is necessary for this; with a very little practice one becomes intuitional about it. My children easily grasp the notion.

The mints have irregular two-lipped flowers, square stems, and opposite leaves, and almost invariably they are aromatic, as neat and discrete and natural and delightful a family as one could want. You can tell an aroid in an instant by its enveloping leaf, and its curious spike; Jack-in-the-pulpit typifies it to perfection; almost any aroid has a stinging taste upon the tongue, as characteristic as the fresh camphoric odor of mint, and, if it does not smell sweet, it will usually smell vile. The crucifers, too—the mustards, cresses, turnips, horseradishes—make a perfectly natural group, with their four cross-like petals, their six stamens and lightly smarting taste. Through some families poison runs, as in the umbellifers, with their celery-like leaves and leaf-stalks, their umbrella-shaped flower clusters; from water hemlock drank Socrates and Hannibal. Innocent open floweriness, winy fruitiness are the marks—besides the five petals, the many stamens and pistils and the thorns—of the rose family, with its brambles and hawthorns and apples.

Thinking in this fashion is loose and general, but it is not unscientific. Every naturalist avails himself continually of family earmarks that are as distinctive as the Hapsburg jaw. It must not be understood by those who are not habituated to natural classification, that a plant or animal family corresponds in rank or grade to a human clan; the genus does that. The family is more nearly analogous to nationality—where that is coextensive with a homogeneous race as, let us say, in Iceland.

JUNE TWENTY-THIRD

S o m e of the families of flowers are hazy of outline, their members externally dissimilar, and the number of them alone makes the beginning of knowledge sufficiently bristly. The same is not true of the birds. One will not readily encounter even thirty families of land birds; if you live on the ocean or in tropical Florida, the number will increase. Ten common species is a large family, at least in this part of the world. The only alarming one of the lot is the warblers, but few small areas will have fifty; of common warblers twenty is the worst one can expect. The finches or sparrows run rather high, but there are no other large families amongst the song birds. One has usually become a bit of an expert before he tackles the ducks, the hawks, the herons, rails and gulls.

Most of the bird families are simply a delight and a joy to learn. Hereabouts the five little wrens, the six airy and sociable swallows, the ten merry blackbirds (of the New World), the seven busy woodpeckers, and the four bold robbers of the crow family, for instance, make charming little groups for study. I have but to mention them and any one will realize how distinctly they are discrete groups with characteristics we have grown up knowing. The actual lines on which the zoölogist draws up family descriptions are quite beyond the beginner; they are based upon a microscopic study of the skeletons. The amateur simply has to acquaint himself with the superficial, and fortunately very easy, outward "look" of a family, its characteristic voice or flight or even its mere behavior. By assigning one's self a group to master, order swiftly comes out of confusion, and one tastes the delights, supposed to be reserved for the most exalted scientists, of being a specialist.

JUNE TWENTY-FOURTH

I F I were going to make a specialty of one family of birds I would certainly begin with the swallows. There are more kinds in the western states, but the very compactness of the group hereabouts makes it accessible and attractive. The identification of the swallows consequently presents practically no difficulties. The barn swallow is steel blue, with a glowing cinnamon-rusty breast and paler underparts; the cliff swallow is similar, but with a whitish patch on his forehead, the tail not deeply forked, and the throat and rump brownish. The tree swallows are known at once by the whitish throat and underparts, and since you almost always see them from below, as they flit in little eddies like leaves, you seldom get a good look at their greenish caps and backs, for against the sun these seem black. The bank swallow is even more modest in garb: white below and grayish above, while the rough-winged is grayish on throat and breast too. There is left for a speaking acquaintance only the purple martins which are steely blue with purple highlights throughout.

Thus easily may one master this little group, which has in common certain family characteristics. Such is the tendency either to nest in holes in the earth, or to make an earthen nest affixed to some vertical support. All swallows are swift and glancing of flight; many of them are highly social birds, dwelling in swallow towns or great rookeries, like the martins, and one and all they live upon insect fare, and so far as I know, upon nothing else.

But the name of a bird is nothing but the opening of a door to knowledge; it is not knowledge in itself, and the pleasures of study consist in making one's self a Sherlock Holmes, intent upon every trace and detail of one's subject's life.

JUNE TWENTY-FIFTH

I NEVER supposed that any place could have too many swallows in it. And watching the light, the free, the deathless ease of our barn swallows, pursuing, wing on edge, the insects in the quiet sky, I cannot believe it even now. But there was a day I spent once on the island of Ste. Marguerite, off the coast of Cannes, that was so beleaguered by swallows that there was no peace to be had in it.

There are two islands there; the littler, and farther out to sea, is a spot of absolute tranquillity, where since the fourth century a monastery has stood. But on the island facing toward the land, the land breeze blows, and brings with it not the odor of the sea, and pine and myrtle, but the dusty smell of earthy things. Here stands no house of chastity and quiet thought, but a prison with triple barred windows, past which the complaining swallows wheel till the head swims. Here, in the court yard, the splash of the whip was heard. Now cobwebs hang upon the bars, and grass grows between the cobbles around the old flint barracks. Forever and forever the swallows wheel and cry, starting out on some important chase with cries not of joy, but of greed and anger. And soon, in despair, they whirl back like some eddy of dust and papers to the spot from which they were lifted on a futile gust. If I had been a prisoner there, like the Man in the Iron Mask, it would have been the swallows which broke my heart or cracked my reason.

JUNE TWENTY-SIXTH

As long as one knows little of Nature save that which impinges upon one sensually, one is subject to the moods it throws, like a shadow, across the spirit. But as soon as one begins to search for knowledge in the thing that dims the light, the power of mood fades. A biologist confined to the prison isle of Ste. Marguerite would soon set up some equipment or technique for studying the swallows—the pulsation of their crowding population, the control of their behavior, their effect upon the rest of the animal life of the island, or something else from which significant conclusions could be drawn.

I accept the challenge of the artists that cool investigation may often be the death of poetry. As knowledge lessens the terror of plague, so it may take some of the soulfulness out of nature. There is a sort of Wordsworthian sermonizing that shrinks before the biological frame of mind, just as the childish abhorrence of insects vanishes with familiarity. But not all poetry is really good poetry (however good it may sound). Good poetry is swift-winged, essential and truthful description—and so is good science.

JUNE TWENTY-SEVENTH

By the time noon came I found myself far beyond the periphery of my usual explorations, over increasingly sandy or muddy roads, down through villages increasingly sleepy and tidewater. I had the exhilarating sense of traveling abroad near home; the vegetation was subtly changing, growing austral, with holly and magnolia and post oak, and deep marshy bays where the lotus stood ethereal and stately above the blue pickerel weed flowers.

At last I found the bank where a tributary to the big river once cut its way through a high deposit of indurated sand; the stream has now sunk considerably below this bank, but still its proximity is perfect for the holes of bank swallows, kingfishers, and the curious burrowing bees, and great colonies of the gregarious sand bank beetle, Stenus.

I was too late to see the birds actually burrowing with their awl-like bills and their sharp little claws, and possibly all the work on the colony was carried on years ago. The bank is pitted so closely in many places with openings not two inches apart, that it seems unlikely that there could be much need now to enlarge the city of these little birds. As they passed back and forth in front of the cliffs, perpetually twittering till the whole sound rose to a loud hum, weaving in and out, seeking their own private doors—or perhaps any door will do—they gave the sensation, in part, of a swarming of bees. Yet the bank reminded me, too, of some oceanic bird rock, and presently, tempted beyond myself, I began to try to scale the cliffs, but I fell down in a shower of sand, as clumsy as a beetle—clumsier far than the Stenus beetles.

JUNE TWENTY-EIGHTH

FROM some of the few burrows in the sand cliff which I was able to reach before I fell, I popped into a match-box, having nothing handier, some curious beetles which were not Stenus. I went home with my head full of the wheeling and wheedling of the little gray swallows, the rattle and swoop of the kingfishers, the flashing of the bees. This vertical little world in itself seems to have the odd faculty of permitting only gregarious beasts to dwell there.

I forgot my beetles until this morning, when intending to light my pipe, I opened the match box and the strange little fellows rushed out upon my hand. All escaped but one, and, no coleopterist, I could not even recognize the family to which he belonged. Though an adult, he ran about like a larva or triungulin, a reddish brown fellow, about three quarters of an inch long, and wingless! Even the elytra or wing covers by which one knows a beetle were rudimentary.

It is ten to one, when you see a wingless insect, that it is a parasite, and so, at last, I found this blister beetle (Hornia) of the family of Cantharides, to be. His larvæ or triungulins lurk in the flowers that the solitary bees, Anthophora, visit for pollen and honey, and fastening themselves to the bees, they are carried back to their burrows where they live as robbers. Significant that the conditions of intense social life, city life, should favor parasitism! The swallows are tormented by bird-lice, the burrowing bees by my Hornia, and, I learn, other blister beetles and even by parasitic bees!

JUNE TWENTY-NINTH

THE merest beginning upon a little specializing in the swallows led me to the sandbank, to the burrowing bees and their beetle guests, and has sent my thoughts straying upon the biology of the social habit, to which life in a cliff seems to give rise. After all, our own ancestors, were cliff dwellers. From there I have strayed in my musings to the nature of parisitism, as it is exhibited by the Hornia beetles, as well as, I learn, several other members of the same family. One may object that all this is reprehensibly diffuse. I should concentrate upon swallows, and not leave them for blister beetles until I know all about the birds.

But the purpose of studying Nature at all, aside from the distraction which it affords, (and it is in the nature of distraction not to dwell on anything to the point of tedium) is that the study should illuminate the relation of living things to each other, to us, to the environment. One thing *should* lead to something quite other. Complexity is the keynote of biology—a fact which those who have been trained first in the exact or physical sciences can never seem to grasp. The goal of biological thought is ramification, many-viewpointedness, and a man who drops his swallows uncompleted because he has suddenly grown excited over beetles is simply a man who is growing.

JUNE THIRTIETH

As a child I did not dream that our meadowlarks were not the skylarks of the poets in whose books my elder sister read. Lord Fairfax, as he sailed up the Rappahannock, released the English skylarks into the hostile New World. There is recurrent a legend around Fredericksburg that skylarks still persist. The skylark has accidentally reached Bermuda, and was once introduced around New York, but has unfortunately failed to establish itself as the domestic sparrow and starling have done. Apparently it is necessary to have some objectionable features in order to get on in this world.

Our only real larks are the horned larks that sometimes come to us in winter. But to what a merry family do our meadowlarks belong, that numbers within its fold the orioles, the grackles, the bobolinks and redwinged blackbirds, a wholly New World family, of which every member known to me has black in the plumage, just enough of it to be smart and jaunty, combined as it is with orange and yellow, and, in the case of the grackles, with green and purple highlights.

At this moment the meadowlarks whistle good-by to June; *ss-wheee-tu-yu*, they call across the meadow where abandoned old apple trunks, orchard grass and Queen Anne's lace all lean one way. Their voices call from the north, and, like an echo, against the hills from the south, but ever out of sight, until the whole blue basin of heaven is ringing with their cries. Though the song bubbles upward from the grass, it sounds as though it fell from the faultless blue of the sky.

JULY FIRST

T H E bobolink is the only bird who never seems to know how to put a period to his musical sentence. All other Aves have a note, three notes, even a phrase that they utter; no matter how many times they may reiterate it, that is all they have to say. But I hear the bobolinks now in the orchard grass, spilling out a torrent of song. When we listen expecting soon to hear silence, he still has more to tell, and with an irrepressible invention he continues as if joy had no end in the telling, until perforce a smile spreads over our furrows and frowns, and we say, "Well, well, *well*, little fellow, is the world really as fine as all that?"

JULY SECOND

O N T H I S day in Geneva was born François Huber, in 1750, whose father distinguished himself not only as a soldier and a member of the great coterie at Ferney, but as an authority on the flight of birds. François was only fifteen years old when he began to lose his sight, the most crushing blow which could befall one who had decided to devote himself to the study of ants. Total blindness finally fell upon him, but desperate handicaps are often the spur to triumph. With the aid of his wife, Marie Aimée Lullin, and his faithful servant François Burnens, who were his eyes for him, he continued his investigations, and laid down the very foundation stone of our scientific knowledge both of ants and honey bees. True, Réaumur had preceded him, but as it happened, Réaumur's work on ants was not published until modern times; it lay in a drawer, forgotten, so that it is from Huber that the great line of ant students stems— his son Pierre Huber, Auguste Forel, C. Emery, Sir John Lubbock, and William Morton Wheeler.

None of us could say that he would have liked to share the fate of François Huber, but there are few of us who would not have been proud to ride into immortality as did his servant or his faithful mate, to be remembered among those who, like the Cyrenian on the first Good Friday, served a great man in his hour of darkness.

JULY THIRD

I T W A S Huber, on a memorable summer day in 1804, who first discovered that some species of ants make slaves of others. But he made only a beginning in this study, and oddly enough it was another Swiss who was destined to carry the subject on. Auguste Forel was only seven years old when he observed one day that an army of big red ants with black bellies was fighting with a colony of black ants with which the child had long felt on terms of special friendliness. The boy tried to come to the aid of his friends, but the enemy were too many for him. The invaders were carrying off the little white eggs of the ants he liked. His mother took him off for a walk, so that when he returned he found, to his grief, all his black friends were dead.

The following year he was able to observe something still more astonishing. In the nest of the red-and-black ants he discovered many of his old black friends, living in a state of peaceful industry. He began to understand that the black ants were slaves, born in captivity.

When he was ten years old he was given a copy of Huber, and was enchanted to find his theory confirmed. But discovering that he already knew several things that were not found in Huber, he determined from that moment to become the historian of the ants, and, as I pen these words, he is still alive, Nestor of formicologists.

JULY FOURTH

LITTLE Auguste Forel's black friends were the common slave ants, *Formica fusca*. Of a fine warm morning you can, almost anywhere, find quantities of them, running actively on their long legs, in the woods, in suburban gardens, even on city sidewalks. They can be told at once by their long legs, rapid gait, large black body, with satiny sheen on the abdomen. The rest of the creature is dull and ashy, as if he had just fallen in the dust.

Every species of ant has its racial characteristics. This one seems to me to be the negro of ants, and not alone from the circumstance that he is all black, but because he is the commonest victim of slavery, and seems especially susceptible to a submissive estate. He is easily impressed by the superior organization or the menacing tactics of his raiders and drivers, and, as I know him, he is relatively lazy or at least disorganized, random, feckless and witless when free in the bush, while for his masters he will work faithfully. I found the variety and the particular colony I studied longest to be superstitiously afraid of the dark. It popped underground at sundown, and was never caught in my kitchen at night, as other species were. But under a broiling subtropical sun at midday its energy was only accelerated.

I found the black ant continually engaged in trying to make petty thefts from the sweet-stocked nests of the golden miners and harvesters of the genus Pheidole. These were not the concerted attacks which highly organized species make on stores of sweets, for the black ants are incapable of doing anything in a concerted way while under their own government. These were single and sneaking attempts to pilfer, like those of the traditional dark thief of the watermelon patch.

JULY FIFTH

W H E N a single slave ant is introduced into the nests of
its masters, even loaned only for an hour or a day, it will
still make shift to serve the entire colony of its natural
overlords. Observation has shown that it will form earth
chambers, extricate young ants from difficulties, gather the
larvæ up and move them up and down as the temperature
and ultraviolet light of the hour demand, clean the entire
city of excrement, and find food for its adult masters as
well as the larvæ.

Our common slave maker, *Formica sanguinea,* is a powerful clan of which the slaves might well be afraid. But there
are some slave makers who are quite incapable or unwilling
to feed themselves unless served by their slaves. They will
starve to death rather than wait on themselves. Aristocracy
could scarcely be pushed farther. In some species the masters have become so enfeebled by long habituation to
slavery, that they are too weak even to make slave raids,
and it is a mystery how they impose themselves upon their
subject race. In some cases they do not even appear to
bring up their slaves from captivity as larvæ, but to succeed, though practically without warriors themselves, in im-
pressing their majesty upon adult slaves. In many instances
slave ants will go out and raid their own species for larvæ
in order to add to the wealth and puissance of their utterly
effete masters.

One may explain these circumstances as due to the natural instinct of ants to collect and nourish larvæ of their
own kind, just as women will not see even an enemy's baby
neglected or un-nursed. Still, first and last, there are some
startling perversions of instinct here, both in slave and in
master. One of these days this sluggard must go to the ant
again.

JULY SIXTH

On this day, in 1766, at Paisley, in Scotland, was born Alexander Wilson, the first great ornithologist of America, the rival of Audubon, scientist where Audubon was artist, luckless in love where Audubon was happy, retiring as an owl where Audubon was gay as a mockingbird, short-lived where Audubon lived long and reaped honors.

Wilson was bound out as a child to weavers, because as a herdboy he was too intent upon watching the birds. In the long years of slavery, humped like a crane over his loom, the iron entered into his soul. Wilson was ever a bitter man, where the world was concerned, but tender to the very few who were ever tender with him. Fleeing the loom room, he became a peddler, who sold stuffs and ribbons and laces for ladies, with ballads of his own composing. In Scottish vernacular, his ballads are often sincere, honest, fresh and genuine. But when he was forced to return to weaving, his libellous lampoons against the master weavers brought him a short prison term, and the humiliation of having to burn his shafts in public.

This was the turn of events which brought him to America, and tramping from Newcastle to Philadelphia he shot and examined his first American bird, a red-headed woodpecker, the most beautiful bird, as he said, that he had ever seen. Weaver, journeyman printer, and schoolmaster, he eked out his first American years amongst Pennsylvania Germans, rutabagas, hymn-howling Presbyterians, as he called them, and general penury.

His first encouragement came from William Bartram, with whose sister he fell vainly in love; Dr. Benjamin Barton, Bachman, Bonaparte, and George Ord, who made up the Athens of science for which Philadelphia then passed, aided him, and bit by bit, from this narrow, bitter breast where a poet had stifled, a great scientist was born.

JULY SEVENTH

It was to an America still partly wilderness, fresh with adventure, that the weary and driven little Scotsman came. You could expect in our woods then an ivory-billed woodpecker, the largest of all its tribe, a creature known to me only as a perfectly incredible specimen in museums. It has a glossy black body almost two feet long, a head crested with scarlet, and a great bill, ivory white. Once widespread in America, it is now all but extinct.

Not so in Wilson's time. He easily captured a specimen in the cypress swamps near Wilmington, North Carolina, and was conveying it, imprisoned under a blanket, in a large basket, to an inn, when it suddenly burst into the most ear-splitting and dismal sounds, like the voice of a baby in agony. Several women on the porch of the inn cast dark looks on the poor little man, as though he had been a kidnaper or an ogre. Marching proudly by them, Wilson conveyed the bird to his room to paint it. But it abruptly left off sitting for its portrait, and violently attacked Wilson about the face with the bill that is made to split oak. Fleeing the room, Wilson after an hour returned to hear the sound as of twenty wood choppers at work. He threw open the door, and discovered that his tropical carpenter had battered his way through the inner wall, and at that moment was engaged in enlarging an opening in the clapboards outside wide enough to admit his scarlet-crested head. Restrained in this, the proud spirited fowl moped and died, leaving Wilson his ivory bill and the innkeeper's bill for repairs.

JULY EIGHTH

WILSON proposed to become the biographer of all the birds of America. Governor Tompkins of New York told him that so far from paying $120 for a book about birds he would not give a hundred for all the birds in the country, if he had 'em alive! In Charleston Wilson wandered the streets looking for houses that would suggest that their owners might be persons of enough wealth and cultivation to subscribe to his book.

Up to his time nothing appreciable on American birds existed in writing, except some lists drawn up by Jefferson, Barton and Bartram, and some descriptions by Mark Catesby. When Wilson's volume containing the biographies of the hummingbird, catbird, mockingbird and kingbird appeared, he was—startling as it now seems—telling the world of science the first it had heard of them. If Wilson was no artist, if he lacked Audubon's power of dramatizing and englamoring each encounter with a new species, the little schoolmaster ("who didn't whip enough," as the parents complained) was at least a peerless observer, cautious, exact, conscientious, methodical—virtues, every one of them, which Audubon exhibited only exceptionally. Nature had not endowed him with the brush of an Audubon, yet he made a draughtsman of himself by dint of perseverance.

Whenever I hear the sweet, swinging *vree-hu, vree-heee* of the veery, called Wilson's thrush, I think of the lonely little weaver, the first bird lover to penetrate the desolate swamps, with only a little parrot on his shoulder for company.

JULY NINTH

A CREATURE that will let an enemy impose upon it is inevitably doomed to slavery, but oddly enough, not to extinction! On the contrary, it seems to be the masters who are likely to become extinct. True, our slavemaker ant shows none of the degenerative signs of a parasitic mode of living, but what of the more effete races? Several of them are among the rarest of ants, and it is easy to see why. The extent to which their sheer existence is limited by the chance that they will succeed in perverting or terrifying slaves into serving them, can mean nothing but gradual attenuation of their race. Just so the orchids, dependent, root and flower and seed, upon a complex series of symbiotic relationships, are individually rare, however much variety they may show.

Why some ants are willing slaves is then less difficult to understand than how the slave-drivers got into the slave making habit. It may have begun as a simple case of head-hunting. The predatory race often eats most of the captured larvæ. A few left untouched may have emerged, and mechanically begun their rounds, serving their masters since they could not serve their own kind.

JULY TENTH

Returning for study this morning to the principal nest of the black ant which my garden boasts, I observed a sharp miniature tussle going on by my feet and bent down to watch it. A very small brown spider seemed to be struggling under the power of a large black slave ant. I used my pencil-tip to pry them apart. The slave ant at once dashed for her nest, distant about one foot, and was actually on its crater when the spider overtook it. Half a dozen sentinel ants were patrolling the top of the nest, or engaged in work upon its ramparts. But from right under their eyes and noses—or, I should say—within touch of their feelers, they allowed their comrade to be borne away by an enemy without making a move to come to her aid. Yet when I passed my hand several inches over their nest they lifted up their jaws and flexed them menacingly.

The jumping spider would seem not to be on their list of enemies, though I was! In any case, all idea that these ants naturally come to each other's aid was disproved by this occurrence. They either could not see, hear nor smell the enemy, or if they did, they were quite unable to have the slightest action-directing thought concerning the tragedy that took place before them.

Nobody would have any justification in assuming, from this incident, that other kinds of ants would have acted in the same way. The races of ants differ more in their psychology and mechanism than the races of mammals—whales, rats, elephants, foxes and moles.

JULY ELEVENTH

THE recognition between individual ants is not, apparently, really individual, but of the nest only. It is not based on any sort of high-sign, since anesthetized ants are readily recognized by their sisters. Presumably its source is smell; it might take the form of sound in some cases, but the most excited ant who has just discovered a store of honey cannot make itself heard an inch away. It must get at its fellows to communicate its intelligence.

I am more and more convinced that the ant colony is not so much composed of separate individuals as that the colony is a sort of individual, and each ant like a loose cell in it. Our own blood stream, for instance, contains hosts of white corpuscles which differ little from free-swimming amœbæ. When bacteria invade the blood stream, the white corpuscles, like the ants defending the nest, are drawn mechanically to the infected spot, and will die defending the human cell colony.

I admit that the comparison is imperfect, but the attempt to liken the individual human warrior to the individual ant in battle is even more inaccurate and misleading. The colony of ants with its component numbers stands half way, as a mechanical, intuitive and psychical phenomenon, between our bodies as a collection of cells with separate functions and our armies made up of obedient privates. Until one learns both to deny real individual initiative to the single ant, and at the same time to divorce one's mind from the persuasion that the colony has a headquarters which directs activity (any more than we direct the activities of our white corpuscles) one can make nothing but pretty fallacies out of the polity of the ant heap.

JULY TWELFTH

O N T H I S day, at Concord, in 1817, was born Henry David Thoreau, the father of all American nature writers, the recluse of Walden pond, who boasted that he had traveled widely—around Concord. It is famous that he went out in the woods with nothing but his carpenter's tools, to support himself in the wild, and that he succeeded admirably, so far as the practical details were concerned. It is less well known that he gave it up after a time, saying that he would not recommend the course to any one who did not have a large fund of sunshine in himself. His hut was built on Emerson's land, in 1845. There was no lock on the door, and no curtain at the window. He needed these things as little as the animal needs them. Like the animal, he had little sense of communal responsibility. He refused to pay taxes because he did not believe in government, especially not a government which tolerated slavery. For this even Concord was obliged to see him in jail for a time.

Said Sanborn of him, "He is a little undersize, with a huge Emersonian nose, bluish gray eyes, brown hair, and a ruddy, weatherbeaten face which reminds one of some shrewd, honest animal's—some retired philosophical woodchuck or magnanimous fox." His portrait reminds me more of a combination of Lincoln and some Marblehead sea-captain of the time.

His days were passed in pencil-making, surveying, and carpentering, but these were not the matters which occupied his mind. He was one of those who "saw beauty in ashes." He believed that "every man will be a poet if he can" and if not, then a "man of science." Thoreau was a poet.

JULY THIRTEENTH

THOREAU in his generation, and Burroughs in the next, were the poets of Nature who brought us all closest to the purely natural way of thinking, the faith not so much in the ways of the wild as in what is nature in a man's self. Of the two I will take Thoreau any day; the difference is that between master and disciple. Burroughs had the art of popularizing himself. Thoreau is knotty, tough, difficult of access, solid grain from root to twig, that no dull hatchet can split. Like Sophocles and Christ, he stings complacency into discomfort, he prods us awake, and cherishes his doubts. The poem called "Conscience" is guaranteed to deal a slap on some very right reverend cheeks, in any age.

As a naturalist he discovered nothing new, I grant you; but he knew (as many men of the past and today, who have turned up fresh facts by the dozen, do not), what to make of what he saw. Fact finding is machine work. Unless the machine has a head there is little excuse for it. Had Thoreau but come under the influence of Darwin and Agassiz as he was under that of Pindar and Anacreon, he might have made an incomparable scientist.

Though we can all pronounce his name reverently, and read him with a steady and gentle glow of pleasure, his view of the natural world will not answer to our needs today. He has no sense of problem. But if he had known what we know—space expanding, elements no longer elemental, life a battle—he would, I venture, have come out of his thicket and joined the fight.

JULY FOURTEENTH

Bees droning; white clouds in full sail for an open sea of blue, and the odor of clover, honeyed and familiar and reminding one of all the summers gone by—that is July.

The clover plant is such a common thing that nobody praises it as it deserves to be praised, this fragrant, hardy, ubiquitous plant that leaves the soil richer than it found it. I am not forgetting that Irishmen have taken the shamrock for their national symbol. But according to the dictionaries the Gael word *seamar*—or *seamroge,* which is the fine old Irish orthography for it—does not mean clover specifically, but any three-lobed leaf. Half the world will uphold the clover and the other half insists that the true shamrock is really the wood-sorrel, oxalis. The three-leaved clover, used by St. Patrick to teach the Trinity to the wild tribes of Erin, seems to me an excellent symbol, for if Ireland were divided into north, south, east and west, then only three of the lobes would be Ireland. Orange Ulster will forever remain the missing fourth leaf in Ireland's luck.

The place to look for the astonishing in Nature is amongst common things. The clover with its dense head of two-lipped flowers exactly suited to the long tongues of butterflies and some bees, sustains a symbiotic relationship with insects quite as much as the orchid. The roots of the clover harbor colonies of nitrifying bacteria which improve the soil, as important or more so than the fungi in the roots of orchids. Where orchids are scarce and useless, clover creeps over the surface of the world, invading our continent and the Antipodes, leaving the world better than it found it, nourishing cattle, alluring bees and butterflies, and trooping down the dusty roadsides where haughtier flowers will not consent to grow.

JULY FIFTEENTH

I CAUGHT the coral triton by a swift dart of my hand, plunging to the wrist in the deep carpet of black moss. Through the nerves in my palm, as the little smooth, muscular fellow threshed about, came the sensation of holding a naked child who is bent on escaping its nightdress. Now I lost him; then I had him, and suddenly I am left with the leg in my hand; bright though his skin is, the little eft has already disappeared before my eyes. Considering his situation desperate, he has parted with his leg. I need not feel too sorry for him. The self-amputation, I imagine, caused him little pain, and he will replace his leg in a short time.

Half the triton's life history is passed in water; it is never far from water in any case. And the manner of fertilization of the triton remarkably recalls the fishes, for the female, when the male has danced and posed to please her, ejects her ova. The male then fertilizes these, after which the female sweeps them up again and stores them for egg laying in earliest spring, while yet the ice is on the ponds.

JULY SIXTEENTH

PEOPLE there are who shrink from touching a creature like the red triton, because he is such an eery, chill and impish little animal. To some minds he seems reptilian, to others fishy; to me he is simply very pagan. There is a sort of cool impudence about him; his grin acknowledges the jollity of his gross little love ways, the irrepressible power of life which has enabled so antique a type to survive into the present.

Also, he slyly implies that he is in the family. It is posted up on the very walls of life that he is an ancestor or very closely collateral at least. Haeckel it was who discovered the great biological law that ontogeny repeats phylogeny— by which he meant that the embryo lives through a telescoped version of the actual evolution of its species through the ages. In its early stages the human embryo passes through a gilled stage like the aquatic newt larva or mud puppy; the adult newt, of course, breathes air as we do, so he bridges the gap between fishes and reptiles. The reptiles link to the mammals; so too the unborn child sketches this history, only losing his tail at the last moment, as it were.

The well tempered mind embraces these kinships without revulsion at the sight of one's ancestors still walking the earth. Appetite for life—that is the symptom of a healthy soul, a readiness to accept its tastes, a disposition to try the new. If newts make you squeamish and you prefer to think about children as cherubim until they lie smiling in their cradles, depend upon it, you are ailing.

JULY SEVENTEENTH

I NEVER hear the thrush now, without wondering if it will be the last time this season that he sings. After each burning day I feel sure that, like a flower of the field, the song will be wilted in the heat. All too soon the thrush will molt. He will be here hopping about silently in the woods and thickets, but he will not sing. Then indeed the dead of summer will be upon us; breathless heat and heavy-hearted silence will settle on the spots where now he still takes up his evening station to refresh the hour when the soul can breathe in quiet, the brief, brief moments between the fiery setting of the sun and the falling of the heavy-leaved darkness.

JULY EIGHTEENTH

O N T H I S day in 1720 was born the naturalist who is better
loved in the English speaking world than any other—Gilbert
White, curate of Selborne, in Hampshire. His parochial
Natural History is the only one of the kind which runs into
repeated edition in fine format. Many people collect any
and all editions of it. Countless are the owners who have
annotated it, and there are many pilgrimages made to Selborne. Some of the pilgrims have been disappointed, perhaps, to find that it is scarcely distinguishable from any
other sleepy nook in England—a quaint but unexciting
spot. They should have realized that this would be so.
Gilbert White's style is also quite unexciting, precise, pleasing without ever once becoming more than slightly graceful, and almost prim and pedantic. His poetry shows how
little of a poet he was. Rapture, emotion, even reflection,
are quite foreign to his tidy soul.

It was in 1771 that White, who had been communicating
all his findings to Pennant, Barrington and Sir Joseph
Banks, first sketched the project of "a natural history of
my native parish, an annus historico-naturalis, comprising
a journal for a whole year, and illustrated with large notes
and observations." But the first edition did not appear
until 1789. It turns out on examination to be a piecemeal
affair of unsystematized material, neither a naturalist's diary
of the year—except for the quaint and lovable calender at
the end—nor a thorough investigation of anything in particular. Yet it is to this rambling character of the book
that we can ascribe its popularity. Dwelling too long on
nothing, it has caught the fancy of many who care little
for Nature; for the naturalist it is still a model in the art
of investigating the commonplace in the certainty that it
will yield up treasure.

JULY NINETEENTH

THERE is little to write of the life of Gilbert White. The man was his book. We know that he was one of those who go into the woods not to collect spoil but to watch the birds and field mice without troubling them from their nests; he would stop and press an acorn into the ground where it seemed to him the landscape needed an oak. A row of hazels so planted by him still stands in Selborne. His style abounds in anecdotes; indeed, it is nothing else; he taught, argued, and thought entirely through anecdotes—never exciting or dramatized or popularized as journalists and editors now consider that natural history should be—but well pointed, lifelike and convincing. His *Natural History* would not now be considered more than the materials for a real and intensive local study. It is his sketch book—and very glad we may be that he never completed the formal pictures.

The *Natural History of Selborne* was the first book in its genre which raised the subject to the rank of literature. It is comparable in its flavor with *The Compleat Angler,* and is the forerunner of Richard Jefferies and Thoreau. But in science White is more nearly the father of Charles Darwin. Like Darwin and Fabre he had the faculty of minute observation; he understood, as they did, how to get the most out of the picture at which he was gazing, without repining for the wonders of Surinam or Cambodia.

White's studies upon migration and nesting of birds, the habits and usefulness of insects, the nature and origin of dew, are commonplaces in our day, and the rambling of his tastes make him seem pre-Linnæan and akin to Nicholas Peiresc, Buffon, Haller, Paracelsus and Boerhaave, but in his time he was a distinct modern, an innovator and, by comparison, concise and systematic.

JULY TWENTIETH

I HAVE no quarrel with the people who long for the sea. The soul craves immensities, fresh emptiness where it can repose. But I would go now, if I could, to the mountains, and I don't mean what they call mountains in the Berkshires. Some gentle hills, a mere unevenness in the land, will not help me. I need a peak to lift the heart, a forest dense as moss upon a rock, laced with foaming brooks.

But on the clearest days the Blue Ridge is not visible here even as a mirage, a high tossed smoky line penciled on the west. Only within me can I hear the song of a waterfall—not the obliterating crash of a Niagara, but an airy cascade, spilling water from tilted ledges. Water poured so fine that it shatters on the air and drifts, as a smoke, as a lightly laden breeze, amongst the filmy leaves of the sweet Appalachian flora. There the maidenhair and the foam flower tremble forever in the breeze of the fall, and the faces of the mountain bluets, deep gentian blue in tiny forests of threadfine stems, are spangled with spray. And over the gleaming rocks creep the mosses—the deep black moss, the frail Jungermannias sending out green fingers everywhere—and the flat liverworts sprawl fast under the overhanging ledges, translucent emerald green, like seaweeds, or graygreen and nubbly, like a lizard's skin. There the gentle wood frog lives, and in the wet moss the little red triton runs, perpetually grinning, a slippery living bit of coral. Who, of a burning day upon the plain, cannot feel the coolness, the repose, of recurring phrases in the dryest of botany books, "in rich mountain woods," "in wet moss," "on dripping rocks," "in cold springs"?

JULY TWENTY-FIRST

A L L about us, summer in all its sweetness, the ants at their labor, the vulture becalmed upon the sky, and in the meanders of the streams, lazing down to tidewater, the tropic-looking lizard's tail, with the green beetles going over and over it. Beauty, indolent and extravagant, a world at ease, that takes no thought of winter, that lives too lustily to remember death.

In all this there is perhaps too much satisfaction, too much of lulled contentment for the strenuous soul. He would arouse me with the cry that the world goes desperately wrong, that crows of war are in the sky, and our fellow men are groaning in new merciless oppressions imposed by those of late oppressed.

"I hear, I come presently." Life, brother, is not all mankind, and it is not sure that we shall not always find a way, even in Heaven, to suffer. Wait with me a little; only listen to the soft, tremendous footfalls of a destiny that is greater than ours; hear a while the hum of summer, for it is not only the scraping of the small chitinous instruments of insects; it is the singing of the world's blood as it runs in your own veins and sounds in your own ears. And if there is any one who comes to help us, it is the listener, the dreamer, the prober. I have no faith in any social theory to bring us happiness, for all are only substitutions of one materialism for another. I will believe only on a Bruno, a Pasteur, a Mendel, a Darwin.

L   E   O

JULY 22 – AUGUST 21

JULY TWENTY-SECOND

THE summer world is the insect world. Like it or not, that is how it is. There are few insects that ever find the day too hot. The more relentlessly the sun beats down around my house, the faster whir the wings of the hovering wasp. Dragon flies are roused to a frenzy by the heat, dashing over the hot brown surface of the ponds with a metallic clicking of their wings that makes them seem like machines. The wasps grow ever more irritable with the heat, their bodies palpitating with alert life.

Just as many chemicals are inert at low temperatures, but rush together with explosive violence in a furnace, so the insects on a November day are easily captured, and seem bereft of their wits. In bleak weather I would pick up a wasp with only a slight wincing of my nerves. Now, when they come near me, limp with heat though I feel, I am galvanized with that tingling sensation of prickly fear such as stinging things inspire.

Of all the rivals of mankind for dominance on this earth no other creatures large enough to be seen with the naked eye have held out successfully save the insects. When we clear the forest, we rid ourselves of the forest insects, only to make way for the field insects. Man sows his crops—and what comes up? A host of long-faced, armor-plated locusts who eat him out of house and home. We strike at them, but it is like striking at the sea. Whatever way we turn we find the insects there before us, in water, in air, on the earth and under it.

JULY TWENTY-THIRD

THERE are no truly wild spots hereabouts unless they may be the marshes—the marshes where no one ever goes save a huntsman, sometimes, or an adventurous boy. Other topography and vegetation yield to man. The marshes are our tropical jungles; there the intense heat, the cutting edges of wild grass, the footing where one can neither walk nor swim but only sink, forbid intrusion. There grows the bulrush, as graceful as the brush-strokes in a Japanese painting. There the wild rice stands, like Indian corn growing in deep water; in the light breezes the reed grass bends like a forest under a great wind, and the great rosy blossoms of the swamp mallow rise in purity. It is perhaps the only habitat in which no foreign weed is found, nor animal inquilines. There I go to look for the blue pickerel weed, and for the leaf beetles that dwell upon it. There the strangest of all our birds are found—the pumping bittern, and the osprey, and on the surface of the water the striders skate as if on ice, and the male flowers of the eel grass drift in windrows and swirling sargassos amidst the female flowers held fast by thin spiral stalks. Everywhere, midsummer silence, save for the snapping flight of dragon flies, silence and a glory of shimmering heat.

JULY TWENTY-FOURTH

Now in the south, these nights, rides Scorpio, the very spirit of the hot month of July. The head and the crab-like pincers turn westward. In the center of the long body glows the brilliant red star, Antares, "Anti-mars," or as we should say today, False Mars. The body trails away to the long tail, then rests on the southern horizon, the stars composing it being rather faint where they cross the Milky Way, but coming out stronger at the tail itself, where it is erect and flung forward as if the scorpion were preparing to sting.

My fondness for the class of insects does not extend to their relatives, the centipedes and scorpions. Something there is about them too strongly suggestive of death in the dust. But I like the scorpion in the sky, and so plainly is he written there that many races, in widely separated parts of the world, call the constellation by the same name. How red and menacing Antares glows! How threateningly the sting is lifted to remind us that in this month, in the marsh and the field and the forest, all that is most tropical is suddenly upon us.

JULY TWENTY-FIFTH

O NE of the commonest little weeds of the red clay banks is the sensitive pea that has just begun to bloom. The children like to touch its leaves to see them close up. The sensitive briars will go through the same performance even more readily, and of course the real sensitive plant, mimosa of Brazil, is the classic wonder among shrinking vegetables.

A Hindu botanist, Sir Jagadis Bose, suggests that the sensitive plant has nerves, and consequently, feelings. And more acceptably, he projects the idea that all plants are sensitive plants, reacting, however minutely or latently, to chemical and physical stimuli. Very careful photography seems to bear him out; the sensitive plant is only one of the more swiftly reacting plants with motions upon a scale visible to our eyes. It was known to Darwin that plants bestir themselves. The poor-man's-weatherglass closes when a cloud passes overhead; the rays of dog fennel droop at night; other plants close in sunlight as if they fear the great gold eye; the leaflets of oxalis can be made to write a regular little design as they open and shut periodically in the twenty-four hours.

Against Bose is brought the charge that he is seeking to prove an assertion in Hindu philosophy, that all things are one thing, that a plant and an animal are but different outward forms of universal soul. For "soul" substitute "life," and I do not see why any one should disagree with him.

Without a brain an organism cannot suffer, and I do not believe that plants have feelings. A perfectly mechanical explantion of the shutting up of the leaves can be proved; the same applies to the opening and closing of flowers. But the evidence that plants do respond to stimuli, however lowly and slowly, is the contribution of Bose to science.

JULY TWENTY-SIXTH

WHEN I touch the sensitive pea I find that the reaction does not take place immediately. I find also that if pinched too often in fairly frequent intervals the ferny little leaflets begin to lose their sensitivity and eventually are numb until they have been given a good rest.

The delayed reaction is one of the characteristics of life. Hit a rock and it will jump, or send forth a spark, or give out a sound, or crack open instantaneously. Hit a man and he may hit you back "at once" as we say, though some expert motion picture photography, or tests of the chemical changes brought about in his metabolism by the shock and his anger, would show that there was a distinct delay in the reaction. Or he may swallow his anger for reasons known to himself, and choose to strike back twenty years later and in some quite different way. The reaction of our systems to an injury may likewise show up many years afterward. A man is cured of malaria, and finally dies of a malarial liver.

It need surprise no one that plants respond in ways similar to animals. They are built of the same elements. There are plants which swim about freely, and animals which are rooted. In the lowest forms of life there are many organisms that could be classed as plants as readily as animals. Many people think of the plants as "lower" than animals in the scale of evolution. Actually plants and animals diverge from the base of life like the two trunks of an ash tree on my woodlot. The steps of their evolution are astonishingly analogous at many points. If man (in his own estimation) is the culmination of evolution, then the production of the social flowers of the daisy family—which seems rapidly to be inheriting the earth—is the culmination of the vegetable branch of life.

JULY TWENTY-SEVENTH

IT IS an old primitive instinct, I believe, to turn over stones, wondering what is under them. The legend of Theseus and the great stone that his mother made him try every day to pull out of the ground is a proof of the antiquity of this curiosity. I find no magic swords underneath the stones I turn. But after some blasting operations, a huge rock has rolled down the river bank, and I have discovered some large scarab beetles, *Anillus fortis,* where the rock had been. They showed none of the inclination to flee from the light which is exhibited by the grubs and silver fish and pill-box bugs that I sometimes find under stones. Not until I took one home and identified him did I learn that he was blind—he and all his race.

There are other examples of the riddle of life's complexity even more startling, but the beetle will serve well enough as a text for the topic of adaptation to environment. This theory was launched in the eighteenth century by Lamarck, a young officer stationed at Monaco. He spent his time botanizing in the strange Mediterranean vegetation, and had the good sense to begin wondering why in dry climates plants have small tough leaves, in moist climates broad and filmy ones. An inheritance of acquired tendencies was the answer he evolved.

Lamarck would have explained the blind beetle in this fashion; living in the dark without use for his eyes, the beetle's optic nerves gradually atrophied; as this went on for thousands of generations the race at last became blind. So, everywhere, Lamarck believed, the great molding hand of environment has taken the plastic stuff of living matter and gradually but inexorably shaped it, until cave creatures are sightless, sun-bitten plants are chary of their foliage.

JULY TWENTY-EIGHTH

I F Y O U have read the *Just So Stories* you will know how
the kangaroo got his long hind legs. He asked the gods to
make him different from all other animals, so Yellow Dog
Dingo began to chase him. The kangaroo jumped and
jumped until his hind legs grew to their present preposterous length. And thereafter, O Best Beloved, all kan-
garoos had just such legs. Kipling and Lamarck agree.

It is objected that the formation of new species by inheritance of acquired characters cannot be observed in Nature nor performed by experiment. There are certain standing examples for argument, such as the binding of Chinese
women's feet, which has gone on for centuries, and yet no
Chinese girl baby has ever yet been born with "lily feet."
But this is an example of injury, and injuries are not what
Lamarck meant by acquired characters, and neither is such
an acquisition as language; that no child, even a descendant
of many English speaking generations, is born able to speak
English, has nothing to do with the case. As for genuine
experiment to prove the theory, its defendants reasonably
declare that since Lamarck announced it, not enough time
has elapsed to make visible the fixing of acquired characteristics.

That the theory is not susceptible either of direct observation nor of experiment is not so fatal to it as one might
think. Astronomical theories about the past and future of
the universe cannot be proved by observation, nor can we
experiment with the stars. Probably new species cannot be
made in the laboratory for the reason that life cannot be
made there. Evolution is not a mere product of life, like
starch or blood; it is a part of life itself, just as flow is
part of a river.

JULY TWENTY-NINTH

CHARLES DARWIN abhorred Lamarck as Luther the Devil. Darwin would say that the kangaroo could not possibly have stretched his legs, not if his ancestors had been on the jump from morning till night. Rather, having long legs, the kangaroo is enabled to make prodigious jumps, and cannot, indeed, otherwise do anything much in the way of ambulation.

In explanation of the blind cave beetles Darwin would tell us that, being somehow blind as a race, they were utterly incapable of maintaining themselves in a world of enemies who saw them quite clearly. Hence they became exterminated, except in the circumscribed safety of spots perpetually Stygian. There, amid blind worms, blind salamanders, blind fish, they were at no great disadvantage. This, in a nutshell, is the theory of natural selection; Nature selects out the variations that are fitted to survive, kills off those that have become unfit, and so, through time, has compelled its own creations by a series of tiny successive propulsions toward the production of new species adapted to live in the environment prevailing in their day. The world has done with pterodactyls and gives us birds; it will not support cycads, except a few relict species, but is in the process of favoring and varying the annual Compositæ.

The work of Darwin's great supporter seems to bear him out. Weismann believed and often succeeded in showing that no matter what characters an individual acquired in his lifetime, he could transmit only those he inherited; his sex cells, as distinguished from his body cells, were sealed orders to the future generations. Heredity is locked up where nothing can get at it, Weismann assures us, and its functions partake of the nature of a stern predestination.

JULY THIRTIETH

My blind beetles tonight are still running about in the glass jar where I put them; in the daytime they are not infrequently at rest, as if sleeping. But they do not permit my mind to rest. The problem they present does not seem to me to be entirely solved by natural selection. According to Darwin they went blind; and natural selection killed them off, except in the caves and under rocks; had they not found that suitable new environment, it would have done for them entirely. In short, natural selection explains how varieties come to an end, but not how they are created. Why did the beetles go blind to begin with? If it happened gradually, how did natural selection *favor* the process until it resulted in blindness?

Indeed, the origin of species seems unimaginable to me without Lamarck, and so it would have been for Darwin, I think, though he never realized the fact. The whole idea of evolution burst on him during a visit to the Gálapagos Islands, where, in an intensive isolation, the animals (obviously chance colonists from the mainland of South America) had come to differ from their ancestors in Peru until they were new species.

What caused them to differ from the mainland species, if the environment of the Gálapagos had no hand in molding them? Darwin would say that natural selection permitted only those already-existing varieties which were adapted to life on the islands to live, and by inbreeding of these isolated animals, the tendencies were accentuated. But how, in the first place, did they come into being?

JULY THIRTY-FIRST

I WAS brought up in my student days to reject Lamarck *in toto*. Weismann and his "continuity of the germ plasm" were once the Law and the prophets. But enough founded criticism has now accumulated to reduce Weismann to the status of an earnest seeker, among others, after truth. It seems to me that Lamarck has his place in the concept of evolution. Of course it is not to be supposed that any animal, much less any plant, has consciously striven to adapt itself to environment, but rather that environment may, after all, penetrate to the germ cells and mold races.

My wife suggests that one could believe Darwin one day and Lamarck the next. I find this a bit too feminine; I prefer to consider both ways of thinking the whole week through. I am entirely convinced that natural selection is a reality, a mechanism by which variations become extinguished. At the same time I am willing to keep a very open mind toward Lamarck's hypothesis and to all other theories of evolution. Before the astonishing development of life can be explained we shall undoubtedly find that fifty theories are necessary and may all be true, in one case or another, no matter how contradictory they may appear.

Lamarck's place in science seems to me, then, not that merely of a pioneer who failed and got nowhere (as I was taught to believe). His ideas appear to be indispensable if we are ever to explain the origin of instincts (which must certainly be acquired), and the similar characters of organisms not at all related, when found dwelling together in specialized environments. And even if much of Lamarck's thought remains untenable, we cannot withhold from him the honors due a man who first bestirred the sluggish mind to ask such questions. It is the question and not the always provisional answer, that is the soul of science.

144

AUGUST FIRST

JEAN-BAPTISTE-PIERRE-ANTOINE DE MONET was born upon this day in 1744 in a gaunt old farmhouse in Picardy, eleventh son of the Chevalier de La Marck. The young Lamarck, while stationed as a soldier at Monaco, first began to question the why and wherefore of life's infinite complexity. Rousseau had interested him in botanizing in a gentlemanly and sentimental way, but Lamarck was made of sterner stuff than Rousseau. He was fortunate, too, in his associates. Buffon procured for him the place of botanist to the King, and the mighty de Jussieu, who can be compared to Linnæus with a compliment intended to Linnæus, made a thorough systematist out of Lamarck. Late in life a change in appointments placed him in the chair of a lecturer on zoölogy, and in order to fulfill it, he made a zoölogist out of himself! To Lamarck we owe the distinction between vertebrate and invertebrate animals, which no one before had had the wit to see, snakes, lizards, and alligators having been classed as insects!

When the Revolution came, several great scientists lost their heads in it. The little band at the Jardin des Plantes —Lamarck, Cuvier, Daubenton, Desfontaines, Latreille, Geoffrey de St. Hilaire—clung on, without salary, without appropriations ("the Republic has no need of scientists," were the famous words of the Directory), wondering when the blow would fall. Lamarck's last days were spent in blindness, only his daughter fending for and attending him, taking by dictation the last lines of this imaginative genius of science. He died in direst poverty; at his funeral Cuvier ridiculed his theory of evolution. No one followed his body as it was carried to potter's field.

AUGUST SECOND

A MAN with a taste for being able to name what he sees will want not only to know the trees and the flowers; sooner or later he will take up the ferns, and I give him no assurance that he will ever get much beyond them. Not that they are so many. But the sirens were only three, amidst all those sailor's skulls.

There are only a little less than sixty ferns and fern allies in my region and it will not take a man a season to know them all, so few, so striking they are, so excellent the many handbooks of fern study in existence. But in the very circumscription of their bounds lies half the charm of the time you first take up a study of the ferns; like the pictures of Vermeer or the signatures of Button Gwinnet, there are just a few in the world, and all of them precious. Gone forever is the age of the ferns, when they ruled the earth. Now, as an experiment of evolution, they are finished; we see of their great subkingdom only the fragments that time has spared. It is that which gives the study of them its classic, its complete and homogeneous character, like the study of a rigid, highly inflected, sonorous and dead language.

AUGUST THIRD

THOSE there are who are annoyed or repelled (or they affect to be), by what they call lush or extravagant beauty. They will enjoy nothing but the bleakest of New England scenery—a few hard-bitten pastures, a rocky wall, a moth-eaten hill that is neither a bold mountain nor a stirring plain, and a stern and paintless old house.

Of this company I do not make one. If it is shallow not to be able to see beauty in the austere, it is monkish, parsimonious and timid to despise the lavish and complex beauty of life reaching its full expression. I liked what little I ever saw of the tropics, and the fact that I was born in a region where Nature was economical of her colors and form begets in me no sentimental feelings about such scenes.

I love the southern landscape, and I love it in summer only a little less than in spring. The South, in winter, is mild enough, but it is little more; it is simply not itself. You probably do not know Labrador until you have lived a winter in it, and to taste the undiluted wine of a hot country, you should see it through a summer. I live in that intemperate zone that is icy in winter and flaming in summer; it blends the tastes of north and south.

And in summer the tropical element in it comes out. Now the heat shimmers above the marshes; it dances over the hills in a haze, engulfs the cool old houses as if they were islands on the landscape. Everywhere the deep blue green of heavy foliage is in full summer splendor; on all the pools the jade green sargassos of the duckweed stretch away across the stagnant water; in the breathless nights the whippoorwill complains, it has been said, that "It is so still, so still, so still!"

AUGUST FOURTH

U P O N this day in 1849 was born William Henry Hudson. We loved him for something, either in his style or his viewpoint, that can only emerge from the soul of a loafer. Hudson was a loafer, it would seem, only partly from choice. Ill health and poverty in London are desperate shackles for a naturalist, and his marriage was unhappy. His wife long kept a boarding house in that city, and she need have been no termagant to find that a husband to whom sparrows and starlings were important, a husband who disappeared, to tramp the roads like a hobo, living on blackberries, was an exasperating mate.

The English readers love Hudson because he saw the poetry in the subtle charm of the English countryside, because he made even more intimate for them the already intimately known beauty of the downs and lanes. In London itself, in Richmond Park, on the housetops and in the gray streets, he looked where seven millions looked, and saw for them what they did not see.

But it is Hudson remembering his lost Argentine that I love to read. There is nothing like nostalgia for producing memorable writing; the poet must go unsatisfied. And Hudson, smoking in the back parlor of the London boarding house, and writing of the birds of La Plata, or the great thistle years upon the pampas, and all that he remembered of the purple lands and green mansions, becomes for me the Homer of nature lovers.

AUGUST FIFTH

THE ants have been called the mankind of insects. Their organization, their great cities, their division of labor, their battles and their kings and queens have all given rise to this comparison, to say nothing of the fact that some ants keep a sort of cattle and tolerate various sorts of pets, while others harvest regularly and some even cultivate fungi, sowing the spores like seeds and eating the matured crop. Without stopping to weigh the worth of each one of these comparisons—and every one may be challenged as a mere analogy—the mind hastens on to the implication behind these comparisons. Are ants intelligent? Before any answer can be given, we shall have to know what we mean by intelligence, and to remember that besides intelligence there are three other kinds of animal activity—instinct, reflex, and tropism.

AUGUST SIXTH

A MOTH, flying to his death in a candle, is obeying his phototropism, his "pull" to the light. He cannot prevent it any more than you can prevent yourself from falling if you are thrown out of an airplane. Even so are tropisms inexorable. As it happens we humans do not consciously experience any; we can only observe them—the positive light tropism of the moth, the negative light tropism of the cockroach, the earth and water tropism of the root, the chemical tropisms in our own bodies when our corpuscles combat microbes.

A reflex may best be illustrated by the fact that even when a frog's brain is removed, he will shoot out his tongue and catch a fly on his snout, or scratch his back if it is tickled. We can just detect certain reflexes in our own muscles, though we seldom give them a thought save when they fail to function.

Tropism and reflex will account for almost everything done by all the lowliest creatures. But not quite! It has been shown that in some cases ants, which are notoriously balked by even a very small trickle of water, or shallow film of it, *can* learn to swim. They do show, upon occasion, that ability to learn from experience, which is the rudiments of intelligence. They exhibit signs of that associative memory by which we can see a baby's intelligence burgeoning.

But it is chiefly by instinct that the ant survives and prospers, to the bafflement of human thought.

AUGUST SEVENTH

OF INSTINCT Fabre says that "it knows all within the never varying tracks traced out for it, is ignorant of all outside those tracks." Voltaire assures us that "we are governed by instinct, as well as cats and goats." In 1858 Kirby and Spence believed that "we may call the instincts of animals those faculties implanted in them by the Creator, by which, independent of instruction, observation or experience, and without a knowledge of the end in view, they are all alike impelled to the performance of certain actions tending to the well being of the individual and the preservation of the experience." Darwin had much the same to say, but admitted that instinct was not the reigning and universal propensity that Voltaire imagined.

All these are descriptions, not explanations. But the fact that we cannot define instinct need not disturb us. Try to define a child, a mountain, a tree, a melody, not to mention abstract conceptions like beauty, morality, justice. That no three of your friends will agree with you detracts nothing from the reality of these nouns.

Even allowing tropism and reflex their full weight in the life of an ant, instinct will still loom large, will, in fact, prove itself so complex, so precisely fitted to take care of the thousands of intricate motions and eventualities which would require intelligence on our part to deal with, that every mechanist shudders away from it, reading the doom of his most cherished principles in it, while a passionate observer like Fabre is filled with glee at the very complexity of the problem.

AUGUST EIGHTH

SUDDENLY, from all over the countryside, the winged ants have emerged simultaneously; the date appointed for the nuptial flight is at hand, of one of the fifty species known hereabouts, and everywhere the ants obey it. The creatures which literally fell under my observation were small, mostly males—unsuccessful suitors, perhaps, for nature launches scores of drones into the air in search of one princess. But even the one triumphant suitor must descend to the realities of earth, after the raptures of mating a mile above it, and I doubt if the nest or Nature has any further use for any of the drones, once they have fulfilled their destiny.

I have repeatedly seen the take-off of the winged ants. The whole colony appears in a state of great turmoil, dragging out its winged or sexual members ingeniously but hastily, like ground mechanics getting airplanes out of a hangar in time of war. The big queen, as yet only a princess, is propelled along the ground, as if she were a plane taxi-ing across the field. At first she seems enormous to my eyes, compared to the workers, enormous and inert and positively afraid. The little males are also trundled forth, and stand about, waiting patiently. Then, at some moment that pleases her, the princess flies swiftly up into the air. In a moment, seen against all the emptiness of blue heaven, she dwindles to a tiny speck, endowed with a joyful frenzy. The males start off in pursuit. The rest is hidden from us by the blinding sunlight.

AUGUST NINTH

How beautiful, cries the mystic, that the queen ant should choose to have her marriage rites performed above the earth, in the clear, pure, sunlit air!

Bah, says the mechanist; she goes up in the sky for no prettier reason than that for which a fly crawls up a window pane. She is simply positively phototropic.

No doubt she is, but it is not so simple as that. The mechanist is forever trying to explain away instinct, because if he does not, it will be the death of him. But he cannot dissipate with his explanations the complexity of behavior on the part of the queen ant and the whole nest at this time, a pattern which does not explain itself save as instinct, no matter of how many tropisms, or reflexes, it makes use upon the way.

Once mated, the queen ant returns to earth. She has become negatively phototropic, explains the mechanist. There is no doubt of it; she tries to hide from the light, like a cockroach. She has also now become positively geotropic, that is, she wants to go down, as directly as a root will do.

Underground, wings would be a curse, and underground is where the queen must now go, a prisoner for the rest of her life. She will have no more use for wings, for a queen never makes but one nuptial flight, though she may live and lay for as much as ten years. In less than a minute she has torn them from her and they lie upon the ground, tiny diaphanous iridescent flakes which carried her toward the clouds for one brief hour.

B U T when she tries to return to her old nest, the queen ant is attacked by her own soldiers. Without killing her, which they could easily do, they repeatedly throw her out, and nip and maul her until she decides (and how is any decision mechanically explained, by the way?) that she will have to obey her positively geotropic, negatively phototropic impulses in some healthier spot. Sternly ejected by her own people, who already have a dowager queen, the newly fertilized matriarch learns at last that she must look for a new home.

She wanders about, very nervous and erratic, hunting for any crack that will shelter her, and there descends forever into earth. She constructs a rudimentary nest and lays her first eggs, and waits while they hatch into larvæ. These children require the most complicated care in the way of food, cleansing, and a constant moving up and down in the chambers of the nest, depending upon the hour of day and the depths to which warmth and sunlight penetrate. At last they pass into the cocoon stage, but often not before the high-born, relatively inept mother has been reduced by hunger to eating more than half her own children in order to survive. But when the pupæ emerge as adults, few though their numbers may be, the queen is at last provided with the beginnings of her colony of slave-jailers. At once these workers and soldiers fall to their complex duties, and so a new colony is founded.

This, in shorthand, is the story, and I submit that it would send any one to the madhouse to explain it without relying upon the fact of instinct, a pattern of behavior that transcends purely mechanical causation as impudently as it surpasses what we intelligent beings call reasonableness.

AUGUST ELEVENTH

TONIGHT the Perseids will be visible in all their glory—
that swarm of meteors whose orbit we encounter tonight
and through which we continue to move tomorrow night.
Sixty-nine falling stars an hour is the average number
that one can see, by keeping a sharp lookout at their
central radiating point, the constellation of Perseus. This
constellation does not rise until eleven, and is really not
well placed for observation for another hour, but as nothing in Nature seems on this breathless night to have any
intention of going to sleep before the witching hour, I shall
stay up to watch.

A meteor is a meteor when it burns itself up in the
sky; when it falls to earth, unconsumed by the heat of
friction with our atmosphere, it is a meteorite. Of all the
astronomical events, the fall of a meteorite is the most
unnerving and yet the most reassuring. Reassuring because
it proves to us that the depths of space are inhabited by
bodies made of the same elements we have here on earth,
that, at rock bottom, a man and a star are built of the
same stuff. Alarming, in the thought that, were a meteor as
large as some that have fallen in Arizona and Siberia, to
crash upon New York or London, a million humans would
instantly meet death.

AUGUST TWELFTH

THE best of summer star-gazing is that it is warm enough to fling yourself upon your back and gaze up at the stars without craning the neck. In a short time the sense of intimacy with the stars is established, as it never can be when a man stands erect. You may even lose the sense of gazing up, and enjoy the exciting sensation of gazing *down* into deep wells of space. Indeed, this is quite as correct as to say that we gaze upward at the stars. In reality there is no up and down in the universe. You are, in point of fact, a creature perpetually hung over the yawning abyss of Everywhere, suspended over it by our tiny terrestrial gravity which clamps you to the side of mother earth while you gaze down on Vega and Deneb and Arcturus and Altair whirling below you.

One can never look long in the August sky without beholding a shooting star, for the trail of the Perseids is spun fine at each end; only last night and tonight we pass through the thick node of them. If we ask ourselves what is a meteor—fragment of the lost planet between Mars and Jupiter, messenger from the farthest stars, or bit of a vanished comet—there seems no certain answer. The Perseids are thought to be traveling in the same orbit as that of Tuttle's comet of 1862, and to be a part of it. But what, after all, is a comet? Nothing more ghostly exists in time or space; it rushes at us out of a black hole of space, trails a fire that does not burn, a light that is no light, and looping close to the sun, vanishes again into space—to return at the appointed time when the sea of darkness again gives up its dead; or, more terrible still, never to return from its Avernus.

AUGUST THIRTEENTH

W E H A V E whole books these days devoted to New England fan-lights, Southern porticoes, hornbooks, wigs, powder-boxes, spinning wheels and covered bridges of the early American past. I cannot see why no one has written about springhouses. There is far more beauty in most of them than in the snuffboxes and rum bottles that folk collect; on many American farms the springhouse is the one perfect piece of architecture, the one structure that exactly fits its requirements, is devoid of every embellishment, and looks as if it grew where it stands. Fitted into the hill or the bank, dappled with the light and shade of the leaves overhead, an old stone springhouse is the first edifice to mellow with time. Dark green moss creeps over its arched roof and its plain flanks, merging in its emerald with the green hollow.

Within—the breath of the icy spring water, the cool, plain smell of naked rock, the odors of maidenhair and moss and lichen, the sunlight dazzling on the surface of the spring. As the door swings open the little blue-tailed skink flits like a shadow from the farthest recesses. The coral newt will rush out of the crevices if he is prodded, and a snail or two will be found creeping over the sides of the wall.

On the shelf the farmwife keeps her butter pats and buttermilk, and the sweet milk, too, or she did in my childhood, before the days of the electrical refrigerator. I knew a springhouse once, large enough for a boy of ten to stand erect in, through which a cool mountain brook shot swiftly on its course. When I buy that brook on which I am always planning, I shall most decidedly try to find one with an old springhouse on the premises.

AUGUST FOURTEENTH

As soon as the green and violet hour of summer dusk is at hand and the bats begin to sweep the sky for midges, the voice of the whippoorwill rises out of the hollow below my house. This will be but the beginning of his whipping of poor Will (that luckless lad) and when first I hear it I can very nearly enjoy it. For it is a nostalgic and intensely American sound, and one that goes back, as we find nearly everything precious does, to childhood.

How often have I wakened gently, to hear, down in the valley, the strange, contented calling of the whippoorwill, and lain awhile to breathe the wind of the night fields, fresh with dew and the scent of sweet clover, and drifted again to sleep, while he sang, thinking of the benediction of night after the burning summer days.

AUGUST FIFTEENTH

THE queen of the summer zenith night sky is Vega, the brightest star in our skies except for Sirius, and, of course, the planets. To find Vega you have only to go out about nine in the evening and look directly overhead. The amethystine star in the small irregular triangle is Vega of the Lyre.

Vega is really twice as brilliant as Sirius, but it is three times as far away—twenty-six light years, in fact. And further, large stars are not seen at their best in the zenith; it is only when near the horizon that their facets glitter with iridescent lights. The luminosity of Vega, however, is fifty times as great as our own sun's. But all these are hard mathematical facts. The limpid beauty of Vega cannot be thus coldly formulated, nor its soft, high-riding queenliness.

But gentle though the great star Vega looks tonight, the thoughts that it brings to me have no certitude in them. For by all accounts our own sun is rushing headlong in the general direction of Vega. Not that Vega is likely to be there when we arrive; it too, will have sped off on its predestined course. We have much nearer neighbors in space, —Proxima Centauri, for instance, in the southern hemisphere. Still, it reminds us that no man knows what celestial encounters may await us out there in the velvet blackness of space. It was once a tenet of all men's faith that the Divine Hand appoints the stars in their courses, so that not one of them, more numerous than all the grains of sand on all the beaches of the world, might molest another. But in truth accidents most certainly occur, and before the very lens of the astronomer. It takes, today, a greater courage to have faith.

AUGUST SIXTEENTH

THE stars of a summer night lack the frost-crystal brilliance of winter. Even by midnight, of a very hot summer, there is no glister to the stars. But if by any chance you wake, or stir abroad in the small hours of the morning, in the sweetness of the dew, in the only fresh and wholly innocent part of the day, the heavens will flash with an unexpected glory. The stars of last night will be setting, Aquila the Eagle flying swiftly down the Milky Way to the west, while in the southeast Fomalhaut will be rising, that mysterious star of the autumn evenings. Indeed, the whole configuration of the skies will present the appearance of the early evening vault of October. So, by rising at that witching hour, you can quite truthfully read the future in the stars.

AUGUST SEVENTEENTH

STAR-GAZING is a common name for harmless futility. But actually there is nobody in either the civilized or savage community, who is looked upon with more tolerance and awe than the man who professes to read the stars. I feel confident that if I were to go out and pass around two hats, one for a foundlings' home and one for a larger telescope than had ever been erected before, I would have my observatory long before I was prepared to tuck the first foundling into a pristine bed. Man is so eager about his great home of the universe, so eager about the secret behind all things, so certain that God is in the stars! That what the seer will tell the rich donor about such things will emerge in equations incomprehensible to him, troubles Mr. Midas not at all. He is rather tickled by the incomprehensibility of his oracle; it makes him certain that they are doing great things under the cyclopean dome.

I think Mr. Midas is a shade more conservative about endowing biological endeavor. Whatever the astronomer discovers—even if he foresees the end of the world—nothing he tells is intimately disquieting. It is all very grand and far away, and everything out there either happened long, long ago or will come to pass indefinite ages hence. But biology is strangely immediate and personal in all its applications, and there is no guaranteeing that its next discovery will be especially agreeable. The mind that would go along with it must have a certain toughness of fiber and a habit of thinking forward faster than prevailing beliefs.

AUGUST EIGHTEENTH

I f t h e word butterfly connotes something fair and frail, a creature of the sunlight hour, so when we pronounce the name of moth we think of something fateful—a creature that will fling itself upon a candle flame to die, a thief of time that, working in the dark, in the blazing heat of attics where we never venture now, corrupts as surely as time and rust. Every association of moths is with night and mystery and death. When in the darkness a moth bats its silver-dusted wings in my face I can never repress the strange little tingle, half of horror, that dances on the nerve ends of my face and through my hair. The moth is a ghost made flesh; the death's head moth can squeak!

The best way to catch moths for study is to set out some of the lepidopterist's "sugar roll" to attract these sweet-mad creatures of night and air. Or set a lamp beside an open window. The moths are relatively neglected by the amateur collector, while butterflies receive all their (rather dubious) attentions. The mind can grasp the butterflies; the hundreds of moths from even a very restricted locality are enough to baffle all but gluttons for toil. If one would know how to tell moths from butterflies, there's a rule of thumb that works well enough. The butterflies have their antennæ tipped with a club-like point. No moths have this; club-like swellings may occur on the antennæ, but never at the tip, save in the tropics. Most of the moths have feathered antennæ. Take but a look at the large antennæ of such common moths as the great pale green luna, the heavy-bodied splendid Cecropia who seems to stare at you with eyes on his wings. Or the sphinx moth, that by twilight or in sunshine hovers like a humming bird above all deep throated flowers. You will see at once what to expect in the way of moth antennæ.

AUGUST NINETEENTH

THERE was once a poor young man in whose breast a scientist was stifling. He lived in the heart of a great city, far from tree and bird, unless it were a few desolate planes and some quarrelsome roof sparrows. This young man had not even a window to look upon the street, but, in his garret room, only a skylight. Without an overcoat, he was often in bad weather kept in his room for days together, with nothing to do but lie on his back and look out at the sky. As he gazed, the clouds in ever changing form drifted by; at first they seemed shapeless and fluid beyond all hope of grouping them into any types, but little by little he came to recognize the sorts you read about in books—the black threatening sheets of the nimbus clouds that bring snow, the cumulus, dream-castle clouds of a fine summer's afternoon, the high, immovable cirrus clouds, like feathers afloat in topmost heaven that promise fair weather.

As we can well believe, having nothing else to look at he soon had observed all the kinds of clouds you and I have ever noticed. And then, one day, he discovered a new kind, the mammato-cirrus, a formation so rare that it has only been observed a few times since. Cut off from every other line of scientific investigation, this genius still found something new that a million other people in Paris could have seen that day if they had had the eyes of Jean-Baptiste-Pierre-Antoine de Monet de Lamarck.

AUGUST TWENTIETH

IT IS the primal constructor, this green coloring matter in the heavy summer foliage, this chlorophyll that directly captures the energy of sunlight and with magic power brews in its alembics, out of air and water and earth, the stuff of which the rest of life is made. It has built up the wood of the table before me, the food upon the plate at my dinner, the linen sheets in which I shall sleep. Without it no animal may live, no animal product were possible. So it becomes the mother, the creatrix of everything living.

All this was known—philosophy for sucklings—even when chlorophyll was deemed an inscrutable mystery. But in my student days it was whispered that somewhere, at the back of laboratories where we never ventured, a great young man was working out the structural formula of chlorophyll, the most complex series of carbon rings ever imagined in one mortal head. And while we shook up solutions of chlorophyll in benzine, or stared at its tell-tale bands and bars through the spectroscope, we wondered if he would go mad, like a chess genius who thinks of too much at once. Today, still young, Conant stands upon the verge of synthesizing this basic sustenance of life, and tomorrow he may hold the quicksilver of creation itself in the cup of his hand.

AUGUST TWENTY-FIRST

N o t blood nor flesh nor hair nor feathers, not the chlorophyll or cellulose of the plants, is stranger than the stuff
called chitin. Chitin is not only the hard shell of the dapper
little beetles in their tail-coats; it is the glistening wing of
the dragon fly, and his thousand faceted eye, the exquisite
feathered antennæ of the moth by which it perceives the
odor of its mate across miles of summer darkness, the feet
of the laboring ant, the heavy armor of the lobster, the
gossamer of the spider, the thread of the silkworm. There
is very little about an insect, or for that matter any of its
allies in the sea or upon the land, which is not chitinous.
One moment the stuff is finer than the tresses of woman,
and the next ponderous and stiff as the armor of a knight,
and all without change in its chemical composition. As a
bloom upon the wing of a luna moth fluttering across the
moon, it is evanescent as snowflakes; encased in drops of
amber where a Mesozoic beetle died, it has seen the ages
pass without a change.

VIRGO

AUGUST 22 — SEPTEMBER 21

AUGUST TWENTY-SECOND

SOMETHING there is about a heron of wildwood nobility. That humped and stilted grace-and-awkwardness, that grand and pensive sorrowfulness that goes with marshes, that touches all marsh creatures, frogs and dragonflies and wild ducks, with the finger of tragedy laid on the tameless, the short of life. That leisurely taking off; that rushing sound in the pinions, that haughty, harsh, and yet haunting cry! Nobility that tempts the fowler's gun, not because the heron is fit to eat, but because he presents an easy mark against the sunset extinguishing its fire in the wild marsh water.

But come nearer to the herons, if only by the binoculars, and even a snowy egret reveals the unsavory ways of the stork family. That endless gormandizing after mud worms, that retching and regurgitating and liming; these things are disillusion itself, and when you actually attain their nests, in one of those heronries where there may be hundreds of families, all that can be inhuman and repugnant in a bird assails you. I would not tell myself the truth if I did not admit that birds can suddenly weary and repel me, just as ants and reptiles or mammals may. The animal lover (self-avowed) will reproach me in this. He *never,* he says, does anything but *love* birds at all times. I say he is a hypocrite; I say, too, that there are attitudes, emotions even, toward Nature, more real and vital and valuable than love.

There is a great deal more stingo, more savor and bite in Nature if you do not try to love everything you touch, smell, hear, see or step on. The disgust which a near encounter with a heronry awakens in me is part of heronness, an ingredient in the whole, that with trailing leg and probing bill, makes up the virtue and staying power of the idea of *Heron* in my mneme.

AUGUST TWENTY-THIRD

ON THEIR great spring migrations the birds look exactly like the pictures in the books. They sang the songs they ought to sing. They were coming back to us—which we can readily understand.

But in autumn the return of the birds takes me by surprise. They come so much earlier, each year, than I seem to remember them, winging down upon a world still in green leaf. The males are in the molt, or in workaday attire, and voiceless are they all, save for a few that whistle mere teasing fragments of their bridal arias, snatches of melody which seem familiar, haunt the memory and cannot quite be placed. And they are leaving us—a fact which we cannot quite forgive them—for lands we shall not see, to feed upon alien banquets.

Indeed, the return to the south has not just begun; it started in July, when the sandpipers, yellow-legs, snipes, woodcocks, black terns and blue-winged teal returned. Many of the swallows and chimney swifts were already on the wing, and a few of the bobolinks. Surely they are not fleeing from cold, for these are blazing days; there is no lack of forage for them, and though the waders have far to go, to South America, others have but a little way to wing. These reflections drive one on further in the search for the mainspring of their clock-like goings and comings.

AUGUST TWENTY-FOURTH

AN EXPERIMENT has recently been performed on birds, intended to confirm a suggestion of the cause of the mighty autumn migration. A bird, in the height of summer, was subjected to gradually shortened days—to a number of sunlit hours that diminished even faster than the declining season itself. The bird showed the most intense restlessness and desire to escape from the cage.

It is not many years since the idea was first proffered that the shortening hours of daylight in the northern breeding grounds produced definite changes in the behavior of the birds, resulting in driving them toward the equator where days in winter are longest. Beyond any question this is the fundamental cause of the autumnal migration. And I do not see why it is not also the cause of the vernal return; as spring advances the birds move with the lengthening days. Instinct—whatever instinct may be—plays its part, but if birds are constituted anything like other animals, from copepods to human babies, sunlight produces definite chemical changes in the metabolism, and penetrates, literally and figuratively, to the very bones and feeling in them. The bird is drawn after the lengthening day as definitely as the moth is drawn to the candle.

So, mysterious as migration once seemed—and the most far fetched explanations, including glaciation, were proffered to explain the origin of the migrating instinct—it is yielding up its mysteries at last; it is not, after all, exclusively an instinct; it is, perhaps, more a case of a very subtle or superior positive light tropism, to which one may add racial gregariousness, imitation, habit, and so far as the habit be innate or hereditary, instinct—probably numerous instincts including the homing—and even intelligence.

AUGUST TWENTY-FIFTH

I T W A S my little son who first discovered the battle between
the ants. His shout brought me into the garden, just at
twilight of this hot summer day. It is the hour at which
ants are reputed to fall to quarreling, but things so seldom
happen in Nature as the books tell you they do!

I had tried to provoke combats by introducing a few
foreigners into a colony, but overwhelming numbers
mobbed and dismembered the intruders before my remorse-
ful gaze. I had discovered that very large ferocious ants will
often simply throw small intruders out, and very glad the
lesser species were to escape. But when I introduced large
species into the precincts of the little fellows, the house-
holders showed no quarter. Their usual tactics were to
hustle the offender down into their narrow labyrinth where
he could not utilize his superior size. This was somehow
more terrifying than a fair and open fight above ground.

I arrived today only at the end of the first voluntary
and general combat that I ever witnessed. The small Lasius
ants were already abandoning their assault upon the strange
hollow dome built by the huge carpenter ants (Campono-
tus) and were retreating, with their faces to the enemy, into
a high forest of horseweed and sow thistle. Dead Lasius
warriors lay all over the plain of battle—about a half foot
square—but a few of the carpenter ants, which had pursued
too fast, were in dire straits, heaving and rolling under the
biting mobs of their enemies, their plight quite hopeless.
Darkness soon put a stop to my observations but I am determined to watch tomorrow.

AUGUST TWENTY-SIXTH

THE varied businesses of my son and myself kept us from the hot and dusty battlefield of the ants until dusk had fallen. Then we went out with an electric torch, and found the tiny Agincourt was littered with legs and heads and abdomens. But the severed members seemed to have come to life; in the ghostly ray from the torch they waved and danced across the battlefield in a macabre fashion horrible to see.

We had to bend very close to discover the cause of this dance of death. Then we saw that the battlefield was being scavenged by a very small beady black ant, a Tapinoma, no bigger, it seemed, than grains of black sand. Each was engaged in bearing away some segment of a dead ant larger than itself, to its tiny hill—a crater scarcely larger than a nickel in circumference.

I have not yet discovered the cause of the quarrel nor how the attack began. The carpenters are very plainly on the defensive, and have my sympathy. Though I have shouted with pain when bitten by them in handling them, they are the most naturally pacific of the nine species in my garden. They never thieve, and simply and rather politely throw out any spiders or beetles or small ants that blunder into their clever mud dome.

Though chiefly nocturnal, they seldom raid my pantry. The Lasius ants, more numerous than all others, are into everything. By day they scatter in search of honey amongst the flowers, or collect aphids on the sow thistles, and by night, tearing along in regular tracks, they tramp through dust and filth and then all through the larder.

AUGUST TWENTY-SEVENTH

THE ant Armageddon is on again! The heavily armored carpenter ants seize their enemies, the Lasius ants, in their terrific jaws, cutting them in two at a single vicious snap. The Lasius fall upon the carpenters in seething masses. The point of attack is usually the antennæ of the great foe. As these are the most sensitive, nervous parts of the creature, his agony must be intense. Though he bisect his tormentors, still their jaws remain sunk in his antennæ. Here, probably, an ant's sense of direction resides. Certainly from the moment his antennæ are attacked, the carpenter is rendered helpless, like a soldier writhing with tear gas.

But now after many hours of watching the battle, my eye muscles have grown strained with the intense, unaccustomed close focus on the Lilliputian world, and my nerves suddenly slip back into a distinct, prickly feeling of horror. Something about ants is too inhuman. I become subject to that hallucination known to physicians as formicaria, the persuasion that ants are crawling on my skin.

It is probably not my imagination that I am smelling formic acid everywhere, and that my eyes sting from it. The underside of my magnifying glass, I find, is flecked with drops of it, and its sour astringency is hanging, though I cannot see it, in a dome over the nest. This is not only a ferocious warning to all intruders, but it may well be the secret of much nest communication, the excitatory alarm by which the emmets take flame and courage from each other.

AUGUST TWENTY-EIGHTH

ON THIS day in 1749 was born the mighty Goethe, who not only walked the sublime halls of epic poetry, but cast his romantic shadow upon the steps of natural science. According to tradition it was during a visit to Monaco that Goethe, upon examining the wild palm which formerly grew as a native of that principality, first observed the fact that a flower is made up not of utterly distinct organs, but of transformed leaves. The green sepals show this plainly, and in the palm these merge into petals. The stamens, next in position, are transformed petals, and the pistils and ovaries are still further modified, but yet one can make out that they are leaves in origin. Thus even fruits are especially modified leaves, and as leaves are mere modifications of shoots, a plant has but two distinct parts; roots and shoots.

Goethe admits that he had read the *Philosophia Botanica* of Linnæus, whence he undoubtedly derived this idea, and it is to the poet Herder, probably, that Goethe owes the mystical interpretation he puts upon metamorphosis, as he owes to him the romantic concept of an "ideal type" of perfection of form in Nature, by comparison with which living beings are to be described. Geothe's Spiral Theory shows us the plant as animated by two *tendenzen,* the vertical and the spiral; verticality represents eternal essence and the male element; it is female to twine around things, and the female stands for the nourishing, cultivating and reproductive.

It has been well said that Goethe's scientific writings have been more admired than read. His reputation for greatness as a scientist was given him by Schelling and his coterie, perhaps to excuse themselves for denigrating his majesty as a poet. Science, which has swept away the romantic natural philosophy, has ever been gentle with this universal genius.

AUGUST TWENTY-NINTH

THIS is the birthday of the beekeeper of Oostacker, the only poet of great merit save Goethe and Chamisso to whom scientists have ever turned a respectful ear. So far as my tastes go, Maurice Maeterlinck in our times is the most acceptable mystic of the western world; to the astonishment of naturalists, when his *Life of the Bee* appeared in 1901, it was not rhapsodic in spirit but only in diction; in fact it was worthy to stand with the work of Huber or Réaumur on the hive, and beyond any question in my mind, it is the finest prose that has ever been used to describe the subject matter of science. Maeterlinck is a brilliant example of what I take to be the ultimate truth, that poetry and science are sister and brother, and lay together in the same womb. Both are forms of description, and when engaged in their highest branches, they seek the essence of things. Maeterlinck, from the realms of poetry, entered the field of science not only educated by a study of the most classical authorities on the life of the bee, but as an apiarist himself. Thus equipped, he turns on us the dazzling brilliance of his power as a poet. His similes ring in the memory, contain the essence of fact, convey reality in the way that only art is able to do.

I know of no more realistic or electrifying description than that of the queen bee after her return from her wedding flight, slaying the superfluous princess nymphs as they sleep in their cells amidst their store of royal honey. Inexorable predestined law operating through an insect's rage is something that neither a poet nor a scientist, but only a man who was both, could accurately describe.

AUGUST THIRTIETH

THERE are two self-styled schools of thought concerning the intelligence of such creatures as ants. The mechanists hold that ants are not intelligent at all; the intelligence is all in the eye of the human observor who reads into their wholly conditioned reflexes, intentions and decisions that are only possible to humans. They raise the cry of anthromorphism and charge their opponents with being sentimental mystics. Maeterlinck retorts that the mechanists are really reacting to the problem in the most emotional and anthropocentric fashion of all: they do not want to think that other beings can share the precious gift of intelligence with them; so they set out determined to prove that only humans (and, really, only mechanists) are intelligent.

The facts seem to be that neither mechanists nor mystics of a violently partisan nature make very careful observers or good experimenters. Albrecht Bethe's experiments on ants of the genus Lasius, which are supposed to have settled the matter in favor of complete mechanistic determinism, when performed over again by a biologist instead of a physiologist, yielded quite different results and conclusions.

Bethe came to the conclusion that ants, like crabs and many other arthropods, are only reflex machines without a glimmer of intelligence. But I am afraid that he went into the investigation already predisposed to this belief, for when he had performed an experiment a dozen times or so, without being able to educate his subjects, he gave them up. Even a dog would appear to be a brainless reflex machine if we gave up trying to teach him to give his paw at the twelfth attempt, and more patient men have succeeded in training the associative memories of insects very highly.

AUGUST THIRTY-FIRST

AUGUST, the aureate month, draws to its blazing close— a month of sun, if ever there was one. Gold in the grain on the round-backed hill fields. Gold in the wood sunflowers, and in the summer goldenrod waving plumes all through the woodlot, trooping down the meadow to the brookside, marching in the dust of the roadways. Gold in the wing of the wild canaries, dipping and twittering as they flit from weed to bush, as if invisible waves of air tossed them up and down. The orange and yellow clover butterflies seek out the thistle, and the giant sulphur swallowtails are in their final brood. The amber, chaff-filled dust gilds all the splendid sunsets in cloudless, burning skies. Long, long after the sun has set, the sun-drenched earth gives back its heat, radiates it to the dim stars; the moon gets up in gold; before it lifts behind the black fields to the east I take it for a rick fire, till it rises like an old gold coin, that thieves have clipped on one worn edge.

SEPTEMBER FIRST

I ONCE began, but never finished, a collection of the beetles in my neighborhood. I began it under the impression that it would form an easy specialty. Beetles are not so difficult to capture as butterflies, and no such finicking job to prepare, nor are they half so perishable. But I gave the collecting up because I discovered that there were almost three thousand beetles already known, from a ten mile square in my own district.

I worked just long enough with beetles to gain a certain feeling for families that is still useful at times. But what chiefly delighted me was the infinite variety of their habitats and their ways of gaining a livelihood. I discovered that there were the powder-post beetles, the odor-of-leather beetles, the caterpillar hunters, the bombardiers, sextons or buryers, soldiers, stag beetles, rhinoceros beetles, unicorns and longicorns, gold beetles, darkling beetles, cardinal, tiger, rove, whirligig and scarab beetles.

Beetles naturally divide themselves as vegetarians or carnivores, but I was more startled to find how many of them had very specialized appetites. One of the several drugstore beetles eats aconite by preference. Now that I come to think of it, this same beetle has been immortalized in Benét's poem *Endymion in Edmonston*. There are fungus beetles, oil beetles, cigar beetles, grain, rice, bacon, carpet, greenhouse and even herbarium beetles.

Before long I was to learn that there are beetles found only in ants' nests, some as parasites or devourers, others as part of the ant's stockyard of cattle kept for killing. There are beetles special to termites' nests, to wasps' nests, to wood mice's nests, to old bones, and beetles parasitic on other beetles!

SEPTEMBER SECOND

IN A desultory sort of way the little peeps, the least sand-pipers, as they are quaintly called, are arriving now from their breeding grounds within the arctic circle. Now they are descending on any convenient pond or stream bank, and even around some mud hole where the farm pigs wallow I see them gathering, bringing life to the ugly slough, and setting it to ringing with their cries. They are never still a moment, continually wandering about on their bright toothpick legs that always seem to be jointed in the wrong direction, and constantly pecking like those wooden mechanical birds I used to buy for my children in Europe.

To me the charm of the peeps is the constant clinking of their sociable conversation. While not actually driving a bill into the mud or sand for aquatic worms and small crustaceans, they talk perpetually between bites. The note sounds like *cling-clang* struck out on a little bell or tiny anvil. The whole marsh will ring with that tiny note, re-peated here, tossed there, taken up on all sides and flung back across the air. Sweet at first, the metallic tinkle pres-ently torments my tympanum by its endless repetition.

Sometimes I see them rise in pursuit of the autumn midges, and again, when I am lying concealed in the grass watching the big water birds, I see the peeps come swirl-ing down amongst them, alighting on the mud. If I make a sound or a motion the herons and yellow-legs fly off with cries of alarm and anger. But the least sandpipers only rise in a little flock, drift uneasily for a few feet, and then, alighting at a run, continue their feeding in a trusting way.

SEPTEMBER THIRD

T H E garden this morning was invaded by a flight of butterflies, and I made sure that it must be the brown monarchs
in their famed autumn swarming. I gave them no attention
for some hours, when I was arrested by one individual who
paused a minute on the window sill near to my elbow. I
saw at once that it was not a monarch but a viceroy, who
has been so named because he so closely imitates the
monarch that he passes for the king.

This is indeed the favorite example of protective mimicry
of one species by another. In size they are close enough, and
there is a general resemblance in the black veining of the
wings, the dark bands lit as with little opaque windows
by rows of white spots. The viceroy has a ground of terra
cotta and the monarch of ruddy brown—near enough alike
to deceive a casual glance. The viceroy flaps nervously between long straight glides, with the wings held horizontally,
while the monarch glides with wings half erect, his actual
flying being performed with a see-sawing motion. The
monarch is notoriously distasteful to birds. The viceroy, it
is said, would be a delicious morsel were the birds not
entirely deceived by the resemblance.

But *are* the birds fooled? Are not rather the observers
persuaded into seeing what they are looking for? As a
theory, mimicry between species dates from a strongly romantic era and today could scarcely be defended save on
grounds of parallel evolution or utmost coincidence. In
either case mimicry would cease to be the appropriate name.

SEPTEMBER FOURTH

T H E example of mimicry between poisonous and edible butterflies that is the most striking is that of the small butterfly Alciope, whose females, on the dry east coast of Africa, resemble an east coast poisonous species, while in the wet rain forests of the Congo they take on the color and form of a noxious kind of the west coast. These females, (the males do not change,) seem to be almost too clever to believe in, or more favored by Mother Nature than any of her myriad children.

The explanation is right at hand, if we would regard it. Already the autumnal brood of our blue and yellow swallowtails, our orange clovers and cabbage butterflies are appearing—the dark, hairy, inactive forms that are characteristic of our dry autumns. The wet season or summer forms are disappearing. Now is there any more astonishment in the fact that a tropical African butterfly changes form on the wet and dry sides of the continent than that a temperate American species does so in the wet and dry seasons of the year?

The resemblance of the edible species to the noxious kinds need occasion no more surprise than that any two species resemble each other. There is no denying that creatures which closely resemble their surroundings (and most creatures do) are aided in escaping their enemies or in capturing their prey. But Nature does not dress her sheep in wolves' clothing. To suppose so is again to postulate design purposive in the manner of human thinking.

SEPTEMBER FIFTH

FIRST in the summer woods they begin with the lady aster, a dainty lavender, its leaves heart shaped. Then on the marsh the rush asters bloom, and so, species by species, they fill up the forests and fields and swamps, New England aster and brown-eyed wood aster with petals like curling lashes. The asters number thirty kinds in the blue hills and green river valleys that I can see from the top of the ridge above my house. The country over, there are hundreds of species.

In England they call them Michaelmas daisies—but Europe has no asters at which an American would look twice. In this our western world the asters stand all through autumn, shoulder to shoulder in forest, on prairie, from the Atlantic to California, climbing up to the snows of Shasta, creeping out upon the salt marshes of Delaware. Here some call the white ones frostflower, for they come as the frost comes, as a breath upon the landscape, a silver rime of chill flowering in the old age of the year. In the southern mountains they are hailed as "farewell-summer." Farewell to August, to burning days. Farewell to corn weather. Farewell to swallows, and to red Antares angry as venom in the Scorpion.

SEPTEMBER SIXTH

ACROSS the boggy bit of meadow, and over the lawn rolling gently to the water's edge, every blade of grass, every inch of space, is covered with a fall of gossamer. It is like the foam upon the sea, like the spray in the air from a mountain waterfall. Millions and millions of threads finer than silk gleam with millions of dew drops like spangles. These are the looms, it was believed in older, simpler days, where are woven the sheer cloth with which fairy women clothe their tiny seductive bodies.

Why is it that a fall of gossamer is almost always seen in autumn? The best authorities seem agreed that at the turn of the year the spider population, like almost all the animal folk, reaches its height. The moment comes when each species has bred and reared, and every inch of its environment is filled. At such times butterflies, locusts, crows, grackles, lemmings and spiders too are moved by some inner emotion that makes them wish to see the world. This is not so much a migration with any fixed goal, but a general exodus, preceded by a swarming. From every bush and blade and hole the spiders sail off upon a thread spun out of themselves. They launch themselves upon a course that is light as air, fluid as liquid, evanescent as a thought.

There is no evidence that the spiders will arrive anywhere save at that bourne where we must all arrive. They must die in the frost and the lake; they must starve in some alien meadow, half a copse away from home.

SEPTEMBER SEVENTH

O N this day in 1707 was born Georges Louis Leclerc de Buffon, whose memory would live, if for no other reason, as an example of the dangers to a scientist of becoming the zoölogist laureate of a great court. Exquisite in dress, an orator and a brilliant stylist, he handsomely ornamented the court of Louis XV, who cared not one damn about anything in natural history. The theological faculty of Paris once threatened to arraign him, but Buffon, who had no intention of becoming a Bruno, parried the accusation with a few elegant genuflections to the infallibility of the Church. The perfect courtier, he speaks often of the Creator in his encyclopedic *Histoire Naturelle,* but in private correspondence he revealed himself as a complete atheist.

Buffon is a man to whom the word magnificent perfectly applies. Resplendent in personality, his works too deal with everything under the sun, giving first place to "noble" beasts like dogs, lions, and eagles, and reserving disparaging remarks for trivial creatures like bees and ants. He had no use for the simplicity which Linnæus introduced into descriptive science. He goes out of his way to attack the Swede, and, for more personal reasons, Réaumur, whom he reproaches for his interest in ants. Ants are all very well, but what a tiresome tendency is "enthusiasm"! There is no use, says Buffon, knocking snuff from his lace ruffles, in giving a creature more space in our minds than it occupies in Nature.

Verily, an epigram may well be the death of thought!

SEPTEMBER EIGHTH

N o t all the courting is done in spring. The nuptial flight of the bumblebees is autumnal, and the whole order of Orthoptera, the crickets, katydids, locusts, and grasshoppers, is dominantly autumnal, like the aster family among flowers. In blue September the Carolina locust, the commonest species hereabout, is shaken by the tender passion, and like other persons in that condition, he is sometimes a comical sight for onlookers unaffected by the emotion. This lusty fellow, whom I always know by his zigzag, choppy flight, is a very inferior flyer compared to his mate. Unlike the drone ant, he would have, I suppose, no chance of overtaking her by speed and sheerly compelling her to his will.

It is by the power of song that the female is won, and complacently she sits on a bending stem of beard grass, while all her swains commend her by moving the hind femora up and down, rasping out what is no melody or serenade but merely an insistent lover's complaint. When she has made her choice the disappointed suitors do not always leave her presence. After all, nothing much awaits them but frost and death, and while she lays her eggs in the ground the males often continue to watch her, satisfied perhaps in some deep instinct that the race goes on, though the individual must perish.

SEPTEMBER NINTH

It is startling enough to learn that the crickets have their ears in their legs. But when I listen to the uproar of the last songs of the male cicadas, it is really too upsetting to be told that the females are deaf. All that stridulation, that insistent wooing—and not one sound can the lady hear! At least, nothing remotely suggesting an ear can be made out in any of the seventy-four cicadas inhabiting the United States.

I am forced to the conclusion that the male does not hear the noise he makes, any more than the female. We are the only ones who derive any sort of emotion from the stridulating of cicadas. With each dying whir I seem to hear the cry that summer is over, summer is over! By to-morrow, perhaps, I shall, for the last time, have heard that familiar sound. And so for the first time in the year I am able to appreciate it, a little.

SEPTEMBER TENTH

IN AUTUMN some of the sweetness of spring steals back again. There are the blessed rains, the sharp nights, the mornings smelling of wet loam and winy air as if blown from the mountains. The woods are filling up with clouds of asters. And best of all, the birds return. Few are the voices of the forest, but the robin has taken to singing again his old "Cheer up, cheery, Wake up, weary!" The grackles gather in the wet woods just as they do in March, and from the fields comes a slender, wistful whistling of the meadow-larks, of all songs I know the most poignant except the farewell whistling of the white-throat sparrow. But there is something sad about these songs, something that merely reminds us of a happiness we once knew, that is gone.

SEPTEMBER ELEVENTH

N o w in the ninth month the great clan of the Compositæ comes to glory in a burst of gold and purple. Of all families it is not only the largest, and the newest in point of evolution, but the very peak and summit of the plant kingdom, as man reckons himself the divine object for which the worm crawled out of the tidal mud and became the first vertebrate.

The seeming intricacies of the composite flower are the despair of the beginner. But in the sunflower each character and organ, as if seen under a magnifying glass, is easily read, and the beholder sees the Compositæ for what they are, a city or society of little florets, the whole enclosed within leaf-like walls. A single visit from a bee may suffice to pollinate every one of a composite's blossoms. Winds bear the downy-tufted seeds afar; or barbs attach themselves to animal's fur, to man's clothing.

So, just as the year opens with the most primitive and ancient families, like the catkin-bearing trees, it ends with the triumph of the newest and most complex flower families. Indeed, as there have been the age of tree ferns, the age of conifers, so we are living in the age of the Compositæ, the plants that for today at least shall inherit the earth.

SEPTEMBER TWELFTH

BUTTERFLIES look dainty enough to be perfumed like the flowers. And the emanations of the male peacock butterfly are strong, even sweet in a rather rank way. The scales within the little pouch on the hind wings of the male monarch emit an odor like honeysuckle. But when I pressed the abdomen of a female at once a strong, unpleasant scent, like that of cockroaches, exuded on my hands. There is just a trace of heliotrope in the odor of the orange clover males, and the gentlemen yellow swallowtails have a sweet flowery smell that I cannot quite place. But their wives have an acid reek which is distinctly rank, while the cloudless sulphurs possess an exquisite, if faint, perfume of freesia.

What strikes me in these investigations—brief as they are —is the fact that I do not like the odor of the females. Certainly no better proof were needed of the fact that our criterion of the beautiful in Nature is utterly beside the point.

SEPTEMBER THIRTEENTH

FABRE's experiments with the odors of moths are famous. So far as he knew the great emperor moth was not found around Seranon at all. He imported a single female, and left the window open to the night. Out of the darkness the males came as if Dis had released them from her cloak. His description of entering the room, to find it a wild flutter of rare wings, is one of the most vivid in all of the marvelous *Souvenirs Entomologiques.*

At the moment when the males entered, the female had, in point of fact, been removed to the next room. But wherever she had alighted, wherever her slender abdomen had rested or her six frail feet had clung, her swains hovered in ecstasy. Even when the lovely lady herself was restored to the room, the males, still depending on some other sense than sight, preferred to worship the ground she had walked on than to seek her in body.

Fabre concluded that they possessed a sixth sense. Sight and sound were ruled out, and of course taste and touch. Fabre endeavored to show that smell was not involved; he filled the room with suffocating fumes of sulphur, and still the males came. But very possibly fumes of sulphur are not smelled by emperor moths at all, or cannot obliterate the odor by which the female calls lovers to her; mosquitoes, for instance, are sensitive to sound at just one pitch, and to no other. A peerless observer, Fabre was behind his times as an experimenter.

SEPTEMBER FOURTEENTH

ON THIS day in 1769 was born Alexander von Humboldt, who has been called the second discoverer of America. In 1799 he put his entire fortune into an expedition to South America where he made collections so vast that much of the remainder of his life was spent in working them up at Paris and in Berlin.

Never did there live a man of more varied attainments. Humboldt is the real founder of climatology, the inventor of the weather map; he was the discoverer of the fact that volcanoes exist in ranges along cracks in the earth's surface; he is the Adam of modern geographers, the model of modern exploration; he experimented, largely on himself, with the effects of electricity upon muscles and nerves; he founded plant geography as a science, and to cap it all he undertook in his old age to write a *Kosmos* that was the *summum bonum* of romantic natural philosophy. He died in the year that Darwin published the *Origin of Species*.

With all these gifts, Nature had yet endowed him with the talents of an artist, and it is to his esthetic appreciation of scenery and his vivid descriptions of the delights of travel that the popularity of his *Travels* is due. The armchair explorer never had a better friend than goodly Humboldt. So far as scenery can ever be reduced to a science—that is, classified by types—Humboldt did it, by combining knowledge of geologic structure with a keen feeling for the types of vegetation. He declares that each latitude possesses its own characteristic natural "face."

I have more than backward looking tenderness for this concept and for Humboldt's versatile gifts; I am of the conviction that a sort of synthetic diffuseness is exactly what science, more than ever, stands in want of.

SEPTEMBER FIFTEENTH

AUTUMN at first is no more than a freshening of morning and evening, a certain sweet and winy odor in the air that blows upon the cheek as one steps out of doors in the morning, or opens the window at night to lean out a moment and look at the stars, before turning at last to sleep.

Autumn is the blooming of the goldenrod all through the oak woods and across the fields. Autumn is the cricket's cry, the swarming of the monarch and the storms of the Lisa butterfly. It is the odor of leaf fires, the smell of crushed marigold leaves, of tansy leaves and the sharp terebinthine scent of walnut husks that look so apple green and leave so brown a stain.

Autumn is the end of vacation, the beginning of school, the gathering of grackles, the dropping of ripe plums, the swarming of yellow hornets in the pear orchards. It is the ripening of the wild rice, the meeting together of bobolink hordes, the first hint of scarlet in the sumac leaf and the dewberry cane. It is the end of one more year's experiment. Now Nature dismantles her instruments and lays them away.

SEPTEMBER SIXTEENTH

N o w this is the season when the bank swallows depart, and in the thickets and from the fields, I hear the cricket-like yet half metallic clinking and whistling of the tree swallows as they wheel and congregate in little parties. Before migration actually sets in, it is their way to indulge in great sociability, like farmers meeting from afar for harvest merriment. Mating and rearing, with their fierce privacy, done, they are possessed now of a specific gregariousness.

Some scientists deny to animals the emotions which men experience, but on what grounds I cannot see. So I am certain that the sensation of jollity, of warmth, of adventure, which we feel when, after a solitary existence, or a purely familial one, we go to a fair, or a dance in a village, or a concert in the city, is only a tithe of what the social animals feel when they congregate, of a misty autumn morning, in adventurous little bands. Over my rooftop I see them drilling in little platoons, as if in martial preparations for their descent upon the south.

SEPTEMBER SEVENTEENTH

Now the autumn dance of the midges has begun, and I distinguish by the motion of their little eddies and spiral nebulæ the different sorts—the tiny fellows that spin in some invisible maelstrom, the larger dark ones that tremble up and down in one vertical plane as if against a sheet of glass, and the clover midges drifting thick as storms of diatoms in the plankton of the sea. But though I swing my hat at them, they are too swift for me. It is the bats, in their goblin flight, seemingly so drunken, in reality so accurate, who catch the midges in the twilight when my eyes just begin to fail of seeing anything but the great outlines of the trees, the humped shadows of shrubbery.

Zoölogists will classify the bats upon the basis of their incredibly convoluted ears, their sometimes preposterous noses, and their always exaggerated toes that appear like the ribs of their wings. No marksman, I seldom get a good look at a bat, save when I have picked up a wounded creature from the ground, jittering angrily and glaring at me from its uncannily knowledgeable black eyes.

I could never see why any one should fear or dislike any bat of the temperate zone. How often I have lain wakeful, in a great old house by the sea, under the ghostly cascade of the mosquito curtain, and delighted in the companionship of the little bats who swept in through the open window, mysterious, soundless, flirting with their own reflections in the dusky pool of the great mirror.

SEPTEMBER EIGHTEENTH

ON THIS day, in Philadelphia, in 1842, in agony and poverty died Constantine Samuel Rafinesque, who was born sixty years earlier, on we know not what day, in Constantinople, son of French and German parents. When his landlord discovered the body he prepared to sell it to the medical college. Friends only prevented this by secretly lowering the shrunken little remains from the window on ropes, and hurrying them away to potter's field. His will was as utterly disregarded as if its executors had torn it up and thrown it away, as most of his writings were treated. Today some of his papers are on the list of the rarest desiderata of collectors.

Careful workmanship, years of patient, well-rewarded search, have characterized most of our American naturalists. But there has not been one among them who was a titan, as Humboldt or De Candolle or Réaumer or Linnæus were titans. The only exception would be Rafinesque, whose unfortunate megalomania, foreign eccentricities and sarcastic tongue earned him enemies in every branch of science that he essayed. How wide were his endeavors can be judged by the foes he raised up for himself. Cuvier began the fashion of rating Rafinesque as a Münchhausen because in the dead fishes he dissected he could not see the colors Rafinesque described in the living specimens. Say and others disregarded his descriptions of the molluscs of the Ohio River, though his names certainly had priority. Asa Gray warned European botanists to have nothing to do with Rafinesque's species. Audubon puckishly tricked him into making himself ridiculous as an ornithologist; Squire and Davis have been accused of practically stealing his work on Indian mounds, and Featherstonaugh, the early American geologist, drove poor Rafinesque before him on the tip of his barbed pen.

SEPTEMBER NINETEENTH

RAFINESQUE's contemporaries were not wholly unjust to him. He was creative, but not conscientious; he described species he had never seen by extracting them from journals of travelers to the western states. The practice was reprehensible, but Rafinesque's scope was so cramped! And his genius was a large, loose, correlative one; had he ever been able to secure good appointments, he might have been a Linnæus of the western world, or, with travel, a northern Humboldt. But his applications were always rejected in favor of mediocre and more respectable and well connected gentlemen of American birth and manners. His thirsty brain hungered for worlds to conquer; fate had placed him in Kentucky, which did not, in 1830, lack for natural wonders so much as for a society fit to understand them. That was the era when centenarian beech trees were cut down as if they were weeds, when hogs were fattened on the bodies of passenger pigeons, and a naturalist was considered little better than a "natural."

That Rafinesque was far ahead of his time may be judged from the fact that he invented, on paper at least, fireproof buildings, artificial leather, steam plows, submarines, regular weather reports. And twenty years before Darwin he wrote: "The truth is that species and perhaps genera also are forming in organized beings by gradual deviations of shapes, forms, and organs, taking place in the lapse of time. There is a tendency to deviations and mutations through plants and animals by gradual steps at remote, irregular periods. This is a part of the great universal law of perpetual mutability in everything."

THE life of Rafinesque has been painstakingly assembled from fragments, scattered on two continents, in the memoirs and memories of the persons who knew him. To a great extent it has had to be pieced out from the accounts of his enemies, and from those of his worst enemy, himself.

"A dark, Italian gentleman," say some of the accounts, "with a fine dark eye." Others recall him as an agreeable talker, a great boaster, a fascinating lecturer. "A most eccentric person," writes one woman, "his extreme absent mindedness contributing to his foreign ways to make him peculiar.... He went into society while in Lexington, and was a good dancer, but had... no conversation save on his favorite topics... Mrs. Holley, the wife of the President, took a motherly supervision over this lone, friendless little creature, while at Transylvania University, and saw that he ate his dinner, that the mud from his various expeditions was removed from his garments and his hair was combed and his face washed."

We find Rafinesque advertising in the *Gazette* to give instruction in French, Spanish and Italian to ladies, offering to lecture (weather permitting) on phrenology. He started innumerable magazines, written entirely by himself; one of them, *The Western Magazine,* with the candid slogan, *Un peu de tout,* was confiscated by the printer for lack of payment. Only three copies escaped. Finally, cast out by President Holley, who had no use for science, we see him selling "Pulmel," an herb medicine warranted to cure consumption. He sincerely believed that he had healed himself by its means.

Not until his death and the reading of his will did the world learn that this sad, mad, and often very great little man had once loved a woman—a Sicilian who had run away with a comedian, and that he had had a son who died and a daughter who vanished into oblivion.

SEPTEMBER TWENTY-FIRST

BEFORE the era of specialization it was permissible for a man to call himself a naturalist and, like Rafinesque or Humboldt, interest himself in birds and shells, caverns and Indian mounds, fungi and ferns and flowers, geology, meteorology, astronomy, and even scenery. Now the systematic zoölogists have practically seized the title of naturalist between their teeth and run away with it, though I am blessed if I can see why a botanist is not also a naturalist. The very name of Nature is now almost in disgrace with the sober-sided specialists. For them it smacks too much of the discarded romantic philosophy of the eighteenth and early nineteenth century, and so they half deny the reality of its existence. So vast has the systematic fund of learning become since the time of the old naturalist philosophers, that the human mind can no longer encompass more than one room of this great storehouse. Many collectors of insects will now take specimens of only one family. The span of human life does not permit a specialist to dally with bees if his business be wasps.

It is my contention that specialization should be left to those who are not mentally gifted at generalization. The specialist is to be called upon for precise information. But there is still a place for the all-around naturalist. His use to the sciences is correlative, his rôle, elsewhere, an interpreter's.

LIBRA

SEPTEMBER 22 — OCTOBER 22

SEPTEMBER TWENTY-SECOND

THE last two have been days of rain and storm. A great tropical hurricane, that must have begun somewhere off the Cape Verdes as a vague "low," a mere depression in the atmosphere, has swept in the groove of hurricanes across the Atlantic, arching up on its typical parabola across the West Indies, flattening the sugar cane, lifting thatches in the Virgin Islands, piling the sea-water high in the everglades, setting the bells of old Charleston churches to ringing doleful warning. It has swept off the edge of the continent at the Capes of Virginia, amidst the frantic signaling of ships, for which the radios have become ominously still, the tinkle of landsman's music suddenly silenced for the crying of the vessels high up on the dials, a sound like the pleading of curlews blown out to sea upon a last, predestined flight.

Inland here the tail of the storm has slashed us in the face. Tattered black clouds skim on a wind of their own, under the rolling, boiling mass of the great nimbus sheet. Of course this will be considered by those who wish to think so a proof of the equinoctial storms—the *"Drei Böse Männer"* of the Germans. Those who believe that the equinox is always accompanied by storms never appear to take heed of the equinoxes when no storms occur. They merely assure you that the three terrible men are late this year.

From an inland biological point of view the interest in the hurricanes lies in the living flotsam which they toss us. The only records hereabouts for Audubon's puffin, Leach's petrel, and the Hawaiian and Wilson's petrels have been made after the hurricanes, while the effect of a storm, followed by sunny weather, is to kill off all the worn butterflies, and to give rise to a fresh emergence of the autumn brood.

How much of any landscape is due to the grasses is a quality in scenery that the best descriptions rarely admit. Orchard grass lends to any land that it inhabits something ample and light and gay. To the marshes the reed, Phragmites, gives long slant rainy-looking lines, and from their grasses the pampas and the steppes must surely take full half of their contour.

It is in autumn that the grasses hereabout come forth in their full beauty; they fill the meadows like some fluid till they are become wind-swirled living lakes. But above all they give the meadow scene its dominant color. There is not one of our sterile upland fields or abandoned farms where the beard grass, Andropogon, does not show its soft terra-cotta sheaths, its glaucous blue stems, and woolly gray puffs of downy seed half bursting from the spike. The misnamed redtop troops across the fields, its purplish stems standing rank to rank, the panicles turning a dull gold as the seeds fall, reflecting the mild sunlight of hazy Indian summer mornings. In the woods and old fields the Indian grass has begun to bloom—as enchanting as any flower that can boast calyx and corolla, with its golden brown spikelets, its dangling orange anthers, the whole plant turning to a sun-burnished bronze in its old age.

SEPTEMBER TWENTY-FOURTH

I TRY each year to disbelieve what my senses tell me, and to look at the harvest moon in a cold and astronomical light. I know that it is a small cold sphere of rock, airless, jagged and without activity. But the harvest moon is not an astronomical fact. It is a knowing thing, lifting its ruddy face above the rim of the world. Even to the thoroughly civilized mind, where caution for the future is supposed to rule all impulse, the orange moon of autumn invites the senses to some saturnalia, yet no festival of merriment. The harvest moon has no innocence, like the slim quarter moon of a spring twilight, nor has it the silver penny brilliance of the moon that looks down upon the resorts of summertime. Wise, ripe, and portly, like an old Bacchus, it waxes night after night.

SEPTEMBER TWENTY-FIFTH

N o w is that opulent moment in the year, the harvest, a time of cream in old crocks in cool, newt-haunted spring-houses, of pears at the hour of perfection on old trees bent like women that, as the Bible says, bow down with child. In this field the grain stands, a harsh forest of golden straw nodding under the weight of the bearded spikes, and in that, it has been swept and all its fruitfulness carried off to fill the barns.

One will not see here, save in the steep tilted Blue Ridge farms, the man reaping by sickle in his solitary field, while his daughters bind the sheaves, nor the bouquet of wheat and pine boughs hung above the grange gable that is crammed to the doors. But we have our own sights and sounds at harvest time. There is the roar and the amber dust of the threshing machines, the laughter of the children riding home on the hayricks, the warfare of the crows and grackles in the painted woods, and the seething of juice in the apple presses. Then night falls and the workers sleep. The fields are stripped, and only the crickets chant in the midnight chill of the naked meadow.

SEPTEMBER TWENTY-SIXTH

ALREADY the woods are filling up with grackles, gathering into bands. They storm like a black cloud through the groves and descend with a sound like the pattering of rain drops, as they alight with their little guttural exclamations in the boughs. They are not going very far—perhaps no more than south of the thirty-first parallel, but they make a much greater to-do about it than many bound for the tropics. All this fussing and gabbling and preening, and starting only to scurry back, reminds one of the New England old maid who said she would rather be ready to go and not go, than go and not be ready. Such people never *will* go far, and the majority of them will never be ready. Only those who start without demanding that they shall be comfortable *en route* and able to maintain a well-preened appearance, will ever see Vineland rising from the wild brown foam.

N o w in the south the star Fomalhaut rises into view. The star maps, cast most of them for the latitude of London or New York, do not show this luminary as it shines for the better part of the world. They picture it as skimming low near the horizon, something that would be half lost in the glare of ground lights, or in evening damps and mists. In more fortunate latitudes it can be seen all through the autumn, rising at its highest full one third the way to the horizon. It shines, a zenith star, upon lands that I shall never see; it bears the name given it by the Arab shepherd astronomers of old, thousands of years ago when, by the shifting of the earth's axis, it was more readily visible in the northern hemisphere than now. To Romulus it rode for perhaps six months high in the heavens; for us it grazes the horizon for but three. It is a lost friend of our race, whose ghost returns to us. It is a glimpse into the past, a peek over the edge of things.

SEPTEMBER TWENTY-EIGHTH

U P I N the fallow fields, abandoned by cultivation and half grown up with pines, where I go to look for grasshoppers and crickets, the common evening primrose is in flower. With its four yellow petals and four drooping sepals and very long ovary and eight anthers teetering on long filaments, it is sweet in the fields, but nothing to carry home.

But the evening primrose was thoroughly impressed upon my imagination in my student days by the reverence in which it was then held as the rallying point for the theory of evolution advanced by the living Dutch botanist, Hugo de Vries.

What de Vries discovered, near the opening of this century, was a field of a kind of evening primroses known, by a paradoxical coincidence, as *Oenothera Lamarckiana,* which seemed suddenly to have "exploded from the inside." Here were giant plants, dwarf plants, broad-leaved and narrow-leaved primroses, flowers with long styles and short styles, a perfect rage of variations.

The idea suddenly dawned upon de Vries that this might be the way in which evolution takes place, by a random series of wild jumps, upon which Darwinian natural selection operates, preserving the fit, slaying the unfit.

WHEN Hugo de Vries came back to look for his field of evening primroses he found that a thrifty Dutch peasant had plowed them under, so that the classic exhibit A of the mutation theory is lost forever. The field of self-sown plants had been garden escapes, but as garden plants are notorious hybridizers, de Vries sent back to America for seeds of the wild plant—since all Oenotheras are confined, in a native condition, to our continent. But a prolonged search here has never turned up one single plant of *Oenothera Lamarckiana.*

Therefore beyond much doubt *Oenothera Lamarckiana* is a hybrid, created in Europe. Now when hybrids are formed by the crossing of two pure species, much the same thing happens to the two sets of heredity-carrying bodies called chromosomes in the nucleus of their germ cells as happens when we shuffle fifty-two different cards together and deal them out in various hands. The number of separate combinations of hands which can be dealt at the bridge table is almost inconceivable, and as in bridge we can receive hands that are worthless, hands that are good for a grand slam, and indifferent hands, so in hybridity there will emerge variations which cannot survive, and others that are more vigorous than the parent species. But, once again like the card game, the next generation of hybrids (if there be any) will constitute a reshuffling of the pack, in which only faint traces of the old hands will be discernible. Hybrids are either utterly infertile and hence without a rôle in evolution, or they show a tendency to a fluidity that rules them out completely as fixed or real species. A living thing that cannot hand down its heredity in an even partially fixed way cannot explain the origin of species.

SEPTEMBER THIRTIETH

MUTATIONS were known before the time of de Vries. Darwin and Huxley called them saltations; the gardener and the animal husbandman know them as freaks. A double rose is a freak; its stamens have been transformed into petals, with the result, of course, that it could not effectively reproduce itself. Indeed, most freaks seem to be in one way or another distinctly disadvantageous to perpetuation. The way of Nature with freaks is frequently to kill them. Seth Wright's famous bow-legged sheep, who could not jump over walls and hence were advantageous to the shepherd of Massachusetts, did show signs of perpetuating themselves by artificial inbreeding, but only under the protected conditions of domestication. Sheep built on the plan of the dachshund would not survive long in a world where wolves had straight legs and long fangs.

If one takes a more moderate stand on mutation than the de Vriesians, and claims only that very gradual changes take place from within the organism itself by a series of minute alterations which gradually accumulate momentum, then one may reasonably be a mutationist, but one is holding to nothing that Darwin and Lamarck did not include in their tenets. The vital point is to discover what causes these slow bendings of the bough of life.

OCTOBER FIRST

Now the autumn colors march upon their triumphs. So still the woods stand, against the faultless blue of the sky, they seem like windows dyed with pigments meant to represent all the riches and display of history—pointed windows blazing with trumpeting angels, blazons and heraldic glitter, intricate, leaf-twined illumination, depths of holy gold within temporal scarlet, soft gleaming chalices encrusted with ruby and topaz, cloths of bronze and ells of green, embroideries of crimson, twist from the vats of saffron and Tyrian and fustian.

The north woods have somehow stolen the fame of autumnal glory from other quarters of the land. But what have they—maples and beeches and aspens and rowanberry —that we have not? Or their fiery viburnums or huckleberries or brambles? We have all their colors and more, and indeed it is the tropical element in our flora that imparts the most dazzling brilliance. The tupelo tree before my door and the persimmons across the valley glow with a somber anger, like leaves that would be evergreen if they might and turn to the color of smoldering charcoal only under compulsion. The sassafras and the sour gum shout with orange and scarlet, and the curious sweet gum, with its star-shaped leaves, exults in crimson and vermilions. Like the gold tulip tree leaf it has a look about it as of some vegetation that does not really belong in the flora of the world today.

And in truth they both, like so many of our trees, are sole survivors of once great families of ages past. In what autumns must the Tertiary have rejoiced, when leaves that are fossils now flamed with colors we can only imagine— flamed upon a world without men in it, to call it beautiful.

OCTOBER SECOND

SOMETIMES, in midsummer, we see a single leaf that has turned yellow or red. A tree, most often a hickory, in a time of August drought, will suddenly color while all its kind stand green. Here is a clew to autumn forest hues. They are not due to frost, as it would seem. The red and gold, the orange and purple, are but the running together of many chemicals in the leaf, held apart when the foliage is in full vigor. With the first retreat of vitality, the withdrawal of sap into the deep cellars of the roots, the raw chemicals, useless now, are spilled together by the tree as it prepares for hibernation.

The maple's orange and the tulip tree's gold, those are but waste products. And indeed most pigmentations, whether in the autumn woods, hung as if with battle flags from some age of chivalry, or in the hummingbird's throat or the coral triton's sleek wet skin, are excretions of a substance that the organism cannot utilize.

OCTOBER THIRD

THE hour was afternoon; the place, the brook, where willows overhang, their leaves still green as summer. I was watching idly the little whirlpools that will continually dimple down a stream, born here, traveling swiftly, and dying, as living things die, by simply becoming a part once more of the universal flow. I sat still so long that the thicket began to resume its life once more; two dragon flies arrived upon the opposite shore, where a thin coast of mud enclosed a stagnant pool.

I must have been looking in their direction for some time before I was aware that one of them was engaged in a rhythmic motion, and poised, not with wings parallel with the water as we are accustomed to see them, but vertically. The creature, a female, was dancing up and down upon the mud, her tail stabbing it with the regularity of the needle in a sewing machine, and, wings glittering as she kept them fanning in the sunlight, she traveled gradually along the mud bank, depositing her eggs.

Beside her, as if to see that the matter were done properly, the male hovered just above the mud, his patience not exhausted as a half hour crept by, while the incredible fertility of his mate was scattered like bread upon the waters. From time to time he turned his head almost completely through three hundred and sixty degrees, while he kept a look-out, it may be, for foes of this rite.

A photograph taken through a dragon fly's hundred-faceted eyes shows a hundred images of the same thing— or so it looks when it has passed through our eyes and registered in our brains. But how does he see things, or rather, what does he think about them? Does he see a hundred wives, or think monogamously? Does he pursue a hundred midges, and devour but one?

OCTOBER FOURTH

EVERY year I see the tansy grow a little commoner hereabout. It is still a rare plant, but not in the sense that it is sought after or prized when it is found. A waif from the Old World, an outcast from gardens, with its ferny dark foliage and golden button heads, it can still claim kinship to a royal line of flowers, for it is but a chrysanthemum without the rays. The aroma of its leaves is closest to that of French marigolds, yet a little similar, also, to the smell of yarrow, of camomile or marguerite. A bitter oil pervades the plant, from which our grandmothers were wont to brew a nasty and I think quite harmful medicament, and it is this that on the quiet dusty airs of autumn afternoons distills that odor that will remind me, wherever I breathe it, of New England walls, of autumn days at college when new friends were made, new thoughts encountered, and the prospect of another year of loved and chosen study stretched ahead.

OCTOBER FIFTH

ON THE question of autumn flowers, our butterflies hold to different sects; one may say they go to different churches, for there is something devotional and religious about the adherence of butterflies to the flowers they love.

The swallowtails and skippers do their worshiping on the great proud heads of thistles. The yellow and orange clover butterflies, the sachem and the painted lady are also members of this prickly Scottish communion.

To the persuasion of the asters belong the yellow clovers, and the monarch and gorgeous red admirals also attend upon them. Indeed, when a butterfly loves asters it usually favors goldenrod as well, for not only are they closely related botanically, but they are pervaded, undoubtedly, by some of the same chemical elements. In both one notes the strong odor of beebread from the disk flowers, especially when the pollen is ripe, and many species of both kinds have glands on leaf and stem smelling strongly of walnut husks and anise.

I find that the yellow swallowtails are devoted to the great mauve heads of joe-pye weed. (And who, pray, was Joe Pye?) But for a completely exclusive place of worship there is none like the lovely balmony, blooming so pure and secretive in the autumn ditches. There a single butterfly, *Euphydryas phaëton,* dances in solitary ritual.

OCTOBER SIXTH

N O B O D Y knows the birth date of John Chapman, known as Johnny Appleseed, so that I shall put him where, I am sure, he would have preferred his biography to be inserted, in apple time. Sandburg and Stephen Benét and Vachel Lindsay have all sung his praises, and from his obscurity John (not Jonathan, as he is sometimes inaccurately called) has emerged as a national hero.

Perhaps the only American who resembles an early Christian saint, he too went his barefoot way in sackcloth, subsisting upon roots, thundering out denunciations of pioneer vanity—store calico and tea drinking—and planting apple seeds wherever he set foot.

Legend concerning him has grown to almost homeric proportions. Many cities and states claim that their apples are descended from his sowing. The sober facts seem to be that he arrived on the Ohio about 1801, being then some twenty-six years in age, a completely daft young Elijah— with a dash of Daniel Boone and General William Booth— who went about in Ohio and Indiana starting orchards from seed. He regarded cutting and grafting as immoral and contrary to the will of God. In flouting horticultural experience he seems to have been motivated by a compassion for apple trees, a devout belief that they should not be deprived of regular sexual fertilization. There is no record that any woman ever looked with favor upon poor ragged Johnny. At sixty-five he died of exhaustion, after a hundred mile trip afoot to one of his orchards. Mad he undoubtedly was, but Saint Paul would have approved of him, and so would Whitman, and Francis of Assisi.

B Y T H E farm door the shell-bark hickory leaves twirl down, a parched ruin. The poplar throws down its round gold foliage like so many coins of a vintage outworn, invalid, called in, as the Treasury would say, to the great bank of mother earth. The grass too is yellowed or browned, and the panting rabbit, even he the soft-footed one, makes a rustling sound as he lopes through the desolate blades and culms of the sedges around the dried pond.

There is a gathering in the south—not yet a cloud, only a density, a vague and undefined mistiness, a breath in the air like a beast's. It speaks of rain to come, of water to fill the ponds dried down to their chalky floor, where the forked skeletons of Chara lie sprawled out in marl. One rush of rain, and swiftly all this waste, this withering, will be turned to use by the silent brown *penitentes* of decay.

OCTOBER EIGHTH

N o w the autumn rains begin, and suddenly, where there were none, the fungi rise all through the woods. Not only the familiar stalk and gilled cap of the agaric family, but the brain puff balls, the little earth-measuring stars, sprawling their six points on the ground like black starfish. The old logs burst out with moon growths of white coral; the wet boughs are flecked with delicate tremulas, like shaking bits of dark wine jelly, and around the base of the oaks a great polypore has pushed out, a rich velvety mass of mouse-gray flounces, each ruffle bordered in deep black.

Wherever I walk, I find more kinds, pushing up their little buttony heads through the ground, or standing just emerged, with bits of the earth's dark caul still clinging to their helmets. When I dig anywhere in rich leaf mold and carry a handful of the dark odorous loam close to my face, the aroma of mushroom spawn comes to my nostrils; I break the loam in my fingers and it clings in little clots bound together by the root-like hyphal threads of fungi.

We speak of the stem of a mushroom; it seems to have roots, and a body. But no true stem or body could be formed like that, overnight, swift and unnatural as thoughts in a dream. The stem is no stem, but only a mass of pale, braided strands, different in nothing from the colorless threads below ground, where the mushroom sucks its living from decay. These gnomish shapes have no real structure; they are nothing but gleaming moonlight softness, texture like flesh, but without the warmth and glow of flesh. They are growth without plan for permanence, mere lunar effusion and invisible fertility, like the thoughts that rise, unbidden and ambiguous, from the dark of our subconscious.

OCTOBER NINTH

AT THE end of a day's most casual collecting, I have rather more than forty fungi spread upon the long table before me, some on white paper and some on black, in order to catch their spores, which may turn out to be almost any hue, irrespective of the color of the fungus itself.

I concerned myself today only with what we are pleased to call the higher fungi. To catalogue the fungus flora of the region, I should have not only to amass something like five hundred toadstools, puffballs, earth-measuring stars, corals, brackets, and other big effusions of the fungus world. I would be required to search old logs for dry rot, twigs for black knot, the tops of trees for the weird proliferation of witch's broom. The leaves of every lilac are overcast with the faint dusty bloom of a common mold; on every dying bramble leaf I can find the orange flecks of a special blackberry rust. Upon the forest floor I notice a caterpillar lying lifeless, a little turret of spores thrust from his body. In the ponds too are fungi, scavenging all decaying matter, parasitizing fish.

All these are but the evidences I can see with the naked eye. If I swing the lens of my microscope upon the world, it seems overcast with fungi, just as the sky, through the telescope, appears powdered over with stars. Here indeed is the underworld of plant life, the underworld and the wonderworld, where death, disease, decay, assault, and robbery are the accepted means of gaining a livelihood.

OCTOBER TENTH

I T I S necessary to make the distinction between parasitism and the condition of being a saprophyte, the first the art of thieving a living by battening upon creatures honestly making their own way in the world, the second applying to those living things that feed only upon decaying matter. The fungi engage in both traffics. Our common toadstools, bracket fungi and others that have large and often handsome fructifications are saprophytes, whose delicate threads or hyphæ dwell under ground or within the decaying log. They consume the leavings of Nature. But most fungi are true parasites, enemies, oftentimes, of man, filling the ear of wheat with ergot and black flag, smothering the young plants in the greenhouse with damp, spoiling the tender rice as it begins to shoot up through the standing water.

Like ghosts, the fungi can occupy the same space as good and tangible beings. Like ghosts, they are no sooner challenged than they turn into something else. You try to slay them on the currant bush and they leap to white pine. You battle them upon wheat, and they hide from you, overwintering on barberry. Manifold, insidious, they attack through all the chinks in our armour, like the insect legions which they resemble in their complexity, minuteness, and polymorphic lives.

If we ask what may be the position of the fungi in the balance of Nature, we receive the grand and sorrowful response that death is a part of life. All things can live only if something else has first been cleared out of the path. Parasitism and saphrophytism are as necessary to the scheme of existence as sunlight and water.

OCTOBER ELEVENTH

THE privilege of lighting the first hearth fire is something I claim in my quality as a husband and father. I have yet to meet that modest violet who does not cheerfully admit that he can build a fire better than any one else. Many visitors politely and kindly take my wood and kindling from my hands. Each has his own method. Some put the kindling on the bottom, some on the top; some stack the wood like a tepee, others like a log cabin. Some will use no paper, others can do nothing without a Cape Cod lighter.

But there is but one requisite of a fire, that it should burn. A fire is like a woman. It needs both love and authority. For myself I like best to woo it with pine, both as kindling and logwood. Pine burns brighter and hotter, and needs less kindling than any other wood. It has the sweetest odor and sizzles contentedly. What good is a cat that does not purr, a chestnut that will not pop, or a log that can not sing?

OCTOBER TWELFTH

AFTER lighting my first fire on the hearth, when the smoke had only just begun to curl up in a fragrant violet spiral, I was startled to hear a rattle of plaster, and a blundering, rushing sound. Only a moment too late did I recall that it must be a chimney swift. I ran outside to look for it, but it had taken its skimming way into the dusk.

Doubtless it had raised a brood here, only a few feet away from my desk, but less known to me than the activities of the wasps in the attic or beetles in the cellar. Like the swallow's, the nest is secured to the chimney by a sort of cement which the bird secretes. There is no soft lining, and, in haste to leave such a rough cradle, the fledglings soon learn to cling by their very tiny and surely weak claws to the masonry, where for some days they must be fed. In this task the parents are sometimes active all the night through.

The swift is a small bird, chiefly crepuscular, and beyond a wiry cheeping, has no song. Shy, humble-colored and domestic, it always seems to me more like a European than an American bird. In the Old World bird and mammal and plant must live intimately with their millions of human brothers. There, where the barley may grow right to the farmhouse wall, the little flowers, the lichens and the mosses dwell upon the wall and thatch, the swallows, storks, rooks, jackdaws and owls nest in the coigns and crannies, on the gables and chimney tops. But on this continent we have much more of the wild and tameless, which must die if it cannot conquer.

OCTOBER THIRTEENTH

LATE in the autumn, when the leaves of the buttonwood
are turning deep as Burgundy and the cat-tails are ripening
their silk, one little frog still sings his rather sad. metallic
threnody. The sound, though small, is piercing, and for
this reason he has been called the cricket frog. Cricket-like,
he is but an inch and a half long, at the most, and he
throws his voice with the ventriloquism of a Gryllus; it
peeps and calls from side to side of the boggy meadow;
though I steal on footsteps that I would make as soft as a
rabbit's tread, silence surrounds me where I walk, mockery
clinks out from behind me.

OCTOBER FOURTEENTH

IT LAY upon a rotting log—a delicate mass, intricate and yet without definite shape, like a bit of patternless lace dyed yellow. I picked it up in careful fingers, and the whole mass came lightly away from the log and lay firm as a fragment of fabric in my hand. Triumphantly I laid it in my vasculum which had only a few lichens and mosses in it, and proceeded on my way rejoicing. There is satisfaction for the student in finding a curiosity he has studied only in theory.

The Mycetoza—unpleasantly known as slime-molds or, sometimes, as flowers-of-tan—would seem upon first view to belong quite obviously to the fungi. They are flat, branched, irregular in form, without definite growth limit, and when they come to reproduce they form themselves into balls, into tiny chalices, feathery shoots, intricate ramified craniform masses like a morelle mushroom, or delicate knobbed forests like a bread mold, which release spores as any fungus will.

But, once liberated in a convenient film of moisture, these spores proceed to hatch out a blob of microscopic jelly like an amœba, which rolls and flows along, engulfing food in its streamers of protoplasm, or dancing along by its whip-like tail, for all the world like a flagellate or a male mammal's spermatozoön. When it meets another such creature it blends; a third is engulfed with total loss of identity into the shapeless mass, and the whole colony moves off, over logs or *through* them, inchin' along, avoiding light and useless obstructions, tracking down prey in the form of fungi and perhaps bacteria.

WHEN I turn my lens on the slime-molds the whole intricate mass leaps to my eye as something more formless, less comprehensible, than it seemed to be when I saw it on the log. I would have supposed, from the brilliant ocher color, the appearance of threads and granulations, that some underlying plan or symmetry must be discovered upon closer examination. But in fact it seems now no more than a sheet of protoplasmic material, without muscles, nerves, or any organs of digestion, as formless as an amœba. More formless! For though I can make out an outer layer and an inner nuclear layer I cannot anywhere distinguish either the semblance of cells nor of individuals living colonially.

I might say it is an overgrown uni-cellular organism, but it would be as reasonable to say that it is a non-cellular organism. The unwalled protoplasm, with thousands of nuclei in it, is in a state of surge, a rhythmic flowing back and forth, that, I suppose, sets more strongly in one direction than the other when the creature is in motion. It is so far from being a single organism that, if made to pass through cotton wool, it will completely disperse into innumerable streams, as it must do when penetrating the log. Yet it is so little a random collection of individuals that on emerging on the other side of such a filter it will reassemble every particle of protoplasm and flow forward again —leaving behind its spores, as no doubt it will do in the log, thus sowing a fresh crop of itself.

The problem is not whether this raw plasmodium is a plant or an animal; it is whether we shall not have to admit that there are at least three kingdoms of living things—the plant, the animal, and the Mycetozoa. Are there perhaps other kingdoms that we wot not of?

OCTOBER SIXTEENTH

IN BERNE, in the year 1707, was born on this day Albrecht von Haller, who was the foremost anatomist of his century and the founder of modern experimental physiology. At the same time he was a poet, and a wonder-child who fulfilled his promise. But I delight in his memory because he was the first naturalist to appreciate the beauty of mountains, the charm of alpine scenery. It is difficult to believe it now, but the Alps were once considered monstrous and horrifying excrescences. Gilbert White speaks of a gentle hill near Selborne as something foreboding and sinister. The Swiss, beyond doubt the most platitudinous folk in all Europe, are said to have shown no interest in scaling their peaks until the English sportsmen taught them to do it. Even today many French seem to me to be depressed rather than elated by alpine scenery.

Not so our wonder-child and poet of Berne, who had a thorough knowledge of Greek and Hebrew at ten, had written two thousand biographies at twelve, and epic poems at fifteen. Not even Saussure himself loved the mountains more than Haller. His face turned to the unearthly *Gegenschein*, the alpine after-glow, the gentians and campion at his feet, the wind of the glaciers in his young hair—that is how I always see him, a melancholy man, even from childhood, one who tried to serve more mistresses, to be more of a giant, than the world will allow.

OCTOBER SEVENTEENTH

IN OPPOSITION to Linnæus's artificial sexual system which grouped plants not into their natural families but merely into a convenient finding key, Haller proposed a natural system based upon the structure not of the flower, but of the fruit. Ray in England had already attempted the same thing, but had failed as Haller failed. Everywhere Linnæus triumphed, with the easy triumph of the provisional hypothesis for which the times are ripe.

Nor was the public ready yet to love Haller's Alps; his poetry was more praised than read, and nothing—not the honors of professorship nor of his career as a diplomat, not the triumphs of his work as an anatomist—brought him content. Though he published more than six hundred works, many of great length, he found no gratification in them. The free-thinking tendencies in the world troubled him and he wrote pamphlets in defense of Christianity. Yet the Gospel gave him no internal peace; he abhorred the vivisections he had performed; he wrestled with his angel over every act of his life. From his childhood a deep melancholy had pursued him. Year by year it ate his soul; he died, in 1777, master of many gifts both in science and art, dissatisfied and embittered.

No one, perhaps, envies the fate of a wonder-child and a man who lived half before his time and half too late. But in one field Haller was a happy pioneer, for he was both the poet and the scientist of the Alps, a man who trod Parnassus where the gentian drinks the shimmering glacial rill.

OCTOBER EIGHTEENTH

ALL day long the monarch butterflies have been swarming in the garden. The children dashed excitedly amongst them, yet the creatures did not disperse. They fluttered around the bird-bath, around a drying puddle; they wheeled about in droves almost like starlings, and toward darkness made for the trees, clinging to the undersides of the leaves.

The days preceding this swarming were rainy, save yesterday which was brilliantly sunny; result—a swift and final eclosion of the last fall brood, as sudden as midges on the first of March.

Many are the books which assure us that the monarch migrates south in great storms in autumn, and returns from the Gulf States in the spring, all the way to Canada. There is no evidence that the monarch really goes south; it is only autumn that goes south, calling into being, in state after state, the fall congregations of this common species. And, if this butterfly be any true migrant, why are there no spring migrations? In April or in May we see no more of this creature than a few tattered females who have over-wintered as adults—exceptions to the rule that winter slays all frail things that do not retreat into the egg or seed.

OCTOBER NINETEENTH

EVERY sunny afternoon I hear the cricket still, sweetly chirruping, and as the nights grow frosty he often comes into my house. From the window he hops by preference into the waste-basket, there to tune his roundelay. He is fond of the bathtub, too, and he hides behind the wood where I stack it by the fireplace. But his favorite room in my house is the cellar.

Now a cricket out of doors is a pleasing sound. Some people fall asleep as soon as the rain begins to fall on the roof; some like the lap of a lake upon stones, or the boom of the ocean on an old sea-wall. I love to hear the crickets chanting when I drop toward sleep. But a cricket under the bed is quite another affair, and there is nothing to do but to get up, on chill feet, and hunt the serenader out, and tell him frankly, by throwing him out of the window, that he has entirely too much to say and says it too loudly.

Out in the night, his small skirl goes sweetly among his fellows'. They sing, I think, of orange moons and meadow mice, of the first hoar frost lying pure and cool as samite on the stubble fields, and of the falling of the dull gold globes from the persimmon tree, the ripening of the heavy pawpaws in the steep woods by the river. By the hearth they speak to my ears of firelight and books, of the cracking of nuts and tucking children into bed. To my cat, his eyes rolling with the fever of the chase, his hair rising with enjoyable terror, they are ghosts behind the book-cases.

OCTOBER TWENTIETH

WHEN the fields are emptied of their insects and the woods of flowers, there is still one delight left to the collector. Winter or summer, the lichens still keep their rocks and tree trunks, and at any season not too cold, after a rain, you may come upon their odd little fructifications. These appear as little scarlet fairy cups, as black warts, as shields or scutcheons or pixy umbrellas or worn-edged coins, or spirals or fantastic little tree-like growths that may be orange, saffron, brown, green or milk-white, almost never identically the same shape even within the species. However a lichen grows, it never grows symmetrically.

There is the utmost charm about collecting lichens for a hobby. Nothing is easier to press and mount. And there is an exquisite fragrance that lingers around even a venerable lichen herbarium, that calls back every mind with any nose for Nature at all—to days of emerald delight in the rainy woods of Maine where the long gray beards of Usnea sorrow over the sad dignity of old spruce boughs, or to sun-bitten, frost-rended rocks above the tree line on Mt. Washington. Or to the tundras of Lapland and the jungles of Surinam, if you happen to have been there!

THE lichens, that appear the most gray and eventless of plants, are in reality a lively partnership. One member is some one of those little green algæ that often stain emerald the north side of a creviced tree trunk, or collect between chinks of a garden walk, or fleck dark, sour, sunless soil. The other is one of certain fungi which half parasitize and half protect their green partners. Though the fungus feeds upon its algal captives, it benefits them too, by maintaining about them a perpetual moist, slimy film that defends them against desiccation, the alga's chief foe. On their side, the algæ provide the parasite with that nutriment, manufactured in the mills of the sunlight, which the fungus, without chlorophyll, cannot obtain for itself.

Thus those elfin fructifications of the lichens, though they have the bright colors and often almost the delicacy of flowers, are not certainly sexual; they resemble fungoid pockets of spores, and yet they are not spores. They are not seeds or buds or slips, though they behave like all of them. Each one of them contains a small pellet of fungus matter to which the alga contributes, or is levied upon to contribute, a quota of its own strands. So together the two partners will roll or blow away, locked in each other's arms in a sort of love and hate, out of which a new lichen will be born, to scale mountain peaks and clothe the lonely forests in sage mourning. There seem to be no conditions that these strange plants will not endure except the fumes of our industrial civilization.

THE pale green maps of the lichens, sprawling across certain boulders that I pass on my regular walks, are as well known to me as the shapes of the five continents. Year by year I never see a change in them. I cannot honestly suggest that they have grown an inch in any dimension, and by all accounts the lichen is the slowest-growing colony in existence. There is every evidence that some of the great lichen patches upon inaccessible cliffs, where nothing could ever have disturbed them, are older than *Sequoia sempervirens!* This ought to deter one before stripping these little gray yet green elders from their niches where they cling with such a desperate grip. They go further north than any other plants, nourishing the reindeer; they scale the cliffs of the Himalayas where men faint and die; yet they flourish most richly of all in the tropics. To them I owe the color and the delectable odor of my ragged old Harris tweed coat, dyed with the lichens orchil and cudbear that the children of the isle of Harris gather. Innumerable are the lichen dyes, of which the most famous is litmus; to lichens many a man and beast has owed his life, on the steppes of Tartary, the muskegs of Athabasca, the tundras of Iceland. Beyond question the lichen is often the first plant upon the barren rock, the first bringer of life to the stones.

S C O R P I O

OCTOBER TWENTY-THIRD

Now the tepees of the corn shocks have been struck. The leaves of the kinnikinnick that the red man smoked are withered. And yet I never see the asters marching shoulder to shoulder under the woods and over the hills, without remembering the Indian who knew them. I never see a thin lilac spiral of smoke rising from a leaf fire without thinking of his camps.

The feel of the corn kernels in the hand, the rime of frost on a pumpkin's side, the contentment of a pipe—he knew them all, as we know them, here on this western continent that was his, this land of sunset and of autumn. He was not the enemy of primeval nature as we Europeans have proved to be; he was part of the American fauna, one with the bison and the elk and the beaver. He dwelt with Nature as her brother. There are few of us that at some time have not had a great longing to know our country as he knew it, and to have led his free and open life. And this nostalgia for the thing that we have killed is abroad in the wistful days we call Indian Summer.

OCTOBER TWENTY-FOURTH

On this day in 1632 was born at Delft Antonj van Leeuwenhoek, that delectable old Dutchman who had the enviable first look at things through a microscope. Not its inventor, he was a self-taught lens grinder who stepped up the power of the microscope from a magnification of ten times to two hundred and seventy diameters.

He remained all his life (which lasted over ninety years) something of the shrewd and self-made business man, and though he would tell his English friends, who elected him to their learned society, how to make lenses, he would by no means send them even the least of his microscopes, and he frequently refused to visitors as much as a peek through one of his vast private collection.

Working so jealously, it would have been easy enough for a charlatan to describe wonders that were not there; but it seems that Leeuwenhoek never misrepresented anything save that in the male spermatozoön he imagined (probably quite sincerely) the outlines of a sort of embryo. First at the high-power microscope, he became the discoverer of the protozoa or one-celled animals, of the sex cells of mammals, of the bacteria, of the crystalline lens of the eye, the striation of the muscles, the structure of wood; he was the first actually to see the circulation of the blood, and discovered that some insects reproduce without fertilization.

He was no scholar, but an inquisitive note-taker. Much of what he saw he knew not how to interpret, due partly to the state of knowledge at the time. But even for his day he was not well educated, and betrayed an obstinate self-sufficiency. Yet in some cases, as the identity of the red corpuscles, he guessed right when Malpighi and Swammerdam, his contemporaries, went wrong in their surmises.

OCTOBER TWENTY-FIFTH

THE keynote of spring is growth amongst the plants, reproduction amongst the animals. In summer it is the reverse; it is the plants that reproduce, the animals that grow. But autumn is the time of fattening. Now the beech nuts ripen their oily kernels; the walnut swells its rich meat through black wooden labyrinths; the wild rice stands high in the marshes, and the woods are filled with their jolly harvest of berries, blue buckthorn and scarlet bittersweet, black catbrier, holly and mistletoe and honeysuckle. The great green cannonballs of the osage orange drop from the prickly hedges with a thud; under the little hawthorns a perfect windfall of scarlet pomes lies drifted, and in the sun the bitter little wild crabs reach their one instant of winy, tangy, astringent perfection.

This is the moment of abundance for all our brother animals. The harvest mouse is now a wealthy little miser; squirrels can afford the bad investments they make. Opossums paw over the persimmons and pawpaws, picking only the tastiest, and like a cloud the cowbirds and grackles and bobolinks wing southward over the wild rice fields, so fat and lazy that the fowler makes an easy harvest of them. Everywhere, on frail bird bones, under the hides of chipmunk and skunk and all four-footed things, fat, the animal's own larder and reserve, is stored away against the bitter months, against lean hunger and long sleep.

OCTOBER TWENTY-SIXTH

IT IS nearly impossible to be sad, even listless, on a blue and gold October day, when the leaves rain down, rain down, not on a harsh wind, but quietly on the tingling air. They fall and fall, though not a breeze lifts the drooping battle flags of their foliage. You stand a moment before a late, last ash, watching. It seems as though the tree were actively engaged in shedding its attire, snipping it off, cutting it adrift. Pick up a leaf fallen at your feet, and examine the base of the leaf stalk. It feels hard to the touch; it is hollowed out. Had you a microscope, and a cut section of the leaf, you would see that indeed it had been cut off. The growth of a ring of callous cells, in a perfect ball and socket articulation, has predestined the fall. Wind need not tear the foliage down, nor decay set in. The tree itself passes invisible shears through its own auburn crown.

OCTOBER TWENTY-SEVENTH

A TREE in its old age is like a bent but mellowed and wise old man; it inspires our respect and tender admiration; it is too noble to need our pity. We take the fading of flowers very lightly; it is regrettable to see them go, but we know they are not sentient beings; they cannot regret their fresh tints, nor know when the firm, fine form begins to droop.

But the old age of a butterfly, the fading of its colors, the dog-earing of its brave frail wings, is a pitiful thing, for if the butterfly does not know that it is beautiful, it certainly knows when it is buffeted by the winds, and weighted and abraded by the autumn rains. It is, after all, an animal, and akin to us; not even the most hard-shelled mechanists have ventured to deny that insects have nerves and emotions, though they may not have intelligence or will as we understand those words. And I for one am convinced, if birds feel the change of season, and little mammals creeping into their winter quarters, that butterflies in some lesser but not inconsiderable degree, are aware that for most of them the term of life is nearly done. Animals often show a sharper sense of the feeling and imminence of death than we.

OCTOBER TWENTY-EIGHTH

THE dominant sound of spring is the song of birds, who are not ashamed at their preoccupation with amorous matters. Any one can hear them, or the sound of running brooks. But to hear the sounds of autumn, one must go into some little aster-smoky wood, and stand very still. At first you come, a great, heavy-booted, blundering animal of the simian branch, and every sound made by other creatures will cease. But you will be observed. The late last pewee whose voice you followed is right in the tree where you thought he was, but he keeps on the other side of the trunk, and will tell you nothing more until he has known you for half an hour.

While you sit waiting on the ground you may harken to the mechanical sounds. There will be the scraping together of two old boughs, and the ticking of seeds in some little wind-rattled pod. Presently a nut will drop. In that there is nothing remarkable, yet it was a sound which rang out in forests before the glacier came, and heralded the march of the trees, as they stole back, a limb's length at a time, after the great winter of the Pleistocene, winning back the thousand lost leagues.

And now at last the animate sounds begin. A squirrel jumps with a splash into a tree. The cottontail stamps, and the little tree creeper emits his wiry *cheep*. Yet these are not the brisk sounds of summer activity.

Nature, these days, is like a great building emptying itself of inhabitants. First the light-o'-works hurry home, leaving the industrious folk to stay and wind up their affairs. Yet at last they too put out the lights, lock doors, go home. Juncos and chickadees, like drab slavies, arrive in the great building with an air of modest importance. Night has descended on the year.

242

D o w n by the marsh, where the cows have trampled the bluish reed-grass, and the wild rose leaves are burning with dark purple-crimson, the bottle gentians are in bloom. Solemn flowers I find them, forever closed, forever in bud; mysterious because they will not appear until the sedge is a yellow ruin, and the marsh milkweed is already wafting silky down across the bog grass, and the great silence of the tenth month lies upon the desolate marsh.

Of all colors, a gentian's blue is the favorite of the bees; it would seem a flower preëminently attractive to those melliferous match-makers. Yet this gentian never admits the bee, nor the long-tongued moth or butterfly; perpetually the great blue bottles remain corked. Within, a perfect mechanism insures self-fertilization—perhaps a lucky circumstance for a flower that blooms when frosts are nigh. They bloom secretive, remote, sufficient to themselves— flowers with a sad dignity, offerings upon the grave of the year.

OCTOBER THIRTIETH

THE day was gray; the wet wind blew the morning long; but in the afternoon the sun came forth in clear green gold, sinking to the blue of distant hills, and cast a forlorn radiance on the burnished copper of the autumn grasses and the bells of purple false foxglove.

I heard the meadow cricket shuffling his harsh, folded wings with the stiff sound of a fan flung open. The common locusts flitted before me with a snapping whir, dropping to the ground again, after a few zig-zag turns. But the leather-wings darted wildly away, flinging themselves toward fiery sunset glow as if they were bent on dying in it.

A sense of the end of things, the last. Of a chant of death, of a final sigh of warmth from the earth. Of frost to come.

"AND what have you been doing all summer," asked the ant, "that you have nothing to eat now? Dancing and singing, master cricket? Well, then, you may go hungry."

So, in many versions, from Æsop through La Fontaine to Walt Disney, runs the old fable, though sometimes its culprit is master grasshopper, and sometimes the cicada. Let us call it the cricket, and pause not so long over the natural history involved in the story (though that is as badly muddled as might be) as upon the moral it has the pretension to advance.

In the first place crickets do not all die with the coming of winter; many pass the inclement season snug in my basement woodpile. In the second place, it is not true, as La Fontaine says, that *"la fourmie n'est pas préteuse."* Maeterlinck insists that there is no animal in the world so generous as the ant, who feeds not only her sisters but several hundreds of other insect species, guests in her house.

But allow the poets their license. It is the moral that I do not like, the self-satisfied little lecture with which the ant of the fable accompanies its stinginess. Were a cricket even as the fable represents it, it is plain that he and the cicada and the grasshopper are artists and entertainers, and the ant of the moral seems to be a banker refusing a loan upon grounds, not of insufficient security, but of the superior morality of being rich, the infamy of poverty.

NOVEMBER FIRST

WHAT I love best in autumn is the way that Nature takes her curtain, as the stage folk say. The banners of the marshes furl, droop and fall. The leaves descend in golden glory. The ripe seeds drop and the fruit is cast aside. And so with slow chords in imperceptible fine modulations the great music draws to its close, and when the silence comes you can scarce distinguish it from the last far-off strains of the woodwinds and the horns.

NOVEMBER SECOND

You will awaken one of these autumn mornings to the sound of a long sweet whistle blowing from the fields. I chanced to hear it this day because I was listening, in the early morning, for a bird of quite another sort—the first call-notes of my youngest boy, who is now at the stage when joy begins at five in the morning. But he chanced to sleep longer, and so I heard the white-throat sing.

I heard it last in spring, in rain. Now, under a faultless blue sky, very high and light, it utters a few notes, in reverie, a silvery attenuation of the bridal song. Perhaps we might think the white-throat is saying farewell to us; but he is in truth only just arrived from his northern breeding grounds, and now, in company with winter wrens and siskins and brown creepers, he will pass the inclement season here, as well as he may.

For the ducks, the owls and falcons, and a few small passerine birds, wintering in this countryside represents a sojourn in the south. Our latitude would appear to be low enough for their needs. For the gulls and ducks all winter long there may be found some open water here; for the creatures of prey there are small mammals that do not hibernate; and for the little song birds the weed seeds still rise above the casual drifts, and there is foraging about the generous unthrifty American barns. So modest are the requirements of this dun and humble company.

NOVEMBER THIRD

THERE was a flurry of small wings, a wheeling about of the whole troupe of little birds, almost as precise and graceful as the turn of swallows or starlings, and a loud outcry from the whole flock as it sailed over the seed-blown thistles. Some one was chasing someone, and their friends joined gleefully in the wrangle, the way the domestic sparrows will do, little ruffians ever ready for a street fight.

"I've cheated ye," came down the triumphant whistle of the leader, as he broke away and winged looping over the withered weeds. The fun over, the rest of the flock settled down to the thistles, making the down fly till it looked as though they were shaking their little feathers off. By one step and another, carefully taken, I approached. The snatch of a song, and the love of thistle seeds, had revealed as goldfinches these sociable small choristers. But how changed they were! The brilliant gold and black males were no more; in their place were creatures toned down from such gaudy display. In their various stages of dull livery, I saw, too, the young males of the season, dressed much like their mothers and sisters. Now while the woods stand leafless, these little wild canaries pass into soft buffs and olives, just as the snow bunting grows a white tip to his feathers when winter comes, or the weasel lopes, dressed in ermine, through the snow.

NOVEMBER FOURTH

AUTUMN is not the conventional season for going out bird's-nesting, but still there is a brief to be held for the idea. The leafless boughs reveal the whereabouts of the empty nests. Astonishing how many bird neighbors I must have had, and so close! I find mourning doves' untidy little platforms all through the osage orange hedge within call of the house; the shrubbery around the door is filled with a variety of little bird homes, there is a wren's cubicle under the eaves—and in the woods every big crow lookout stands forth now black and spiky in the wind-racked oaks. The cat-tails and bulrushes reveal a village of redwings' nests.

The autumnal bird's-nester may sleep o' nights with an easy conscience, since he knows that he has not affrighted or driven from their eggs some little pair fluttering with parental anxieties. Against this must be weighed the in-dubitable fact that it is a bit difficult to identify a nest whose owner has departed for the tropics, leaving no name plate on his doorpost. Still, there is always the delight of watching to see whether next year some one will not return to the summer cottage, abandoned now to weather.

THE first winter which the young Audubon spent in America revealed to him a deserted village of stout nests secured to the sheer walls of a shallow cave. All winter long the young ornithologist, fresh from France, waited eagerly for the return of the inhabitants, wondering what strange New World species they would prove to be, going again and again to look at the nests, dreaming upon the personalities of their occupants.

He was lucky in the nests he chose, for they belonged to phœbes, who return, with infinitely precise instinct, to the self-same habitation. An ordinary bird, you say? But to the young and thoughtful, the clear-eyed, nothing is ordinary.

That year he banded the little travelers before they left in autumn, intent on learning if indeed the identical birds returned to their nests. Now this was the first time that man had ever thought of trapping the secret of a bird's flight. The idea of bird-banding had occurred to no one, not studious little Wilson, at that moment teaching school less than fifty miles away from Audubon's cave, not even the precise Gilbert White whose passion was bird migration, nor Linnæus with his peasant good sense for practical investigation by simple means. The inventor was Audubon, Frenchman and artist, a bird-hearted man, whose thoughts followed after the flying wings in a way not conceivable to the parochial White who, for all his interest in migration, let the motile restless essence of the Aves elude him through his inability even in his mind to travel far.

NOVEMBER SIXTH

O N T H I S day in 1848, in a fine old farmhouse near Swindon, was born Richard Jefferies that naturalist and poet of nature whose works in influence and literary quality stand in English letters with those of Gilbert White and Hudson. Of the three he is the least known in America. Hudson was a cosmopolite, and Gilbert White almost universal—universally parochial. Jefferies stands deepest rooted in the soil; he melts into his scene and becomes its voice, speaking for it, as a dryad speaks for the oak she inhabits. He has the intense awareness of the genius of a spot that the classic nature lovers had, and in *Round About a Great Estate, Life of the Fields,* and *The Gamekeeper at Home,* he stems straight from Theocritus, the Sabine Farm and the *Bucolics.* He can make an acre of ground ring with lark song and glitter with dew. More than all other peoples, the English appreciate their nature; Jefferies is this love in its pure fonthead.

A failure as a novelist, Jefferies in his nature writing benefited by a novelist's powers of self-expression. He has that choice of the fresh word, that eye for the quietly dramatic, with which White was entirely unacquainted. Yet he wrote out of a conscientious naturalist's first-hand information, with religious fidelity to truth. If, through all his work, and most of all in his autobiography, *The Story of My Heart,* there is a strain of the melancholy, a way of narrating things as though he were remembering happy days, it is because much of his life he was writing of Nature from hospital beds, from poor city windows. Consumption, the malady of poets, slowly and very painfully destroyed this poet of the wild breeze on Beachy Head, of the hearty health of farm and soft-breathing beast, of granges packed to the door with sweetening hay.

NOVEMBER SEVENTH

THE saddest feelings evoked by musing over Richard
Jefferies' tombstone are not that disease so crippled and
embittered a life intended for manly health and great
fertility, but that his works have since been buried with
him. Yet the influence of Jefferies, not only as a nature
writer but as a novelist with a deep and exciting sense of
the elemental, is felt in modern literature. He had a way of
peopling his Nature with human figures that throws the
scene into a most comprehensible relief—the men, the children, the girls, just such as we would expect to meet on a
wild down, in a copse roaring with the autumn wind, in a
poacher's cottage. Some of the ache of *A Shropshire Lad,*
some of the grand leisure of *Lavengro* and the imagination
of *Wolf Solent* are in Jefferies. The primal idea of *After
London*—an England after the cracking of western civiliza·
tion, with London in ruins, and men fighting amidst the
brambles and the forests returned, indicates a fine sense of
true time as Nature ticks it off. And *Bevis,* that small boy
Crusoe, that hobbledehoy Julius Cæsar of the Great Pond
and the Down, just too old to allow himself to be beaten
and just too young to make impudent compliments to
lasses, stands out for me as a classic of a boy in Nature and
Nature in a boy.

NOVEMBER EIGHTH

Now to their long winter sleep retire the batrachians. A warm-blooded animal, even one who purposes eventually to hibernate, may still keep the field for a few weeks more. But the cool spring newts, the earthy toad and the frog who looks like the lily pad he sits upon, make off to their winter quarters.

The wood frog hides beneath old logs, and the others plunge under the chill waters, there to burrow deep in the mud. But the toad begins to delve under shrubbery or an old board or flagstone, and when I catch him at the business he is usually working behind his back. For his very tough hind feet, provided with conspicuous spurs, are his spades, and with these he digs his own burrow, almost his grave, and so, inch by inch, he backs into his house. When he has gone deep enough to escape the bitter surface frosts, he pulls his hole in after him, by drawing the earth down over his head.

Now with toes curled up under him and his head bent down, he prepares to sleep. A great darkness comes over his jewel-like eyes, a numbness through his limbs. Like one dead, he lies with heart almost stopped, breath practically suspended, an earthy thing gone back to earth, a cold thing blended with the cold clod. Life flickers very low at this moment; it sinks into an icy torpor not readily distinguishable from decease; even a sort of *rigor mortis* sets in; the sleeping toad may be cut up in sections without arousing him to consciousness. So to preserve itself from death, life will feint with it, even lie down in its black arms, in order to rise in the morning the triumphant creatrix!

NOVEMBER NINTH

RAIN upon the face; rain in long slanting lines, blowing in veils through the dead reeds. A paddle in the hand, the swirl of cold yellow water. The smell of a fine old pipe, a wretched old leather coat; a stout boat, a gun smelling of clean oil and shining with blue highlights along the barrel. You must love these things, and love them much, in order to learn anything about ducks. Whether you are a hunter or an ornithologist, some marksmanship is required, and hardihood for wet. Ducks and rough weather seem nearly inseparable.

All this explains why it is that ducks are birds for men. It is natural that women should like the birds whose domestic affairs can be observed under the eaves; they love the sweetest singers, the brightest plumage, the species not too shy to be seen at close range. For them the waders and swimmers, the awkward of leg, the harsh of cry, the wild of soul, have seldom the same appeal. But that which flees from men, that will men have. Women of all people ought to understand this, but they do not, quite.

NOVEMBER TENTH

THE folk who want to shoot ducks, and the naturalists who would protect them, meet, occasionally, in conventions and in the lobbies of legislatures. They have this much in common, in the present day, that they are both interested in duck conservation, for sportsmen have begun to understand that unless they restrain each other, there will soon be nothing to shoot. It is the contention of the fowlers that the ladies and professors who make up the conservative ranks are as incapable of understanding why a man wants to shoot as pacifists of seeing how a soldier can find war ennobling.

Hunters, like pipe smokers, are recruited from two antipodal types of men—gentlemen and worthless loafers. I will say this for them all, that as I know them, they are naturalists of a sort. They know the ways of a rabbit as a dog knows them, the ways of a duck as a hawk does. They have a fund of intimate observation upon Nature exactly as it is, that might be envied by the behaviorists putting caged creatures through mazes and paces. Without the least poetry in their way of expressing it, they are none the less appreciators of the wilderness in a fashion scarcely possible to the city dweller, for when they go into the marshes, or in the brown fields or the silvered woods they must proceed to their quarry by accurate observation. They know what to expect as the norm and what is out of the way. The very fact that the hunter is following a trial to kill arouses instincts in him that observe more than the diffident, tolerant student can hope to notice.

NOVEMBER ELEVENTH

I REMEMBER the first baldpate duck I ever saw, floating upon a marsh, in a cold evening damp—floating motionless, with speckled and green head, and blue bill outstretched lovingly upon the water, the exquisite mantle of brownish gray laved by the wind-driven dark ripples, the green and black-bordered wings outspread as if in an ecstasy to catch the wind. So, like a lovely boat, this creature of beauty drove on before the breeze, toward open water, more graceful and more silent than a swan—and dead. Gone was the fowler who had wounded him, but failed to retrieve him. With the bullet in his body the wild thing had still fought for its life, got clear away—to die unconquered, its proud plumage still unplucked; to drift, like this, a Viking's funeral, between the water and the sky.

NOVEMBER TWELFTH

In Normandy or Piedmont or the Schwarzwald, such a forest tract as the one that stretches all the way from the village past my house, and many miles down to the river, would never be permitted to lie so unprofitably idle. At this season of the year, when the forest floor is littered with thousands of twigs and branches and fallen nuts, this wood should be full of industrious children, collecting the branches into faggots, the nuts in sacks.

But I am eyed askance here when I go out with my children to gather patiently the twigs and break up fallen boughs. This appears as cheese-paring upon my part, a menial evidence that I have somehow acquired in my European years a low and foreign standard of living, reducing my children to the estate of peasants.

Now I know of no one who has all things better ordered for a truly high standard of living than a good peasant, who knows how to find the greatest possible satisfaction in an acre of black earth, a barrel of wine, an armful of wife, a big horse and a fine ripe wood lot. To all he gives back the gift of being needed, used, garnered and brought to appointed fruition.

But all about me I am presented with a people, blood of my blood and dear to me, who have no capacity to enjoy that which they have. In place of the forest turned to account without injury, I have the spectacle of my neighbors who burn off the woods every year from sheer incompetence to enjoy their blessings, from an innate hostility to Nature.

N o s m e l l so sweet as the reek of wood fires. And more than sweet—exciting, quietly, some depths of my feelings where I am not easily stirred. I am speaking of that sense of Nature that is enjoyed in human fraternity, in the pleasurable sensations that always accompany simple obedience to our instincts. Nor do I suppose that only men enjoy gregariousness. The swallow must feel it when he joins in the autumn flocks, and the bee dies of loneliness when isolated.

The evocative djinni of this emotion for me is the smell of wood smoke, down blowing on the air, stealing out of the home chimneys, curling up to a bedroom while the evening is yet young, from a just left hearth below, whispering across twilit miles of tranquil villages and old farm houses warmly inhabited. Even a miserable hut, a black man's cabin, or a gypsy's bivouac stirs me to a blind emotion, half wistful and half lusty. I have descended at nightfall on a hamlet in a strange mountain valley, or entered an old city standing in a long silver rain, and caught a whiff of men's hearths that has stirred up in me the loud call of, Brother! For it speaks of hospitality, of women, of children like apples good enough to eat, and, perhaps, of music, wine, and books—all those aspects of greater Nature that are particular to human nature.

NOVEMBER FOURTEENTH

G o n e to seed. They are drear words, and men have turned them to imply failure. In Nature they mean success. Now the wild yam in the woods has torn open its tropical papery pod, and from its fine symmetry upon the immemorial plan of three, the seeds escape. Old warty milkweed pods, silvering from their summer greeny purple, split open now, and a glistening mass of down around the flat brown seeds emerges between the valves. The goldenrod is a turret of inflorescence in fulvous and gray tones; a breath of winter wind will bring the cobweb castle down. The heads of the cotton-grass, that is no grass, but a sedge, fleck the horizontal scenery of the bog with their great puffy tufts, some white, some brown, borne on very tall slim culms, delicately and disdainfully above the burned out peat. Summer's prettiness is gone to seed, and become beauty.

Beauty, great beauty, is for me the fitting of the object to its use, the truth of things. And the truth about this season is that now the very birds are in their winter molt; the colors of the little mammals' fur are one with the bronze and silver of the wood, and that, happily, in the fields the flowers have gone to seed.

NOVEMBER FIFTEENTH

WE GROW a double larkspur in the garden, and exaggerated double dahlias so heavy that they cannot hold up their own heads. But these are like idle, childless women demanding to be young perpetually. In the marsh, on the steppe, in the crevices of cliffs, the purpose of life is fruition. I could never see why a man should rebel against this law, or imagine that the best of his dreams would be more precious than the children for whom he must compromise them.

Do you object that this is a weary round—soberly to beget, in debt and fear to house and raise, in order that my sober children, early yoked, shall continue dully to repeat my life, and work out for the benefit of some monarchical or socialistic society a gray and featureless Utopia? But I ask you, what is dull about the fulfillment of biological destiny? At every moment in that destiny the beauty and terror of life confront a man—still more a woman—and round the circle of the days the eyes of Death move watchfully, pondering on children running in the light, on woman in the night, on man at labor.

NOVEMBER SIXTEENTH

O N A FINE balmy day like this, just after rain, with a breeze blowing as steady as a Trade, silken argosies from aster and goldenrod, thistles and dandelions, drift past continuously. They seem to light, to have reached a destination, only to be borne on again by another wind.

It is worthy of note that the newest, the most highly developed and successful of all plant families, the thistle family, is especially given to plumose seeds. The goatsbeard has so much feathery stiff surface of down, proportioned to the weight of the seed, that should it start from a high mountain altitude on a continuous current it could, it has been estimated, travel sixty miles before once touching earth or water. In this fashion the composite family has made its way around the world, a conqueror particularly of the steppes and prairies, the veldt and the pampas. It has invaded Hawaii across thousands of sea miles, from North America, whilst all the rest of the island flora derives, with the prevailing ocean currents, from the southeast. It has reached the Azores from Europe, the Canaries from the peaks of Atlas.

And yet the idea is nothing new. Nature has tried the winged seed experiment a score of times in many families —dogbane, milkweed, clematis and some anemones, trees like willow, poplar, sycamore, maple, linden and ash, and some grasses and sedges. It is found in the cat-tail family, one of the most ancient and primitive flowering plants still alive, and wafted it successfully round all the marshes of the world. So in the end there seems to have been a return to the beginning, as if nothing more competent could be devised.

THE sky chanced to be cloudy here upon the nights when the Leonids were scheduled to appear. But in regions where the sky was naked, astronomers trained their gaze upon the constellation of Leo, during the early morning hours when it had risen out of the east, for a glimpse of the meteors that seem to radiate from the heart of that configuration.

The great Leonid shower of 1833 appeared to those who saw it like a display of celestial pyrotechnics. In 1866 the mighty host reappeared. The fourth jubilee within a century was scheduled to take place this year, with that mathematical regularity of heavenly bodies which assures us that our terrestrial mathematics are not abstractions without reality. But the Leonids this time were a disappointment, save for the fall of a few meteorites to earth. Astronomers do not, today, make mistakes calculating the year in which an event within the solar system may be expected, so we must conclude that the Leonids, like guests expected to dinner, were unavoidably detained—no doubt by Jupiter, the giant of the planets within whose terrible sphere of pull they must have passed.

The estimate of the astronomers is that the sun pulls two thousand tons of meteoric matter per second into its fiery furnaces. Small wonder if, coming too near the sun's mightiest child, the Leonids have been decimated. Be it understood, such an accident to the career of this superb meteoric swarm is no accident at all; it happened by the law of heavenly mathematics. Nor will it be any accident if our sun should some time plow into one of those dark clouds of inert matter that lie in space, as dangerous as sunken reefs. If it does so, sun, planets, earth, man with his dreams, will crash into destruction, all in strict accordance with the letter of the law.

NOVEMBER EIGHTEENTH

ON THIS day in 1810, in Oneida County, New York, was born Asa Gray, often called the father of American botany, though we might have to go farther back even than his teacher, John Torrey, to bestow that title. I would be dead to gratitude, did I not honor this teacher of my first teacher. But a life so blessedly uneventful as his, expended rather in education than history-making discovery, scarce lends itself to anecdote.

It was Gray's influence on his times in America that rings significantly. Asa Gray it was who, almost single-handed, fought the battle of Darwinism in America, fought it, that is, with his intellectual peers. It was perhaps not too difficult to influence Emerson and Thoreau; but so far as Boston and Cambridge were concerned the crux of the matter was not the scientific one, of whether it were possible for the teasel family to have evolved into Gray's favorite Compositæ, or the eohippus to have brought the horse out of its loins, but whether Darwinism meant atheism. Asa Gray's prominent pew in the Congregational Church, and his chaste and solvent life, carried the day amongst the Brahmins.

What Gray considered his own monuments, the *Synoptical Flora of North America*, and his revision of the genus Aster, mighty enough in their scope, are not the kind of science about which most of us would now be excited. Pure classification has neither the implications nor the applications that we hope for now from a life's labor. But Gray was not merely a systematist; his many popular text books, including *How Plants Behave, How Plants Grow, Field, Forest and Garden Botany,* raised up a great generation of well informed nature lovers—an admirable class of individuals that has notably diminished since such books grew weightier and duller.

NOVEMBER NINETEENTH

THE second-hand book dealers often endeavor to sell me a first edition of Gray's *Manual of Botany*. But in scientific writings first editions are seldom worth last editions. The first five editions are the only ones that Gray actually edited, and we should now consider them intolerably provincial; they serve one at best only in New England and the Middle Atlantic states. But the reverence in which our forefathers held their "Gray" was comparable to that of schoolmen for Theophrastus.

Yet roaming the dealer's shelves I often take down one or another of the brown-paged early editions, that begins in the old style with the buttercups and ends with the ferns or mosses. I finger the leaves affectionately, not so much for good Asa's sake as because I respect the one-time owners, whose names I like to read in the covers of these books—the sterling Felicias and forthright Amasas of a bygone generation. I like to shake the faded wisp of a jewelweed or a birdfoot violet out of the leaves, where it was pressed some summer long ago. And I always turn over toward the back to the Euphorbia family, fairly confident that there I shall find a sprig of flowering spurge, the amateur's stumbling block. And there I find it, where it was left, a landmark, a triumphant monument to persistence.

NOVEMBER TWENTIETH

In 1762, on this day, was born the French entomologist, Pierre André Latreille. He is famous for a work on the mutillids or velvet-ants, those parasitic wasps so exactly like their brothers of the Formicidæ that I once picked one up in my ignorance and received a sting that set me to shaking my fingers in agony. But the incident that lingers in my mind concerning Latreille is that which concerns the beetle that he named Necrobia—"life out of death."

Latreille failed to take the oath of allegiance to the First Republic, and was cast into prison, in Bordeaux, if memory serves me well. There, awaiting deportation with other priests to the hells of French Guiana, he was nursing a sick bishop when some visitors entered the convicted men's cell. Latreille, kneeling by the sick man's side, suddenly saw a curious little black-headed, green-backed and red-tailed beetle, one of the sort that invades larders and has a fancy for stored hams, run out upon the foul floor. So intense was his interest in this specimen that the on-lookers stood amazed, marveling at a man who, on the verge of life exile and death in tropical miasmas, could forget all for prison vermin.

Among those bystanders was a relative of the well known naturalist Borey de St. Vincent. This little beetle seems to have been a link which connected Latreille with the powers that be and brought him reprieve. But the hell-bound ship was weighing anchor, Latreille among the rest of the manacled passengers, before the letters of reprieve arrived at the barnacled dock.

Our first reader would have climaxed this tale with the moral that even a little beetle could save the life of man. But in truth it was not the beetle, but the confraternity of science, which saved Latreille—that guild that recognizes no politics or religion but only intellect.

NOVEMBER TWENTY-FIRST

IN a guest-thronged old Southern house, of a stormy November night, I was put as a child to sleep on a couch downstairs under the short blankets and old coats that make up an extra boy's bed on such occasions. At first it was very novel and pleasant to lie on the brocaded cushions in the fire-lit room. But I wakened, in a windy midnight, to a fire gone out. And somewhere there was a curious ticking sound as of a clock, but intermittent. I knew there was no clock about, and I tried hard not to recognize the sound.

But all the time I knew it well, for a young servant who liked to make children's eyes grow large had once told me what it meant. *Tick, tack, tack,* it came—that sound that the death-watch beetle makes in old woodwork, as he counts out the minutes that are left to some one who has not much longer to live. By day I knew that beetles do not occupy themselves with the span of human lives. But in the night I saw how logical it was that some one at this hour was living out his last minutes. With the first signs of dawn I gathered up my chill clothes and fled to the comfort of the old black cook just lighting a kitchen fire of fat pine. Does any one else, like me, feel again the eeriness of the beetle's pendulum when he listens to the stroke of the bedside watch in Strauss's *Death and Transfiguration?*

Sometimes I find the beetles still, up in my attic. The warmth that steals up to them from the heated house keeps them unseasonably alive, these hammer-headed Anobia. I know their presence by the tell-tale pile of sawdust on the floor though I never catch them in the open. But the uncanny associations with a creature which slowly devours my rooftree while ever remaining invisible, have not faded; they tremble like an eidolon across my scientific knowledge.

266

NOVEMBER TWENTY-SECOND

THE end of autumn comes, and one by one the plants in their little stations and many small creatures hole up and turn to sleep. We feel a great longing for that sleep, in the woods, in the very air and the soil that nightly grows colder, a little less kindly. The year's great living settles to its close, and not alone because the harsher cycle demands it, but because it is in the nature of most things to rest. Winter has a meaning beyond the meteorological one; it is that surcease must compensate all this perfervid existence.

For many beings in the great packed store room, autumn represents finality. They will be thrown out complete as waste, all the annual plants, the ephemerid insects. They have their chance at immortality, I know, through seed and egg. But individually the time for them has come, the time to go. For species on the wane, each autumn, perhaps, represents a step toward extinction. So be it; it is written.

But out of all this great débris new forms will be made, as in the first place life took its origin in ways mysterious to us, and alighting like light from a star upon a dark dead world informed the water and the rock with itself.

SAGITTARIUS

NOVEMBER 23 — DECEMBER 21

NOVEMBER TWENTY-THIRD

ONLY three explanations of the origin of life have ever been suggested by the mind of man.

Either it came into existence as the special creation of an omnipotent Providence whose dispositions are inscrutable, or else it reached this our earth in the form of spores or bacteria-like organisms from some other world, or else it was an act of spontaneous generation which took place long ago on the earth—in some instant when a pinch of dust and a drop of water became a living thing.

Each one of these explanations is accepted by groups of highly reputable scientists, as well as by a public at large. The scientific adherents of a special act of divine creation are recruited mainly among the astronomers, staggered by the immensities with which they deal. The physicists and chemists are prone to belief in spontaneous generation, for it is their instinct to proclaim the oneness of all things, and to explain all things in a purely mechanical way. Most reluctant to venture any hypothesis are the fellows who know most about the subject—the biologists. Some of them, with a rather grand simplicity, wave the question away to the stars, with the suggestion (by no means wholly fanciful) that life has reached our earth from very far afield in the cosmos.

ALL three of the explanations of the origin of life remain unproved and, moreover, they create as much mystery as they clear up. A special act of divine creation, a special suspension of the laws to permit of spontaneous generation, or a wafting of the seeds of life across the cold hells of space, will require, as creeds, an act of faith that simply staggers one who is not already the lucky possessor of it.

The astronomer's primal and creative God, who set the stars in motion and decreed that all motions shall obey one law, who plays out the drama of the universe from its titanic beginning to its inert end (which man unhappily foresees) is surely omnipotent enough. But He has so little spirit, as the astronomers picture Him; He seems to be so limited by His own laws, or He simply is those laws. He can be expressed in equations, which the astronomers, probably quite rightly, call sublime.

No need to point out how the inexorable working-out of mathematical sequiturs differs from an Old Testament God of wrath or a New Testament God of pity. I can understand how the mathematical God of Mr. Jeans would *cause* the smallest sparrow's fall, but not how He could mark it with compassionate eyes.

I have recently been reading many astronomers' and physicists' new pictures of the cosmos. I follow them as well as my comprehension allows until they get down to earth, to the naked sphere of it waiting to receive life. Here the mathematical God breathes upon the dust—one thinker suggests He struck it with a bolt of lightning—and life begins. From this point on the astronomer and his God seem to take no further responsibility for all the disharmonies and tragedies, the loss and wastage of that which might have grown full straight and brought the world more swiftly to the spiritual goals.

NOVEMBER TWENTY-FIFTH

THOSE who assert that there is no essential difference between living matter and dead save that of degree are generally styled mechanists. For them the simplest living organism is not divided by a tremendous gulf from the most complex inanimate form of matter, and they are able to make out a strong case for their contention. They show how many of the functions of life are imitated by matter certainly not alive, and how all living creatures obey the same laws as the non-living.

When they come to explain the origin of life the mechanists have no philosophic difficulty in accepting the idea of spontaneous generation. One day, they assure us, inanimate matter became living substance, and the change was probably no more than a little increased atomic or molecular complexity, no greater than divides some of the elements from each other.

Now the difficulty with this classically simple belief is that Louis Pasteur showed for once and for all that a sterilized medium never gives rise to any living organism or substance. He put the burden of proof of spontaneous generation upon the mechanists who can only beg us to believe in it without evidence. They urge that spontaneous generation did once take place under conditions which we know nothing about today since they no longer exist. The history of the earth, so far as we know anything about it, gives no clue as to what these conditions might have been. On the contrary, it indicates that the farther back in time we travel, the less livable was this our home. If proofs like Pasteur's may be wished away at any time by asserting that at some other time they would not have obtained, there is no limit to what we may imagine, for law, and necessity to obey it, no longer bind either the germs of life nor the stars in their courses.

NOVEMBER TWENTY-SIXTH

FOR days now the skies have let down torrents of rain upon the land. The fire logs have sung upon my hearth, and I have been house bound, deeply happy in the instincts that flower beneath a roof, content with a philosopher's existence. The sky is still heavy with unshed drops, but the human frame would stand no more confinement. I walked in the woods, with boot and stick, hunting that fresh surface of experience, that actual touch and smell of reality without which a philosophy soon becomes metaphysics.

Of birds there are very few about—not nearly so many as I see on a fine day in snowbound midwinter. Without snow, the tracks of little mammal neighbors are invisible, though my dog follows their eery trails upon the air, yelping and crashing through the thickets after every rabbit, warning the entire wood that I am coming and spreading silence and absence around me as a stone spreads ripples. If I shut the dog in, the crows from their signal lookouts forewarn the world of me as if I were a dangerous public enemy.

Everywhere now in the woods, the signs of sleep, and death and decay abound. I break off the bark of an old stump and discover shiny beetle larvæ scurrying in embarrassment down the labyrinths they have made, small spiders tucking themselves into silk coverlets, a soft florescence of mold at work upon the wood. The wood itself is but a damp and rusty sawdust, reduced to that condition by innumerable insect carpenters, by the bills of woodpeckers, the teeth of little rodents, the dissolving power of the fungi and the final break-up wrought by those indefatigable little junkmen, the bacteria.

NOVEMBER TWENTY-SEVENTH

No PICTURE of life today is even worth a glance that does not show the bacteria as the foundation of life itself, the broad base of the pyramid on which all the rest is erected. We know them well enough as our most terrible enemies. But man's power over the pathogenic forms advances with a certainty of purpose, a display of courage and intelligence that heartens us back to a belief in ourselves. And in truth the deathy seeds that slay us still are the least significant of the whole lot; they are expensive hothouse parasites, so finicking in their requirements, so overspecialized in their adaptations, that they have written their own doom in time.

The bacteria which fire my imagination are those that I smell as I walk these days through the dripping woods, where the sodden leaves no longer rustle. I call it the smell of loam, but of a truth loam is no more than ordinary earth rich in soil bacteria. It is their gases which I scent, as it is the emanations from other sorts that generate the fetid odor of a bog, the stench of a carcass in the woods, the delectable reek of ferment in the hay-crammed barn.

It is among these harmless sorts that there flourish species which assist to break down the naked rock that once was the five continents thrust out of the seven seas; they have made them habitable for the rest of life. Green plants —the source directly or indirectly of all the food, fuel and apparel that we use,—would find life unendurable but for the bacteria. And but for the kinds that inhabit symbiotically the digestive tracts of animals, the tough cellulose of plant food could never be dissolved and assimilated. Men, as well as insects and legumes, live out their days in an unconscious dependence upon organisms so minute that, like the angels of metaphysical monks, ten thousand may, (and frequently do) stand on the point of a needle, and so numerous that they surpass all the stars in heaven.

WE HAVE the geologist's word for it that the oldest rocks that bear a fossil testimony to the existence of life show impresses of bacterial scars. The biologist is not soaring on reckless wax wings of fancy when he imagines that the bacteria may have rained upon earth from distant space. Germs, we call them when they invade our bodies; germs of life, too, primordial seeds, they may well have been. For harsh as the astronomer's outer realms may be, hostile to all delicate life forms like ourselves, the bacteria (some of which are anything but delicate) may well have been fitted to pass between the Scylla and Charybdis of the astronomer's ice and fire. These specks of dust, these particles fine as smoke, boast members which can endure prolonged subjection to the temperature of liquid hydrogen, that is, 260 below zero Centigrade. Most of them prefer to live in the total darkness that is the natural state of nothingness, in which the stars struggle like wavering candles, destined at length to burn up their tallow of allotted energy. Many are the bacteria which lead their darkling existence totally without air, and right here on earth there are still others that live in hot springs, or can, by walling themselves up in tough, dormant spore cells, resist repeated boilings. The only way in which the laboratory can rid itself of such stout foes is to incubate the spores until they are tricked into emerging as the vegetative, active and more delicate phase. As yet little is known of the longevity of such spores. Seeds of lotus, found in lakes dry two thousand years, have been made to sprout. But any seed is frail flesh indeed, compared to these pallid germs so fine that some will drain through a poreclain filter as wheat through a sieve, roll round the world as an invisible breath, spawn by the million in a few hours, or rest in dormancy no man knows how long.

NOVEMBER TWENTY-NINTH

BEFORE a man has done with such a wild horde of rock-eating savages as the bacteria, all easy notions of what life is may break down as completely as the Newtonian physics before the onslaughts of the Einsteinian.

If I try to fix a vital temperature range between the freezing and the boiling points of water, the bacteria confound me. If I maintain that the very focus of vital forces is in the cell nucleus, there are certain bacteria that leap to my sight in the microscope, devoid of nuclei.

It is even a mystery in what kingdom to place them. The zoölogist will generally not admit them, the botanist is embarrassed to know what to do with them. He tucks them in somewhere near the fungi, because they are without green coloring, produce spores, and because so many are saprophytes or parasites. But the bacteria are without the double cell wall of plants, and whatever their cell wall may be composed of, it seems not to be cellulose, the very brick and mortar of plant life.

It is perhaps simplest to say that there are four kingdoms of living things, plant, animal, slime-mold and bacterial. How many more kingdoms may there be in this or other worlds? One of the startling discoveries of the modern age was that of the bacteriophages, organisms so small that they have never yet been seen, which disembowel bacteria and eat their vitals. They may be bacteria also, but just as possibly they are not, they may be something even stranger.

THE end of the bacterial paradoxes is not yet. They have members of the guild which ply their trade without air, and others that take free nitrogen out of the atmosphere and utilize it. We think of the element carbon as the very stuff of organic tissue, blood of our blood and bone of our bone. But the bacteria might subsist in a world where the marvelously versatile element of carbon was extremely scarce. For some will ingest a diet of iron, or in default of it will substitute the element manganese.

There are not only sulphur bacteria, but certain ones of this persuasion have developed a pigmentation screen, absorbing and utilizing the sun's energy through it in the red and orange end of the spectrum, as green plants are able to do in their own color range. In this wise have these Lilliputian workers anticipated and rivaled chlorophyll, the green blood of the world.

No other organisms show so great a range of adaptability, from sun-utilizing species to others that live in total darkness, from aërobes or air-breathers to anaërobes. True, no one bacterium combines all these modes of living. But it is not necessary that any one species should be so versatile in order to imagine in them something very close to universal seeds of life.

The bacteria are only the most primitive, and adaptable-to-the-primitive beings that are at present known. They may have had—may still have—antecedents even more hardy and fitted to digest the raw stuff of the universe, perhaps even the interstellar calcium that is one of the recent discoveries of the watchers of the skies.

DECEMBER FIRST

NATURE in winter is like a great toy shop at night. The doors are locked, and only at the mysterious depths of the shop does some cold light burn. If we press our noses on the pane we can just make out the forms of bigger objects. All the tenderer delights have been taken from the window —flower and moth and bird. What is there left for us to play with?

Winter is a study in half tones, and one must have an eye for them, or go lonely. Trees, skies, and even the black, white and gray and rufous colors of winter birds and little mammals, all are subdued, modest, economical of a lofty beauty. Now one may make friends with owls and mice, with the different colored stems of willows and cornel and sassafras and spice bush, with winter buds in their furry scales, with the berries that the birds seek out, with the bark of trees and the prints of the four-footed.

DECEMBER SECOND

So FROST is on the land at last, the stiff rime of it dusted across the grass, treacherous on the stones, exquisite along each vein of the leached-out skeleton leaf. Frost is in the golden crown of that beggar king, the dandelion; frost pushes up out of the red clay in a gleaming forest of curving icicles, so strong that it has lifted the earth and even little stones high on its cold prongs, so frail that at a touch of my cane I can slay it as easily as so many glass flowers. Sickles and spirals and curls like a carpenter's shavings are shooting out of the stems of the frostweed, that modest little member of the rock-rose family, and from the dittany, which has the same odd property of extruding the water in its stem.

DECEMBER THIRD

Now everywhere in the woods, silence. The brown tree creepers utter not a note as they spiral round and round the tree trunks, hungrily foraging for their lives. So quietly do they flit to the base of another trunk that I do not even hear their wing beats. There is not a single hum from the fields, of insects tuning up their tiny orchestras. I cannot think what can have become of even the crows; the squirrels today have fled the boughs; there is no scampering of chipmunks; there are no brooks that speak, only a slow dwindling of rivulets, and no pods that click, no sudden whirring of pheasant or grouse from under foot. The sky is heavy with unshed snow, and even when it falls, it will make no sound, spinning down in the first great, starry flakes, in silence. Everywhere, only silence...silence.

DECEMBER FOURTH

TIME now for the long sleep of the four-footed brethren. The frosty nights, the days so brief and so subdued, the cold and voiceless emptiness of the ruined woods, have warned the woodchucks, the pine mice, the chipmunks and the bats. And now in couples, or in families, they creep away to their lairs.

When I am troubled with insomnia, I think not upon those foolish sheep, jumping heavily and wearily over a stile. I think instead of the sleep of the white-footed mice, in their burrows and hollows, warm flank to warm flank, clever little paws folded over sensitive noses and whiskers, as they doze away the days and the nights together, secure in their retreat, contented with their lot. They sleep as the plants sleep in their roots and bulbs. Their hearts beat so slowly that they scarce suffice to force the warm blood through the chilled limbs; minds are a blank, all hunger, desires, impulses and fears in abeyance for days and days, for weeks and weeks. So do these little fellows sleep, five and ten at a time, fallen upon each other in little furry windrows of drowsiness.

DECEMBER FIFTH

N o t a flower now, and scarce a berry. Birds flown south, and insects gone; leaves all fallen, and the very sap in the trees descended to the roots; mammals and reptiles stolen away to their winter's rest. Everywhere life in recession, life like a flame turned low.

Now, perhaps, is the moment to catch napping the phenomenon life, and examine it to discover what it is. For of a brilliant summer day, with the air humming with midges, with every great tree expanding a full acre of green leaf surface to catch and employ the power of the sun, with mating and birth going on all around us, and the waters bringing forth and the very earth astir, a man can make little enough of it all. There is too much in summer —too much green, too much spawning, too much profusion of kind and form.

But in winter here is the problem in its least common denominators. No ant or bee is abroad to distract with questions of instinct and intelligence. The vine has ceased to grow; no need now to concern ourselves with tropism. The maggot is numb; touch him how you will, no reflex stirs him. Life is so still, almost we are persuaded that we can reduce it to structure and protoplasm, look up in the brilliance of the winter constellations and behold what structure they too have, sort out the elements of which life and the home of life are made, and test the poet's notion that

> "All things by immortal power
> Near or far
> Hiddenly
> To each other linkèd are,
> That thou canst not stir a flower
> Without troubling a star."

WHEN the woodchuck sits up at the door of his burrow, the sunlight shining on his coat and his gentle eyes watching us warily, he is a fellow of ours, divided from us only by species. In the brain under his low furry skull glimmers a consciousness like ours; through all his body run indecipherable instincts, reflexes, tropisms.

But the woodchuck asleep, under the ground, is a creature remote almost as the dead, one shorn of thought, instinct, action. The mind contemplates the sleeping subterranean animal coolly, like a specimen. One faces the problem of what is alive in an animal who is not moving, growing, reproducing, eating, nor excreting, and is neither acting instinctively nor is in any way conscious. Buried and motionless as a corpse, he is yet alive, I know. I know it because he is warm to my touch and I can distinguish his heart beats, though so slow.

But the little mechanism down in my cellar by which I operate a country lighting system is also warm to the touch; it too has something very like heart beats; it too is combusting an energy supply, as the woodchuck is slowly oxidizing his autumnal layers of fat. True, my machine will not, next spring, climb up and run around and look for a mate, but neither would the woodchuck, if by the turning back of time the glaciers returned and summer were no more. He would lie there until the fat supply was used up, and then die in his sleep.

DECEMBER SEVENTH

T H E woodchuck in his den, the acorn in the soil, both hibernate—to use only the zoölogical word. Close to death they sink, into something very near to suspension of all activity. The marmot, of course, if you could dig him out, would be warm to the touch; the seed, if you wish to know whether or not it lives, can be shown to be breathing, taking in carbon dioxide and exhaling oxygen after the way of vegetable life. If you place a sunflower seed in water it will, presently, begin to give off bubbles of oxygen, provided that it is alive. A dead seed gives off none. The animal too breathes, very slowly; it is that combustion of his reserve of fat which generates the heat of his furry body. This storing and combustion is that strange thing, metabolism, the very chemistry of life itself.

Metabolism, if you wish to be precise, may be divided into two phases, the katabolic or burning (energy releasing) process, and the anabolic or up-building of combustible material. The fascination of metabolism is that nothing remotely like it is found except in living beings. The living organism is able to maintain the constant relation of katabolism and anabolism; constantly broken down, it is constantly reëstablished.

But in non-living matter, though chemical interactions occur, they will do so only until an equilibrium has taken place within the system. Then total inertia reigns.

DECEMBER EIGHTH

A SURGEON may cut brain matter in any direction without finding a thought. He cannot even tell what part of the tissue it is that thinks. Even so evasive and pervasive is metabolism in the cell.

Mechanists and vitalists agree that the cell holds the secret of life, and by cell they mean not the cell wall but only the protoplasm itself. Protoplasm is a colloid—that is, a suspension of particles in fluid, a suspension which however never settles like mud in a glass of water. It is also a sort of gell; it will pass from a liquid into a solid state and back again, or rather it acts like a solid when solidity is needed, a liquid when it needs to flow. It has spontaneous powers of movement; it assimilates the environment and converts it into its own substance, oxidizing it to form carbonic acid gas and to release energy or heat. It grows or reproduces when its store of energy surpasses its loss. It deposits, excretes, and gives rise to everything else in the living body. In short, it performs every known function of life; it is the very seat of life, as the brain is the locus of thought. Now either life is an ineffable thing like thought, or it is a mechanism in some way different from or more complicated than inanimate machines.

The mechanists who conceive of protoplasm as a machine merely differing from all others in fundamental structure, postulate, to explain it, all sorts of bodies, granules, or special life molecules, which they call biogens. No one has ever yet actually discovered a biogen. Other mechanists there are who hold that the matter of life differs from other matter in no way save its complexity. But none has ever succeeded in unraveling a complexity so insuperable.

DECEMBER NINTH

IF I WISH to know what protoplasm is really like—to use a vague but very real colloquial expression—I hear a clamor of voices from the men of the microscope, of the chemical laboratory, and from experimentalists. I hear that protoplasm is a foam, protoplasm is a network, is a soaked sponge, is granules, is fiber-like thickenings through a fluid-solid colloid. In truth, at one time or another it may be any of these. Or more exactly, protoplasm may act *as if* it were of any of these structures, and to some extent you may actually see it in some one of these forms—depending, perhaps, on the angle of the section you are looking at.

If I ask the theorists to explain these appearances to me as they explain the structure of the atom, they are ripe with suggestions. They assure me that a protoplasmic molecule is something of comparatively immense size allowing for immense complexity. I am ready to believe it! But if the peculiar properties of protoplasm have to have a molecular explanation, such a molecule would still have to be complex beyond anything a physicist could hope to represent by any sort of a model.

For protoplasm not only produces absolutely everything seen in the living being—chlorophyll, hæmoglobin, chitin, cellulose, flesh, horn, bone, hair, eye, brain, even thought and heredity—but the molecule must have the power to make absolutely different compounds out of the same material. You may feed a man and dog on beefsteak, but with what different results! So complex will this molecule have to be that it will not only make different species of animals and plants, but account for the difference between individuals—every individual living thing that ever lived or ever will live!

DECEMBER TENTH

WROTE Jacques Loeb, high priest of mechanism, "Unless we can make protoplasm artificially we must admit that a deep gulf yawns between living and dead matter."

Many an attempt has been made to synthesize the protoplasmic cell. The results have all been imitations—though with an imitation many minds seem to rest content. Bütschli compounded a mixture of olive oil drops and potassium chloride salt, which is extremely avid of water. With this he imitated that drop of naked protoplasm, the amœba. When intimately mixed with water, the oil film and the drops of water taken up by the salt worked themselves into a fine froth. In this wise was the surface tension lessened, and the delighted experimenter had the satisfaction of seeing streamers, like the pseudopodia of amœbæ, put out to engulf synthetic bits of food.

There are other spectacles which the mechanist may stage to amaze the onlooker. A drop of chloroform can be induced to ingest a sliver of glass coated in shellac. The drop devours the shellac, but the glass is spewed out like indigestible matter. Mere changes in surface tension account for these remarkable simulations, and for the way in which an artificial sperm can be made to penetrate a synthetic egg, or a drop of mercury will stalk potassium bichromate like an amœba on the hunt. So, if you like, you are left with the inference that a similar lowering of surface tension explains the amœba's characteristic locomotion and activity.

DECEMBER ELEVENTH

Now the trouble with chemists and physicists when they begin to experiment in biology is that they are careless observers of life processes. The surface tension of the amœba engulfing its food is not lowered, like the surface tension of Bütcheli's mock amœba; it is actually increased. The currents within living protoplasm are almost precisely the opposite of those in the artifice, and the animalcule does not shoot out a streamer and draw in its food as its imitation does. It sends out arms on each side of the food, which meet around it, and then the whole animal wells up about the prey.

One by one the imitations of living protoplasm that seek to show that growth, reproduction and metabolism are completely shared by the inanimate world, have come up for examination and are found guilty of argument by analogy. The mechanists were so bold as to state, at the height of their influence, that all appearances of volition within the organism were delusion. Thus even man's consciousness would be but the mechanics of the brain; a slight storm in the endocrines might be all that was necessary to account for a religious leader. This sort of thinking, with sociological implications, has been popularized by brilliant and superficial minds.

But mechanistic predeterminism is itself the delusion. Perhaps some may be able to conceive a robot which would grow from the inside out, produce perfect little robots, maintain within itself a continuous and reversible chemical interaction, and perform purposive actions. But if even a mechanist came upon this conception in a story book, he would dismiss it with a shrug as fantasy.

DECEMBER TWELFTH

I KEEP always on my desk a bit of an old olive root that I pulled out of the flames, one cold December evening on the Riviera. Intricate as a finger print, that root, in its fantastic whorls and devious involutions. Intricate as the history of Europe, which it very possibly witnessed, for the grove from which it came was planted by the Romans.

Between what the physicists call an organism, such as a fluorine atom, and what the biologists admit as an organism, there is this mighty difference, that a fluorine atom must ever remain the same and identically the same, lest it be fluorine no longer, while the root of an olive, and the finger tip of a man, are never twice the same. I do not say it is impossible to conceive in life the accidental occurrence of two perfect identities, but everything in our experience points in the other direction. Mendel showed once and for all that nothing is so unlike as two peas in a pod, and observation tends toward the belief that even one-celled animals have individualization.

In the bit of root nubble is written the history of the tree, the obstacles it met, the tropisms it followed, the lean years and the fat. So easy to touch a match to it; so forever out of reach to recreate a bit of wood like it!

As the fire glances from the burning log around the room it falls upon the faces of the people seated round the hearth with you. What do you really know of them, your own children, and the wife who bore them to you? All are locked mysteriously away in their individuality. So I guard the old olive root upon my desk, to keep myself humble as a scientist and, as a man, full of wonder.

DECEMBER THIRTEENTH

I STAND in the quiet woods, conscious that under my feet, in the soil, are millions of dead, millions of living things. That all around me are trees, half dead and half alive, and looking alike. I myself am perpetually dying. I do not mean that I am simply drifting ever nearer toward that right hand bracket that will ultimately close up the dates in my biography, but literally dying, cell by cell, artery by artery.

Scratch a live twig, and a bit of the green cambium layer will shine forth; scratch a live finger and blood will flow. These are cheery, colorful pennants of living things. But so much that is alive flies no flag, and wears the expressionless mask of the lifeless.

As I see it, the great and distinguishing feature of living things, however, is that they have needs—continual, and, incidentally, complex needs. I cannot conceive how even so organized a dead system as a crystal can be said to need anything. But a living creature, even when it sinks into that half-death of hibernation, even the seed in the bottom of the dried Mongolian marsh, awaiting rain through two thousand years, still has needs while there is life in it. The bacteria have needs, and it cannot be said too often that merely because a living creature is microscopic there is no justification for thinking that it brings us any nearer to the inanimate. The gulf between a bacterium and a carbon atom, even with all the latter's complexity, is greater than that between bacteria and men.

If you object that this criterion of life is chiefly a philosophical one, I reply that in the end the most absolute answers concerning every problem of matter, energy, time and life, will be found to be philosophical.

DECEMBER FOURTEENTH

It is the habit of scientists to speak contemptuously of philosophy, the Greek mother out of whose womb came all the sciences. When one reaches the momentary limits of scientific deduction or construction, the periphery of empiricism, one "turns the matter over to the philosophers." This implies that the subject has grown too airy to be weighed or even seen. It suggests that philosophy is guess work, and that as the sciences advance, philosophy must retreat in an ever shrinking realm.

It is easy to understand the scientists' discontent with philosophy. Leibnitz argued himself into a corner with his monads and sealed himself up. Spinoza did enough thinking about God and the universe to make ten Moses and Mohammeds, but came to ethical conclusions that showed he was only a hurt, sick, lonely little Jewish bachelor, with no knowledge of life at all. Kant proves conclusively to himself that there are no atoms, if I recall him aright, and the irreproachable Comte is humorless enough to try to found a religion on reason.

One wonders if there be anything which philosophy might still do amongst the natural and exact and social sciences. It seems to me that it could synthesize, not in the person of one philosopher, for accumulated knowledge has grown too great for that, but in a peripatetic school, a perpetual conference of large-minded representatives whose task it should be not to codify and embalm the laws, but to keep them fluid.

DECEMBER FIFTEENTH

A PHILOSOPHER with a biological turn of mind has to ask himself three questions. How does life do what it does? What is it made of and how put together? And where does it find itself in the universe? You might take these questions in any order, but that is the order in which they occur to most of us, and in which they have occurred to me as I "watch things grow from the beginning," from the first pale upshooting of spring till the frost upon the head of the dying year. First the performances of life startle us into a questioning frame of mind, a discontent with all our old ideas. So that to understand function we go back to structure. But structure turns out to be so complex that inevitably we return to environment, the inanimate world out of which life somehow builds itself. And the environment is the earth, and yet not the earth only, but the cosmos.

What is the nearest star? That is a famous catch-question in astronomy. Some young students will answer that it is Mars, some Proxima Centauri. But the correct response, of course, is the sun, our mother. The table on which I write, the pane of glass through which I look, the cloud bank out of which the westering sun is just dropping, all were once in the sun itself, and so was the petal of the rose and the brow of Helen. All were once in the fiery womb of a star.

So, though I have no passport to the infernos of astronomy, I must journey there, in fear and trembling, to seek my answers. I shall not go alone, but, like Dante, take some Virgil's hand. The astronomers must tell me what it is I see, explain the laws by which the cosmos works, and reënact for me the birth of worlds.

DECEMBER SIXTEENTH

I HAVE no telescope, and in truth scarce time even for star gazing with the naked eye. I see what I can, as I walk home in the night, breathing gulfs of the tingling dark air. Or I do my celestial traveling in bed, and watch the glittering wheel of the heavens turn slowly past my window space.

When I seek my pillow Orion has already risen and, as my window faces south, I see the silver-shod hunter mount into the sky; it is midnight, I know, when he stands due south, and he sets before dawn, at four-thirty. By the end of the month he will be setting an hour earlier, and pass the center of my window at eleven.

So each night the value of the characters on my clock shifts a little. Everything about the heavens perpetually shifts. But in any one wakeful night the rolling of the great dome is so slow that the mind, winging straight out of the window to the Pleiades or Sirius, has all the time it could require for contemplation upon the miracle of the heavens, and one constellation provides as much meditation as another.

But I learned Orion in childhood, and still on winter evenings I journey to it first, like Barrie's old gentleman who never set forth without first going to Charing Cross. Orion points me the way to all stars, all constellations in the winter sky; it marches in majesty, heeled by the Dog, with Sirius; it flings an arm up toward Capella, gestures portentously to red Aldebaran, and sweeps before Procyon and the Twins.

DECEMBER SEVENTEENTH

WHEN I try to look at the sun my weak eyes flinch away before the light from our bright particular star, like an animal that cannot meet its master's gaze. But a man may look at Orion, and stare its brilliance down the sky, because, in truth, he need not see it as it is. One can recite the musical and ancient names of the gems that compose it —the three stars of the belt, Alnitak, Alnilam and Mintaka; Betelgeux is for the head, Rigel at the forward knee, and Saiph at the hinder foot, and in the outflung arm the glorious Bellatrix.

No constellation in all the sky is so vast, so dazzling, so heroic and exciting as this mighty hunter. The heart lifts up at the spectacle of those three perfectly matched jewels of the belt, at Rigel the color of glacial ice, and Betelgeux like some topaz flashing its splendor across the depths of space.

One of those strange variables that now is dim and then again is bright, is Betelgeux, that in 1852 blazed out in such splendor it surpassed Capella, Vega and Arcturus, and was second only to that stabbing shaft of violet radiance, the dog star, Sirius, at the hunter's heels. The hue of Betelgeux appears to vary with its brightness, deepening to the color of embers as the star grows fainter, leaping to a blazing yellow as if it found fresh fuel—a sun that is flickering out, yet one still a thousand times as brilliant as our own.

But Rigel, in its youth, is ten thousand times as brilliant. And these intensities are not mere appearance, like that of Sirius, which is so bright largely because so near to us; they are the true measure of the size and heat of two great hells seething and pitching on through icy blackness.

DECEMBER EIGHTEENTH

T H E mind of simple man, beholding Orion, conceived almost everything about that great configuration save the awful truth. The three belt stars are three steps cut in ice by the Great Eskimo, for little Eskimos to climb into heaven. To the Arab, Orion was a giant, to the Jews he was Nimrod, to the Egyptians Osiris. In Greece he was that hunter who dared boast that he could slay all the beasts, whereat a scorpion stung him in the heel.

But no sooner did the telescopes swing upon this giant, god, or brute, than thousands of thousands of stars sprang forth to the view of man—stars, and the Great Nebula, and the Horse's Head, that dark impenetrable mass behind which, as behind a hill, a blaze of brightness peeps. And between the stars were seen the looped festoons of light, like cirrus clouds upon a fair-weather sky, like spindrift brilliance washed up on the black shingle of nothingness.

Now indeed are we gazing at our own spiral nebula, the Milky Way, in one of its most terrifying and chaotic perspectives—black dust reefs of dead matter on which a sun might speed to ruin, streamers of incandescent gas, wandering fires of the air, and suns so vast that our own might drop into them and be lost as a stone is lost in a crater's pit. This is the inner circle of inferno in which our poor mortal planet spins about, bearing its freight, to us so precious, of life and hope.

DECEMBER NINETEENTH

M A N , that most inquisitive of mammals, has not stopped his searches within the Milky Way. He knows now that our sun is traveling in it, in a saraband, circling, maybe—but there has not yet been time to know it surely—round and round some core or nucleus whose awful heat and brilliance are mercifully hidden from us by a great cloud bank of inert matter somewhere in the constellation of Sagittarius.

But the telescope has revealed other nebulæ than ours, and there is one that even with the naked eye I just discern. To me it looks like a faint luminosity between the great W of Cassiopeia in the zenith and Andromeda at Cassiopeia's feet. Before me as I write I have a photograph of this other island universe in space, that shows me what astronomers see—a wild swirl of smoky light in which no individual stars appear but all seems like an act of creation coming out of chaos contorted with birth pangs. Only if the picture were enlarged to the size of this continent would a sun like ours be visible upon it, as a small speck.

Such is M 31, the great nebula of Andromeda. It is none other than a Milky Way, our nearest neighbor star city— so near that light, traveling from it at 186,000 miles a second, has only taken 900,000 years to reach us! Has it some destiny of its own? Are we, our Milky Way and M 31, two ships that pass in the night, who see each other, sides glittering with porthole lights, as they plow their way through space, turning a luminous furrow in the ultimate dark?

O NE star city will do as well as another for a poor biologist, for every one looks as hostile as the next. The astronomers and mathematicians eagerly invite our admiration of cosmic law and order. They show us all things in motion, all motion obeying one law, all suns moving in majestic dances around their galactic hubs, and—who knows?—perhaps all galaxies swinging round some center of it all, some terrible abode of a mathematical God, some lawgiver for all these laws. Or else there is no center save as a centrifugal locus from which all matter rushes away, stretching itself apart, expanding at furious speed like a bubble recklessly blown out.

Some celestial philosophers ask us to believe that intelligence must move behind all this, intelligence with an ultimate purpose previsioned from the start. It may be so. But ask them to tell you about the end that they foresee, the ultimate inertia, the disassociation of everything into an infinitely expanded chaos, the running down of the time clock. Is it for this that some purposive intelligence behind it all plays out the drama of the ages?

Verily before a man clasp astronomical law and order to his breast in the comforting hope that it somehow makes all things right, inscrutably resolves disharmonies, it is well to reflect that what is called order in heaven might look like pandemonium on earth. If the elements here behaved as those in the sun we should certainly call it chaos. And the physicist's laws are not laws at all in the sense of some fiat from on high; they compel no thing; they are but subjective descriptions of the way that things take place, up there where, so far as we know, there is no thought nor life to give rise to thought. Unless, mayhap, dead suns and planets that we cannot see may give life sanctuary, or the interstellar space carry it in the black of its womb.

DECEMBER TWENTY-FIRST

ON THIS day in 1823 was born Henri Fabre, the sage of Serignan, who entered the world of the insects like a transmogrified elf to spy upon them. The monstrous matings, the cannibalisms, the unnatural appetites, the hunts, the deaths, the smells, the fabulous eyes, the snatchings, gluttonies and rapes—he describes them, mildly scandalized, but like a Christian, loving all. The drowsy corner of Provence where he had his roof and taught physics in a boy's school, for him was a teeming jungle, a land of Lilliputian marvel and adventure, in which event was the trembling of a moth's feathered antenna, the knotting of a thread in a spider's web.

With all this wealth of observation, amassed over Fabre's very long life and flung before us in the most captivating, witty, readable style ever given to a reporter, the reader is surely carping to find a fault. Yet there were faults in Fabre's work. As an experimenter in animal psychology, behavior and mechanics, he was naïve and crude. His conclusions were too frequently *non sequiturs:* obstinate village piety made him forswear evolution and the door of interpretation that it would have opened for him.

But behind his words works the kindly spirit of Fabre himself, a valiant old man who for much of his life never owned a miscroscope and yet saw more than twenty microscopists, a man who lived, not the unnatural ascetic like Spinoza or the irresponsible wanderer like Audubon, but the whole man, taking a wife, keeping a rooftree, begetting children, and struggling to make their shirts meet their little breeches.

CAPRICORNUS

DECEMBER 22 – JANUARY 20

DECEMBER TWENTY-SECOND

Now is the darkest hour of all the year, the winter solstice. We are arrived at the antipodes of brave midsummer, when it was once the custom for men to while away the few hours of the short night with bonfires and a blowing of conches and a making of wild young marriages, that men might hold the earth for the sun god during his brief descent beneath the horizon. But at this season of the year, when the sun was a pallid blur behind a junco-colored sky, a darkness fell upon the spirits of all men, and a splinter of ice was in their hearts. To some of us the winter solstice is an unimportant phase of terrestrial astronomy; of old it must have produced an emotional reaction which a Christian can only experience on Good Friday, and the breath-held Saturday that follows.

It is not the cold of far northern lands that drives the human animal to despair; cold is tingling, exciting, healthful, and it can, in a limited way, be overcome. It is the darkness that conquers the spirit, when the northern sun does not rise until late, only to skim low upon the horizon for an hour or two, and set. Now indeed is Balder slain of the mistletoe. Now life is at its lowest ebb, and the mind conceives a little what it will be like when the sun has burned to a red ember, its immense volume dissipated by constant radiation, and the earth drifted far out into space, the shrinking sun no longer able to hold her child upon a leash so close.

DECEMBER TWENTY-THIRD

W H O will tell us why only in winter do we see that strange chill apple green in the sunset sky? Is it gold diffused on the very clear light blue, giving us the illusion of green? I call it green, but as soon as I look at it, it turns into something else, some shade that I cannot name. Our visual range is impoverished, limited to the narrow octave between red and violet. It is tormenting to reflect that even in a sunset there are colors, perhaps almost an infinity of them, which we shall never see.

Yet the physicists and astronomers give us reason to think that in one sense the sunset colors are not there at all. Ascension to the stratosphere has shown that darkness prevails as the air grows rarer and space clearer of particles. Out in the wastes of space all is perpetual night. The sun and the other stars must stab through the darkness with blinding shafts, like searchlights. So, after all, it is not the heavens, but little earth, dear, dusty, ill-behaved and mortal earth, that diffuses all this bombardment of the photons that we call light; it is the evening damps, the restless dust, that give us sunset.

Yet not even this is quite literally true. For when the astronomer looks at the sunset with his telescope, blue turns white, clouds look dingy yellow, purple becomes insipid pink, and all the sky is a tawdry mixture. The beauty of the sunset is, then, in reality only in the human eye, and in the mind behind the eye.

DECEMBER TWENTY-FOURTH

WHEN I set out to buy a Christmas tree, I have my choice of long-needled pines, red cedars, and fragrant spruces with narrow spire-like tops, the branches beautifully up-curved at the dark tips. But I am looking for a balsam, which has this inestimable advantage over all the spruces, that even in the warmth of the house its needles do not drop.

You may know a balsam from a spruce in this way, that the leaves of the balsam are flattish, and the cones are borne erect; on many of the branches the leaves are two-ranked, so that they appear to form a flat spray, while in the spruces the needles are scattered, bristling out in every direction from the stem, to the touch seeming four-sided; and the cones of a fir always droop.

Time was, not long ago, when a man bought a Christmas tree in all innocence, feeling that it was no really material expenditure but a symbol, almost intangible, which gave beauty and good cheer to all who beheld it. Now come the tree conservationists, to reproach us with the forests that we slay to make a brief holiday, to let them die then ingloriously upon the rubbish heap. But balsam is only used in a small way in the crafts and sciences, while the spruces, by far the commonest holiday trees, have, otherwise, only the pulp mill for their destiny.

And the Christmas trees cut for the city across the river would not suffice to put out the combined Sunday editions of its newspapers in one week, bearing into every home their freight of unchallenged intellectual poison—the brutal humor, the worldly inanity, the crime and pseudo-science.

IT WAS Francis of Assisi, I believe, the man who called the wind his brother and the birds his sisters, who gave the world the custom of exhibiting the crèche in church, where barn and hay, soft-breathing beasts, flowing breast and hungry babe, shepherd and star are elevated for delight. One who has spent a Christmas in some southern country, where an early Christianity still reigns, will understand how all else that to us means the holy festival is quite lacking there. It was originally, and still sometimes is, no more than a special Mass, scarcely as significant as Assumption, much less so than Easter. Out of the North the barbarian mind, forest born, brought tree worship, whether of fir or holly or yule log. It took mistletoe from the druids, stripped present-giving from New Year (where in Latin lands it still so largely stays) and made of Christmas a children's festival, set to the tune of the beloved joyful carols. It glorified woman and child and the brotherhood of men in a way that the Church in, let us say, the second century, dreamed not on.

You will search the four Gospels in vain for a hint of the day or the month when Christ was born. December twenty-fifth was already being celebrated in the ancient world as the birthdate of the sun god Mithras, who came out of a rock three days after the darkest of the year. His birth was foretold of a star that shepherds and magi beheld. The ancient Angles had long been wont to hold this day sacred as Modranecht or Mother Night. Thus still do we flout old winter with green tree, and old mortality with child worship.

DECEMBER TWENTY-SIXTH

THE old Saxon name of *mistl-tan,* from which we have the name of mistletoe, has debated meanings. One of them is "different branch," because, though it sprouts from a tree like one of the tree's own branches, it is in reality a parasite, a very different branch indeed. I find no mistletoe about my house, but it grows thickly nearer to the sea, on gum and maple. In Europe it is the missel thrush that carries the berries from tree to tree, wiping the seed from its beak off upon the bark. Here the waxwings perform the same involuntary office. Once upon the tree the viscid pulp soon hardens fast like a sucker, and instead of an honest root this green parasite thrusts a claw down into its victim.

The druids considered that the mistletoe represented pure spirit, since it never touches earth—quite a different view of it than we take either of its aspect as a parasite or as an opportunity. Druids cut it with a golden sickle, and caught it in a clean white cloth; Keltic women wore it in the hope that they would soon go freighted with child. Pseudo-Aristotle's *Golden Cabinet of Secrets* mentions it as a love powder. But wicked Loki put it as an arrow in blind Hoder's hand that he might kill Balder the young god of light. And here, if you like, you may read an allegory of the winter solstice—the sun god slain upon the twenty-second, revived upon the third day, after the mistletoe had promised never again to slay but only to bring life.

All this is legend, one may say. But legend concerning events of earth and heaven is part of the natural history of humanity, and you may pity the man who has so blunted his perceptions that he can feel no old racial associations with the things that grow and the things that creep.

DECEMBER TWENTY-SEVENTH

U p o n this day in 1822 was born Louis Pasteur, the type of man that we devoutly hope will be the hero on the pedestals of the future, instead of the Bismarcks who now stand there. France, at any rate, has the sense to put Pasteur and not Napoleon on her postage stamps. The account of Pasteur in *The Microbe Hunters,* more widely read in America than any other story of his life, was something so superficial, so nearly hostile, that we can only suppose that the medical profession has not yet given up its intense annoyance that a layman should have to set them all to rights, and convince surgeons and obstetricians against their will that they themselves carried septic fever from wound to wound, from one woman in childbed to the next.

Pasteur, who as a boy student was rated merely one of the *bons ordinaires* by his dominies, had already distinguished himself in chemistry when he began to investigate the common blue mold, *Penicilium glaucum.* He was led on to the diseases of beer and wine, as brewers then called them, and it was then that he discovered that sweet beer contained mysterious globules of a nearly spherical shape, while sour beer was infected with elongated microscopic objects. It seems very odd that men should have been seeing bacteria in their microscopes since the seventeenth century without an idea that they lived, multiplied, and could devour or ferment. But it was Pasteur who, still in his youth, made this discovery, and in seeking to find a way to exclude the elongated microörganisms, developed the first technique of sterility and gave spontaneous generation its death blow.

DECEMBER TWENTY-EIGHTH

THE blood of a healthy man and the juice of a sound grape contain no bacteria, Pasteur showed. Break the skin of man or fruit, and the seeds of decay have entry. But sterilize the wound, and life is saved. This was Pasteur's discovery, the greatest biological triumph of the ages, which Lord Lister carried to victory among the medical men.

The result of this glittering achievement was that on all sides Pasteur's aid was sought. A disease of silkworms was ruining the south of France. When Pasteur consented to undertake the problem he had never seen a silkworm. In four months he had quenched the malady. He conquered chicken cholera, and in the attack upon the dreaded anthrax disease of cattle developed the principles of antitoxin to a science.

It is a story that needs no retelling—how he stamped out rabies by this means. The terror has gone out of the dog-days, and never again need any one die in its inhuman agonies. But all great men must wrestle with their angels, and in the early days, before his cure was ascertained, there arrived at the chemist's door two peasants bearing a child in the last stages of hydrophobia. "But I cannot save him," Pasteur protested. "It is too late." They begged, but he resisted. Should the cure fail now, disrepute might blight the whole undertaking. But the agonies of the child were too much for him. He plunged in the needle and watched—the failure. The peasants ran crying to the village, to all the world, that Pasteur had killed their child. That was the darkest hour of all his life.

DECEMBER TWENTY-NINTH

On november 14, 1888 the Institut Pasteur was founded, Pasteur's greatest triumph. Now, all over the world, similar institutions carry on his work, lighthouses of safety for humanity. It was at the inauguration of this institute that Pasteur closed his oration with these prophetic and Christ-like words:

"Two opposing laws seem to me now in contest. The one, a law of blood and death, opening out each day new modes of destruction, forces nations to be always ready for battle. The other, a law of peace, work and health, whose only aim is to deliver man from the calamities which beset him. The one seeks violent conquests, the other the relief of mankind. The one places a single life above all victories, the other sacrifices hundreds of thousands of lives to the ambition of a single individual.... Which of these two laws will prevail, God only knows. But of this we may be sure, that science, in obeying the law of humanity, will always labor to enlarge the frontiers of life."

I often wish that that group of people who decry the progress of science—dilute orientalized mystics, fantastic Chestertonian Christians who imagine that life was gayer, more spiritual and clearer-headed in the Middle Ages, and others of that ilk—would recall that whatever chemistry and engineering may have done to make war horrible, the biological sciences have never done anything but render life nobler, and free man from his miseries.

Louis Pasteur died at St. Cloud in 1895. He awoke from one of his final torpors and gazed around at his students clustered at his bedside. *"Où en êtes vous?"* demanded this tireless admiral of the ship of humanity. *"Que faites-vous?"* And then, *"Il faut travailler!"* he said, and died.

DECEMBER THIRTIETH

THE first great snow of the year is falling, long presaged in gray skies and sullen weather, in a brooding and sad silence. First it fell in a few great flakes, swinging leisurely down in the damp still air, one white star and then another drifting down so slowly that with the naked eye one could see each crystalline form etched out in gleaming white against the gray of sky and stone and ground.

Then thicker they fell, and now they sweep in a white horde, wind-driven wolves leaping on the woods, raiding in long hungry lines across the mystified fields, gathering up from the ground again, like ghosts whipped up by the wind's command, in arms. I see the trees that take the wild assault like grim old warriors, and the naked bushes that kneel before it, their backs to the lash of the storm, their fine ultimate withes and twigs flung forward like woman's hair, upon the ground.

Now that the storm is actually descended, there is a sense of relief and lightening abroad. For days even the winter birds had moped in silence. Now they are whipped into activity; they scud around the angles of the house in little excited flurries. A red bird and his pretty wife, nuthatches and downy woodpeckers gather sociably around the feeding tray outside the window. Within, the human animal sits by the clear pane, the possessor of fire and light. It is a fine thing, of a winter's afternoon, to be a man, a fortunate man, reading in an old Greek's stately thoughts, out of a well bound book, while the snow falls, pure and decent, and the birds, his friends, come to his door. But only the accidents of life have placed him there, and not in a smoke-filled street where in others' eyes he might be forced to read his own despairs, his own brute thoughts.

DECEMBER THIRTY-FIRST

EACH little year that passes is one more grain of sand slipped through the narrows of the hour glass of our universe. Physicists suppose that matter and energy in the universe are finite; I cannot imagine time in a cosmos that reached ultimate inertia and dissipation; the supply of time, too, then, may well be finite—particularly terrestrial time.

What did mankind do with the sand grain that is even now falling? He discovered new stars, and one more chemical element, the last with a chair reserved for it at the Round Table of the elements. He averted another great war—at least momentarily. He discovered several new methods of destroying his brothers with the utmost cruelty. He reëstablished in some countries tyranny, torture and religious intolerance; in others he toiled on, unencouraged but not discouraged, with the age-old problems like poverty, disease, prostitution and crime.

The best that we can say is that some of humanity shouldered the old loads; some hindered, hung back, even attacked the burden bearers. Most of us did nothing, neglected to raise a cheer for the struggling, passively permitted the wolves to go on devouring their hideous banquet of men and women, wolves of war and greed, vice and drugs.

Biologically considered, man is the sole being who has its destiny in its hands. And few of his species feel any sense of racial responsibility higher than the fundamental one of begetting children. Yet now and then, as the years pass, comes a Noguchi, Pasteur, Beethoven, Lincoln, Asoka, Marcus Aurelius or Plato. They are humanity as it might be.

JANUARY FIRST

IT WAS the habit of an old scientist of Göttingen to inaugurate the new year's work by sitting down ceremoniously at his desk upon the stroke of midnight. My own temperament is more indolent than that, but the first hour of the new year finds me still awake and, in spite of cheer, cold sober, in that frame of mind where the spirit stands alone in the night and asks, What now? Where now?

When I go to the window and look out, I see nothing of the new year save the wild flying of the snow as it swirls, whiteness born out of blackness, into the brief warm rhombus of light from the window, and then, brief as life, it vanishes into darkness once more. It flies upon a level wind; it is hurled as if a spirit were behind it, some dark force that has these arrows without limit in his quiver.

For those no longer very young the snow will always speak a little of death. For soon or late it comes to us all to bury some one in it—a friend, a father, a sister. And the heart does not forget these things. The soul, that looks out on a wrapt world of night and cold, demands its ultimate answers, or if it have them not, it will know at least, where lies the hope of man?

I say man's hope is in himself, and when I say it I do not deny that God may be the font of all resource man finds within himself. But any one who has read thus far will know how little I would lean upon that chill God in which the physicist finds it easy to believe—some Being that embodies the first and second laws of thermodynamics. Who cares for sheer bulk in a God, compared with accessibility? No, I say, man's hopes, like his faults, are not in his stars, but in himself, and not alone in our rare noblemen who live or die that others may the better live, but in the whole blood brotherhood with all its scars and weals.

JANUARY SECOND

THERE was once a boy of eleven who heard that the Pole star is the only one that always remains in the same position—the fixed, the guiding star round which the whole of the bright firmament appears to swing. The child decided to find this star, and he had no instruments with which to do it. But a dearth of instruments, the despair of the mediocre, is the making of gifted persons. So he made himself a cardboard tube (quite without any lens, of course) and put it on a stand. He fixed it upon star after star, but they all moved rapidly from the field of vision. Yet his patience was the equal of the task he set himself, and at last he found the star that did not alter.

The moral of this story should be that he turned out to be Copernicus. But he didn't; he was in later life the librarian to the Empress Maria Theresa, a position as exalted as you choose to think it. The real moral, I suspect, is that every one who discovers something for himself is the richer for it, and richer in inverse proportion to the equipment with which he started out.

But there is a moral back of this, and that is that the distant and terrible sun Polaris has not always been our Pole star. Uneasily shifts our temporary planet on its axis, like a top wavering as it dies. For, thousand years ago, it was Thuban, one of the bright stars in the Dragon, that was the zenith star above our Pole, and the tombs of Egypt were so constructed that from the low door of the house of death one could behold it, the one star, as man supposed, that would ever remain in its place. Tomorrow—only twelve thousand years hence, that will be Vega of the Lyre.

JANUARY THIRD

T H E true lover of nature does not complain of his mistress that now she turns a colder cheek. He takes his luck abroad like the small birds that all through the leafless woods scurry in little gusts before him. They are not merely weathering it out till spring, but have a song for it—*tsick-a-dee-dee-dee*. The first syllable is like the click of a seed in a weather-beaten pod, the rest a twanging of wind in old treble wires. Gray, black, and darker gray, they and the juncos flit past in their little unsymmetrical groups, making a moment as lively and dainty as a Japanese print.

Even in mid woods there is no sadness in the silence, only an immense and thoughtful gravity. The skies are prescient of snow; the air is still, awaiting it; the cycle is at its perigee. Life after death, fruit after flower, decay and again resurrection—like some conjurer's trick it is all performed time after time, and still we wonder how it was done, still we are intent upon the magic.

JANUARY FOURTH

N o w we are in the very lists of winter, and what a winter, with the Atlantic coast lashed with storm on storm, with ships crying at sea through the lost staccato of their wireless. Cold blowing out of the Arctic, out of Keewatin, on the wings of cyclones that engulf a continent in a single maelstrom, vanish in the east to be followed by another. Frost reaching a finger to the tender tip of tropic Florida. And here, fresh ice thickening upon the unmelted old; ice on the loops of the country telegraph wires, every tree locked in a silver armor, a sort of a white Iron Maiden that breaks their bones and listens with glee to the cracking sound. Something there is in our North American winters peculiarly sadistic—with a pitiless love of inflicting suffering for its own sake wherever the poor are huddled in the smoky cities, wherever men, and women too, battle against the cold in lonely prairie houses. We have no Alps from west to east to block the way of roaring boreas, no southland protected against our north. Our mountains march with the north wind, and in the drafty gulfs between them, and along their outer flanks, raids the pack of the howling white-fanged days.

JANUARY FIFTH

U P O N this day in 1786 was born in England Thomas Nuttall, who yet belongs to the New World, for it was America he loved, and America that in return made Nuttall famous. He enjoyed the enviable distinction of being both an ornithologist and a botanist, and those were the great days, in the first quarter of the last century, when all our continent called to the naturalist, called him from the gannetries of the Gulf of St. Lawrence to the heronries of Florida, when the white man had never trod the alpine meadows of the Rockies, nor the redwoods of California.

In person Nuttall was a shy, eccentric bachelor, shabbily dressed and parsimonious from necessity. His associates in the old Academy of Science at Philadelphia, then the Lyceum of America, scarcely knew where he lived or what he did with himself. During his curatorship of the botanical garden at Harvard it was his fancy to cut in his house all sorts of secret doors, which had for their purpose only his privacy; as a result, a man might enter Nuttall's study and find there nothing but innumerable cages of birds, with which this elvish little man continually experimented.

Toward the end of his life Nuttall was left an inheritance, one of those British legacies by which the dead lay hold upon the living. It provided that Nuttall must dwell nine months of every year in England. He accepted the bequest because he wished to give the money to a sister; but it meant, as he put it, exile in his native land. He returned to the field of his great endeavors but once, when by sailing for America in autumn and returning in spring, he circumvented the provisions of the will. But it was winter, and the flowers were dead, the birds were gone.

His travels took Thomas Nuttall first of all in the footprints of Rafinesque—upon the Delaware Peninsula, all about Philadelphia and Washington. But before long he set out for the untrodden prairies, in company with the Scotch naturalist Bradbury, whose journal is on the *desiderata* list of American collectors. West of the Missouri they were captured by Indians, and only saved from torture when Bradbury took his watch apart and distributed the wheels and springs among the childishly delighted savages. Nuttall, wandering afield, was lost, fell unconscious with hunger and fatigue, and was paddled back to camp by a friendly brave.

In the years that followed he traveled from the Great Lakes to Florida, explored the Arkansas country, suffered countless hardships and capture by the Indians. Finally he resigned his post at Harvard to accompany Wyeth's expedition to the Pacific, and trod, the first of men, the bright elysium of the mountain meadows of the West. As almost every European flower bears the Latin name Linnæus gave it, so do the fairest of the western blossoms owe their names to Nuttall. From California he journeyed to the Hawaiian Islands, and returned by boat around Cape Horn where he begged in vain that the captain would set him down, if only for three hours, to collect. But when Nuttall came to pay for his passage in New York, the ship's owners waived away the gentle scholar's money.

In the actual description of the new species Nuttall left his mark chiefly upon American botany. He completed Michaux's splendid book on the trees of North America by adding the western species of which Michaux could know nothing. But the work he will longest be remembered by is the *Birds of the United States and Canada,* a volume treasured, I am sure, by thousands of bird lovers as I treasure it.

JANUARY SEVENTH

F E A R rises out of all darkness, fear for us who are diurnal, not nocturnal animals. But I do not experience this sensation out of doors, as many people do. Night terrors are bred in closets, beds, cellars, attics, and all those traps and pits and sinks in which civilized man houses himself, blunts his senses and breeds his own ills. Out in the open night it may be cold, or windy, or rainy, but it is never anything in which a bogy could endure.

Indeed, if you think of night in the true, philosophical proportion, you must realize that it is the prevailing, the absolute thing. Light, day, burning suns and stars—all are the exception. They are but gleaming jewels spattered on the black cloth of darkness. Throughout the universe and eternity it is night that prevails. It is the mother of cosmos, capacious womb of light.

I F I T were true that the star under which a man is born determined his destiny, how does it happen, asks St. Augustine, that people born upon the same day endure such disparate fortunes? How account, we would add, for the fact that Charles Darwin and Abraham Lincoln were both born on the 12th of February, 1809, when it would have been so much more reasonable for Darwin and Alfred Russel Wallace, the co-discoverer of the theory of Natural Selection, to have seen the light together? But Wallace was born on this day, in 1823.

When Wallace was twenty-three and traveling in Borneo, he wrote down this sentence: "Every species has come into existence coincident both in time and space with a pre-existing closely allied species." The question of how changes of species could have come about continued to torment him, and three years later, while he was lying muffled in blankets in a cold fit of severe intermittent fever at Ternate in the Moluccas, he began to think of Malthus's *Essay on Population.* "There suddenly flashed upon me," he wrote, "the idea of the survival of the fittest." The theory was thought out that night, and as soon as the fever had abated he sat down and wrote out his ideas. After several succeeding evenings the paper was finished and he sent it to a certain Charles Darwin, of whom he had heard.

"I never saw a more striking coincidence," wrote Darwin to Lyell, on the day he received the paper. "If Wallace had my MS. sketch written out in 1842 he could not have made a better short abstract! Even his terms now stand as heads of my chapters." On the advice of Lyell and Sir Joseph Hooker, the essay was read, with Darwin's as a joint paper, before the Linnæan Society on the memorable first of July, 1858.

JANUARY NINTH

THE great coincidence of the theory of Natural Selection discovered by two men at once is but one of the many such in the history of science. It is notorious how many inventors may lay claim to one invention—the airplane, for instance. Of a truth, many inventors are probably necessary to bring a scheme to fruition; inventions and discoveries come when the times are ripe for them; when telescopes improve, new stars are noticed at once everywhere.

In the case of Darwin and Wallace it is easy to see how they came to arrive simultaneously at their conclusions. Both were self-taught men with an interest primarily in systematic zoölogy. Both had explored a tropic island region and had been tormented by the need to account for what would seem like special acts of creation for insignificant islands, and both had read Malthus's essay on population pressure. But for that coincidence we might know natural selection not by the alternative of Darwinism, but Wallace-ism. In some ways Wallace's ideas were sounder that Darwin's. He did not fall into Darwin's error of "sexual selection," nor rely as Darwin did on so unstable an argument as the man-made evolution of domesticated animals.

With the naturalist Bates, Wallace is co-author of another theory of natural selection—that of protective resemblance, which, whatever its exaggerations, has a fundamental truth about it. He was also the father of geographical zoölogy. In his old age—he lived for ninety years—his kindly temperament departed from the paths of science, and he turned to the problem of man's destiny and happiness, which, he seems really to have believed, were marked out respectively in the paths of Spiritualism and Henry George's Single Tax system.

JANUARY TENTH

THE brooks are locked now, even in this climate; never before have I seen them frozen to the bottom; the wood ponds too are frozen deep, perhaps to their beds, and on their little bleak shores the ice has pushed up in its strange expansion. Very odd, that property of water, unique amongst the elements, that near its freezing point, instead of continuing to contract, it should suddenly expand. An inconvenience when it bursts a pipe or cracks a garden fountain or a wall.

Yet as water is the absolute essential of every living thing, every property of water will have tremendous significances for life. If ice contracted like other substances at freezing, it would, for its volume, be heavier than water; it would sink to the bottom of every pond and stream and lake and there, isolated, it would lie unmelted. Year by year the ice deposit would increase. The seas too would long ago have filled with ice and become great reservoirs of cold, chilling all land life to its marrow, coagulating all protoplasm.

But because ice floats it forms only at the surface of all the larger water bodies. Never may the temperature at the bottom fall below the point of its density, for upon cooling further it begins to expand again, and rises. So the first warm weather will find the key to the brooks.

JANUARY ELEVENTH

IT IS an old saw that as the days grow longer the cold grows stronger; the heartbreaking part of winter comes upon us when it would seem that surely, with perceptibly lengthening days, the sun should take some pity on us.

But the ice-locked world that rolls away before me outside the window has great arrears in heat to pay before the spring may pass this way again. For to melt one part of ice without raising its temperature—merely converting the constant cold substance from a solid to a fluid—man in a laboratory, and the sunlight in the laboratory of the cosmos, has to apply such heat that it would be sufficient to raise the same water up to one hundred and sixty-seven degrees on the Fahrenheit scale. This, in the meteorologist's way of speaking, is the "spring lag." I find that a mild epithet indeed for the inherent and unregenerate vileness of January.

Yet there is a biological value even in the cantankerous latent heat of melting. There would be no winter but for that strange property of water, and winter has its value to living things—the value of sleep. Every gardener knows that bulbs and stocks must rest; autumn bloomings and sudden growths in winter thaws exhaust the plant. The seed, the spore, the leaf, the whole metabolism of plants requires surcease. True, in the tropics no winter intervenes; but biologically the dry season is the winter of the tropics— the adverse season when trees shed their leaves and seeds lie ungerminated.

JANUARY TWELFTH

Out of the southwest, a sluggish "low" has crept across the map of the land; the whistling "highs," with their peeled blue sky and icy breath, have shifted up, and in their place are gray skies again, heavy with snow. How kind is gray! Beautiful, delicate, elegant. And now, quite quietly it has begun to snow again. A new mask falling over the old one, a sense of deepening of mysterious winter, of an adventure in experience through which we shall not too swiftly see, as we see through the autumn's intentions from the first.

There is only one way to study snow crystals, and that is to take your microscope—or take a hand lens if nothing better offers—out of doors, or into some long-chilled room, as I did today, an attic where I opened a window to the damp drift, and caught the flakes upon a glass slide.

There is no telling of the beauty of snow crystals; one look is worth all words, and no comparisons are adequate—not even the tracery of a rose window, or altar lace on which old women have worn away needle-numbed fingers and a life-time of fading sight. But there is one charm which the snowflake possesses that is denied to most crystals, and above all to that emperor of them all, the carbon crystal or diamond, and that is that it is evanescent. Nothing in this world is really precious until we know that it will soon be gone. The lily, the starry daffodil, the regal iris (and these, too, are built upon a symmetry of six)—are the lovelier for their imminent vanishing. The snow crystal has but touched earth ere it begins to die.

JANUARY THIRTEENTH

THAT about snow crystals which confounds all understanding is how so many variations—millions perhaps—can be schemed upon the unvarying fundamental plan of six. Be it etched out to elaborations as fine feathered as a whole pane covered with frost designs, still there are always six rays to each delicate star, and one can still make out in the finest, the ultimate details of attenuated ornamentation, the same fundamental symmetry. There can be no chance about this; some cause underlies it, and I am no crystallographer to explain the details of a snowflake's fine-wrought surfaces, its internal tensions and stresses, its perfect equilibria and balanced strains that distend each fairy tracery and give to these flowers of the winter air their gossamer strength.

But one may hazard the guess that the six-sidedness of the snow crystal is in reality a doubling of three, just as the symmetry of the lily and the amaryllis is. Of all the magic numbers in old necromancy and modern science, three is the first. Three dimensions has matter; three is the least number of straight sides that will just inclose a space. Three legs is the smallest number that will just support the equilibrium and stresses of a stool. Two would not do; four are superfluous; and twice three points are required, and just required, to keep intact the frailest of all solids—a flake of snow.

CRYSTAL—the very word has a chime of delicate bells about it, a clash of shattering thin ice; it has a perishable sound, which enchants the poet, as its meaning does the mathematician. For the crystal is matter in its most organized form, wherein all the molecules are so disposed or polarized or deployed like a perfect regiment, that they stand equidistant from each other along planes of symmetry that may be simple or exquisitely complex. And the result is that, unlike the rest of inanimate matter, a crystal turns a definite face to the outside; it is discrete, organized, has a specific form. When you crack a crystal it does not break up in a jagged fracture like ordinary poured glass; it breaks along lines of its own symmetry; in effect, it merely becomes two or more crystals of smaller size; it can almost be said to reproduce, as the simplest organisms do, by fission. For given the wherewithal, each fragment crystal will increase and grow, as the living cell will do.

Now frost is on the morning window panes, upstarting in intricate primal forests of moss form and fern form and tree and fungus. The growth of a forest of window frost is oddly like the growth of some fungus that springs up over night. If the temperature keep falling outside, and the relative amount of moisture increase on the inside, the frost flowers will continue to grow, and may be detected in their spread across the glass. Like living things, they branch like a tree, grow usually from the bottom upwards. If they cover the pane entirely they add thickness, as a tree does. But there is this vital difference, that the tree grows from the inside out, transforming its raw materials into something else, while the frost crystal can only add to its outside the chemically unaltered water vapor of the atmosphere.

JANUARY FIFTEENTH

WITH its internal stresses and specific properties of elasticity and cohesion, properties magnetic and electrical and optical, the crystal has elaborate organization. It seems but a slight step, then, to call it an organism, for indeed it is easy to see in what way the most complicated crystal is organized. But difficult, cantankerously difficult to analyze the organization of unicellular animals or plants. The crystal, with its elegant mathematics and its orderly molecules, is the mechanist's dream and ideal of organization. If only, if only living matter were so transparent! The mechanist cannot help feeling that somehow opaque, unpredictable protoplasm will yet give him a chance to see through it.

Haeckel, the great tower of mechanistic strength, did not hesitate to proclaim that the distinctive nature of life is due simply to its molecular and atomic structure, and needless to say all crystals threw him into an ecstasy. He firmly believed that the crystal and the living cell were in all ways comparable, both as to their chemical and physical makeup, their growth and their individuality. He practically classified crystals into genera and species, and then went on, with a mania like a numerologist's, to show a crystalline form in pollen grains, corals, infusorians and the arrangements of leaves and flowers around their axes of growth. The poor fellow—a man of the most romantic morality in private life—was faced, of course, with the old Aristotelian dilemma as to where spirit (or soul or God or vital force) dwells, when there is no difference save of degree (as he asserts) between living and non-living structure. He was in consequence driven further than was Aristotle who bestowed soul on a jellyfish; Haeckel had to assume that there is spirit and vital force in the inanimate rock, and he crowned his life work with a book entitled *The Souls of Crystals*.

JANUARY SIXTEENTH

A PHRASE like "souls of crystals" is calculated to entrance many minds; it seems to have put Ruskin into transports of delight, for in his *Ethics of the Dust* he is perpetually telling the little girls for whom he wrote the book about the goodness and beneficence, the symmetry and divinity of the inanimate. In spite of his savage but childish attacks upon Darwin, Comte, Mill, and all other scientists, he was fond, as Burroughs was, of making use of the mechanistic explanation of phenomena for ultra-romantic purposes. Indeed, the mechanistic and the sentimental viewpoints seem to have a way of meeting, by traveling in opposite directions around a circular argument. To account, for instance, for consciousness in a mechanistic way, it is necessary to throw the origin of consciousness back at the stars themselves and it becomes impossible to deny it to plants. This will fit Wordsworthian poesy and Hindu mysticism very nicely and many minds will construe this as the highest praise.

I realize as I write that mechanism and vitalism are terms which I have not defined to myself, and that I seem to be heaping abuse upon the mechanists without a hint of all that mechanism has accomplished. "If to be a vitalist," wrote the distinguished mechanist Bateson, "is to assert that here and now we cannot explain the phenomena of life by physics and chemistry, who would not be a vitalist?" To this I make the retort courteous, that if to be a mechanist is to seek the mechanical explanations of the way in which life functions, then every biologist should be a mechanist. Beyond a doubt life does function through physical mechanism. Common sense and every scrap of evidence confirm it.

JANUARY SEVENTEENTH

T HE old warfare of the mechanists and the vitalists runs back almost indefinitely into the history of philosophy. In biological matters the mathematical Descartes was a mechanist; a man who started with the axiom *I think, therefore I am,* was unwilling to extend thought to beings not strictly like himself. I doubt if Descartes could logically have maintained the reality of the existence of even his own cat, further than that he had the sensation that he called a cat on his lap. Moreover, whatever his cat did, must have been performed by mechanical predestination; Descartes never for a moment admitted a cat to his own august rank as a conscious creature with free will.

Vitalism, in a correspondingly extreme form, has taken up the attitude that life is not only unknowable, but that, as Thoreau felt, to investigate it is somewhat irreverent and destructive of beauty and morality.

The shifting points of attack and defense between mechanism and vitalism are mere phenomena of the history of science, or, really, of the temperaments and personalities of the men who made that history. The old mechanism was frigid, the new is iconoclastic; the old vitalism was superstitious and pietistic, the new metaphysical and lost in an exclusive terminology. It may be one's emotional nature that determines which of these two camps you will belong to, or whether you prefer tc stay outside them.

THE mechanists have been recruited either directly from the ranks of the exact sciences or from men intellectually disposed to them. So brilliant have been the triumphs of the physicists and chemists in their own field that they carry with them the prestige of their arms. It is the instinct of the man of physics, for instance, to find a single simple explanation of a vital phenomenon, something to him as soul-satisfying as an equation, some abstract by which he can make rigid order out of the slippery protoplasm. He wants to show that surface tension, or other simple and comprehensible causes, underlie the seemingly supernatural ways of life, such as fusion of egg and sperm rushing together, the vitalizing effect of that contact upon the egg, the dazzling transmission of thousands of hereditary characters bundled up in a single cell, the forwarding of their separate individualities from a single mother cell to millions of daughter cells. The process of reducing all to simple causes has worked so well in the exact sciences, that it seems incomprehensible that there could be anything more to biological problems; the opacity of life is the only obstacle in the path, thinks the mechanist; however, by trying he hopes that a cell may some day be made as clear as crystal.

The day was when the mechanists were top dogs, but the new vitalists have a strong case for us. They warn that simplification, so successful in the mathematical sciences, carries you further from the truth in the natural sciences. Many, not a few, explanations are needed to explain any vital phenomenon, just as many causes must be sought to explain a war, if you are writing a history of it. And to extol the crystal will not belittle the cell.

JANUARY NINETEENTH

Y o u may believe in X-entities or entelechies or biophores or any other sort of imaginary plastid that embodies life and carries its purpose within itself. Or you may disbelieve in them all and deem that life, like thought, is an ineffable thing, not physically discoverable in living matter but merely emanating from it impalpably.

The fundamental issue between mechanism and vitalism has been put most clearly by one thinker when he argues that if life were only a special way of putting inanimate matter into a system, a random or chance system that happened to "work" or perform the life processes, then we ought to see fragments of such systems that didn't quite work, lying about in Nature—chains of molecules that are almost life molecules. The mechanist believes that he can point to such fragmentary systems in the carbon rings, and in the marvelous adaptability and cohesion of the carbon atom. He points to all the triumphs of synthesizing based, one and all, on the chemist's handiness with the versatile element of carbon. He knows the very alphabet of life, C, H, O, N, that represents the four elements, carbon, hydrogen, oxygen and nitrogen, out of which he will build you the Tyrian dyes, rubber of Brazil, camphor of Formosa and all the perfumes of Grasse.

But the vitalist is undeterred by these facts. He maintains that the products of living plants and animals are not themselves part of life, and their imitation is not life. Things have all the characteristics of life, or they have none of them, he says, and it seems to me that, up to the present, this argument is unanswerable.

JANUARY TWENTIETH

THE rôle of biology today, like the rôle of every other science, is simply to describe, and when it explains it does not mean that it arrives at finality; it only means that some descriptions are so charged with significance that they expose the relationship of cause and effect. It may be an ingrained trait of the human mind to look for a first great cause of all natural phenomena such as some poets and some mechanistically disposed scientists believe in, but it is a far nobler thing to be able to suspend your judgment—for your whole life time, if necessary; to observe without the will to believe some particular thing or the intention of proving some preconceived belief.

That is the stand that every honest modern man, scientist or otherwise, must take, and mechanists and vitalists alike ought to be found assembled on that hill, lifting up their arms to heaven and praising truth.

AQUARIUS

JANUARY 21 — FEBRUARY 18

JANUARY TWENTY-FIRST

I WONDER how much of fatality has come to the birds in the past week that I have been house-bound, while storm after storm swept the fields and woods, with alternate thaws followed cruelly by sleet. The papers tell of airplanes brought down with their fuselage ice-incrusted. It is not the cold that kills the birds, and somewhere, somehow, they always manage to find forage; it is the winter rains that ground them too. For the titmouse that I come on stone dead in the woods, how many more small winged creatures are lying for the hawks and weasels to find, in the hills and on the fields!

Yet today, when I trudge abroad, just breaking through the stubborn crust at each tiring step, I hear the brave whistling and clinking notes of many little birds rejoicing in the noon mercy—though the mercury is below zero. I turn this way and that, trying to see them, but wherever I look the intolerable glare of the crusted snow, of the trees glittering in silver mail, parries my sight like a cutting sword. I cannot look into the eye of this ice-armored day; I can only bow my head and listen attentively, to the small indomitable voices of tree sparrows, white-throats and chickadees, ringing as bright and delicate as frost crystals become audible on the tingling air.

JANUARY TWENTY-SECOND

THE moment when a fresh fall of snow is on the ground is the opportunity for finding out what your animal neighbors do with themselves and where they go. If you follow up a field mouse's dainty tracks, with the characteristic mark of the dragging tail, like a little sled mark but with only one runner, you will run him literally to earth. Today I pried up the crust where the clew to a field mouse disappeared under a snow bank, and discovered that beneath the snow there are runways now like those he has beneath the sod in summer. One hall branched into two, two into four, and so on into a labyrinth it would take his nose and whiskers to unravel, and I concluded that my small neighbor was at home to no one.

Squirrel tracks always begin and end at tree boles, and you may know them further by the great leaps between the prints, and the smallness of the actual footmark, where the little nut-cracker lands with all paws close together.

But cottontail tracks differ from all others in that they are regularly trodden, like village lanes; indeed, all this wood hereabout is one great cottontail village. A hare in full flight will streak across the ground in any direction, but under normal conditions it traverses regular lanes, as if it were not the feckless creature it is but had the most serious routine business. I know where these lanes run in summer, by the beaten grasses; in winter the tracks precisely overlie the same place, and the goshawk is said to walk calmly along them, stalking unwary youngsters. But though cottontails must be the staple on which the entire carnivorous diet of the wood depends, they are still the most abundant mammal in the countryside.

JANUARY TWENTY-THIRD

T HERE is—or there was once—a charm of the wild and the untouchable about the mammal fauna of this continent of ours. But from the very first it began to shrink at the touch of European man, and not of man alone and his gun, but of the tools and creatures that he brought with him. The ax and plow have changed the face of the land; the bison had to go before the useful Old World cattle; the beaver could not live in a tamed river; we have no room for the deer, for even if hunters did not slaughter them, we could not let them raid the woodland farms and nibble precious crops. The wood rat gave way to the house rat who came hidden in the hulls of ships. Bears and cougars were too dangerous and we slew them. But the sad result is that we have driven off most of the beasts that might be called noble or at least exciting; we are left with a tremendous numerical predominance of the smaller creatures that the lost lords preyed on—the rabbits and rodents and weasels, prolific, ratty, night-thieving nibblers or killers.

Men feel a craving for intimacy with the best of their fellow mammals. Their bright-eyed, bewhiskered, keennosed, furry warm ways and forms attract us physically as children do. But we have shown them the worst sides of our character, and they have shown plainly that they will have none of us. Mammals of all groups are the least accessible for easy study. They live by flight and stealth, in the night and in their dens. So we come reluctant and baffled to the realization that we are close to our native mammals in systematic zoölogy, but in no other sense. They have intelligence, but not like ours. Theirs is unsocial intelligence, the wile of flight, the cunning of pursuit, the vanishing wisdom of the wilderness.

JANUARY TWENTY-FOURTH

In the gray of the year, to our green-hungry eyes, the pines come into their greatness. The deciduous woods in winter have a steely and shelterless appearance, but even in a blinding snow storm pine woods have a look of warmth about them. Alone among trees, evergreens keep up their sap in the winter; the fires of life still burn in them.

I like our loblolly pines for their long glittering foliage, full of warmth and light at all seasons, bringing back to me the very smell of the South, the feeling of those grand sad lowlands of Georgia and the Carolinas. I like the yellow pine for its generous armored trunks built up of laminated plates like the leather shields of Homeric foot soldiers. But it is in the pitch pine that you have all that was ever embodied in the name of pine—the fondness for growing on craggy ledges, the wind-molded, storm-blasted shape, the dark and pungent foliage, the tears of silvery rosin bleeding from the rough male trunk, and the clusters of cones black against the sky. When it dies, it dies standing. And even as a skeleton, it has grandeur.

Its perfect complement is the white pine, a feminine tree with silky, silvery and perpetually talkative needles. Adorned by long shapely cones with delicate flexible pink scales, clad in a smooth and lustrous bark, it rises in a delicate pagoda-like shape. Instead of the bold ledge, the white pine loves the glen, and there it consorts, in the damp, shadowed air and the earth mold of the color of tanbark, with hemlocks in groves where the pine siskins unite in little flocks, conferring together in voices fine as the whisper of a small watch.

JANUARY TWENTY-FIFTH

THE hardwoods, those trees that shed their leaves, are withdrawn from us in winter; without their leaves they seem no longer to have faces by which to know them; they are headless trunks, nude trunks. To those not used to country sights it seems almost necromantic how a woodsman can walk through a snow-filled forest and with confidence lay a weathered hand upon one bole and another and say this is a black jack oak and that a hornbeam. Only gradually one finds that he too is learning the subtlest differences, where at first all seem alike. The branches of ironwood, like the muscles of a straining wrestler, the shapes of elms like a falling fountain, the mottled bark of sycamores, the alders with their little cones, the hickories with their buds almost like flowers—out of the silvery winter ranks individuals step forth, are marked, remembered.

After familiarity with twig and bud, scar and lenticel, bark and stature, comes a love of wood itself—first the dark stain of it, or the light and living gold, and the raw fresh smell of it; then a feeling for the very touch of it in the hands; a knowledge at a glance whether a face of lumber has been quarter-sawed or cut on the radial section or the vertical side slice called tangential. A love of grain and pattern, a hatred of stain and veneer, a preference for mahogany in its natural ruddy brown, and the understanding that American woods like black walnut, yellow poplar, and cherry birch are as fine as any mahogany.

But indeed I am talking here rather about the man I would like to become than the one I am—about the fellow who can weigh a block of wood in his palm and with precision tell you what it is, how long it has been seasoned, and to what account the precious stuff of centenarian vegetable toil may best be turned.

JANUARY TWENTY-SIXTH

ONE of the sharpest wild hunters in this countryside is the domestic cat. Her tracks in the snow are often to be found well away from habitation, where she has been stalking small birds feeding on the ground. But her chief quarry is the rodents. I have often pondered upon the astonishingly similar equipment of this hunter and these hunted, a similarity not explicable on the grounds of any closeness of kin. Both have the same pointed and wondrously acute ears, the same eyes that see in the dark, the same delicately sensitive whiskers which play a part almost like the insect antennae in giving advance knowledge of objects in obscure places.

It is plain enough, and can be explained by natural selection, that there will be a rough equilibrium between the fleetness of the hunter's foot, for instance, and the speed of the hunted's. But remarkably similar equipment is carried out to such detail, not only in the case of cats and rodents but of so many other animals, that we must admit a plain case of responsive evolution—life responding to the needs that occasion and environment create. I feel that natural selection and Darwinian pre-adaptation are not sufficient to explain such elaborately sympathetic responses. The fit between shoe and foot, all through living structure, is far snugger and more elegant than that, and it requires conscious effort to resist the temptation of the old idea of an intelligent design behind it all.

JANUARY TWENTY-SEVENTH

So AFTER centuries of struggle on the part of science to free itself from the Aristotelian cosmology, the old concept repeatedly revives. Even Walt Whitman, who bared his head so bravely to the elements, begged of God that whatever else be denied, it be not denied to find in Him some ultimate plan.

The new believers in the Great Design sound for the most as though they were in a high state of exaltation about it, bordering on religious conversion. I confess it is a lonely thing to stand apart unbelieving from those who sing hosannah. Others, astronomers and humanitarians, poets and churchmen, can see complete perfection where I cannot. They ask me only to admit their primal contention—that all is moving to its appointed goal—and my soul shall be saved. I shall be turned free then to investigate anything I choose from a glow-worm to a star.

But every experience in the history of truth-seeking has shown that really strenuous investigation withers at the touch of predeterminism. If we are to accept its rule, then Galileo endured torture in vain. Then the man who collected his pieces of silver for burning Bruno at the stake earned his pay well. Then science may just as well fold up its 'scopes and agree that it is already the best of possible worlds and there is nothing left but to extol its perfections.

JANUARY TWENTY-EIGHTH

WHEN man begs that he may find a Mind Behind It All, he is only asking that God shall be made in man's image.

To mathematicians, God is a Mathematician, to priests he is a High Priest, to intellectuals he is Intelligence. But intelligence, will and purpose are merely the human tools with which we attack the problem of our maintenance.

If bees have a religion, they might well demand a picture of the cosmos in which instinct keeps the stars in their courses. Their God would be a female god, a Great Queen, with an all-seeing eye, seated on a throne of honey. To us the idea of instinct ruling the universe is sheerly brutal and terrifying; vestigial in us, instinct is ordained by us to a lower rank than the powers in which we excel.

These are will and intelligence, but all that we honestly know of them is what we can discover in the human brain. We infer them in some of our brother animals, but in descending degrees. Outside the animal kingdom, no one can point out a purposive intelligence.

Is it possible then to presume that intellect as we know it moves among the stars? Can we really suppose that it could do anything at all with a reeling hell like Rigel or Sirius?

JANUARY TWENTY-NINTH

WHAT, asks one of the Designists, is the development of an embryo, if it is not growth directed to a purpose? This sounds plausible enough, but the author of that argument forgets the famous law of Haeckel, that embryonic development is merely a recapitulation of descent. The fœtus develops as it does, not in order to produce the babe, but because all evolutionary past has stamped its impress on it. Man is a result of the past, not the purpose of it.

He is like the law, which has become what it is today, a mass of preposterous anachronisms modified by recent adaptations to circumstances. It works well enough, but none too well. So the human body is a mass of organs that, as the nimble George Dorsey said, work just well enough to "get by," and not one whit better.

Life's adaptations are, however, so marvelous that, though rejecting intelligent causation, you may demand explanation. If you are fond of 'isms, you may like Max Verworn's "conditionism." Embraced in this term is a view of life that sees all phenomena as due to a multiplicity of circumstances concurring. The World War, for instance, was not part of some purposive plan either in the collective wills and intelligences of Europe or in some great Intelligence hovering outside it. It took place and assumed its terrible character owing to a series of concurrent circumstances, some of them running back to the inventions of the Iron Age.

There is this beauty about conditionism, that it explains the multiplex and highly adaptive nature of life's history at the same time that it easily accounts for all the disharmonies, imperfections and the unfinished look of life's experiments. Those imperfections are the bitter mouthful that the argument for design has never been able to gulp down.

343

JANUARY THIRTIETH

FOR myself, I do not care particularly for any catchword or camp slogan like "conditionism," and I shrink from learning to repeat any hardened credo by rote. But I can say at least that I believe in what "conditionism" is meant to stand for—the historical view of biology. This is, if you like, the old philosophy of cause and effect, but without seeking for a First Cause. The dilemma of the First Cause is that of the Indian who was asked what held up the world. "A great elephant," said the Indian. "And what is the elephant standing on?" "The back of a great turtle." "And what does the turtle stand on?" But of this the Indian had no idea, and neither has any one else.

What I like about the historical—or I might better say, the evolving—view of vital phenomena, is that it does not lead to self-satisfaction, but to a bracing discontent. On the purely humanistic score, it leaves us no sneaking hope that because we are next in rank to the angels we are predestined as a race to salvation. Rather it reminds us how new we are. It gives us, if not certainly free will, the opportunity to impose our will upon the future—the opportunity, and the fateful responsibility for so doing. On the biologic side, instead of closing the subject it opens up questions. This, the aim of all science, is the bane of all dictatorships, whether hierarchical, political, or pedantic.

JANUARY THIRTY-FIRST

T H E whole crux of the argument for the Great Design exceeds the bonds of science, or indeed of Nature as we can discover her. From Aristotle to the present, the Designists have been compelled to rely upon divinity, from the very nature of their predicates. Their defense is that, after all, the greatest task of science is to find God in all things, from a star to a sensitive plant; that knowledge of God is the ultimate knowledge. But I had always understood that it was, from the time of Galileo on, the first rule of science that the scientist may not try to commensurate God, nor may he call Him in to cover the deficiencies of present knowledge.

Science does not suggest that a man should try to dispense with God in his private belief. But cast out the idea of purposive design, and then look at the world! Does darkness, in consequence, fall across it? Spring water tastes just as pure, woman's body as sweet; children's arms around your neck clasp tight as ever. And, at the end of it all, when you are wearied, will you not sleep as deep?

FEBRUARY FIRST

SCIENCE is a ship afloat upon a wide waste of waters. Less than Columbus does it know where the world is bound. It does not even know from what port we have set out.

These thoughts inspire the landlubber with terror. He begs to be allowed to dream that he knows what lies ahead. But for those whom William James called the "tough-minded," by which he really meant the stout-hearted, the search itself is the thing, the shore is perhaps but an illusion.

The beauty, the rightness, the excitement of the search are facts which even the humblest naturalist understands, though he has never done anything more than pursue an unknown bird in the woods for half a day, or climb an alp to find a saxifrage.

FEBRUARY SECOND

On Groundhog Day that chubby marmot is supposed to poke his head out of winter quarters, to see if his shadow lies upon the snow. If it does, he ducks in again, prepared for another long bout of winter. But if it be gray, he ventures forth, so they say, hopeful of an early spring. According to Chambers' *Book of Days,* our American groundhog superstition is only a New World variant of the badger myth of England. It is thought to be of ancient pagan origin, and to antedate by far the Christian feast of Candlemas which happens also to fall upon this date.

You would think it more logical if the groundhog, upon seeing the sun shining, should conclude that spring was on its way. But if so, you know nothing of the country-man's pessimistic philosophy. Things that begin too well must soon end badly. Early peach blossoms, early geese, early beauty, early love—all will come to some bad ends, like whistling girls and crowing hens.

Perhaps if I were a farmer I would, after a little experience of the malevolent spirits that dwell in the weather, in the earth and in beasts, come to this persuasion myself. As a philosophy I should call it being afraid of the fairies. But I think it ill becomes those who are fortunate, those whom life gives its fairest gifts, forever to hang back, to groan, to doubt, to be afraid of the fairies. What right have they to teach youth to be afraid, to hoard happiness, hide delight, and discourage venture?

FEBRUARY THIRD

I WOKE in the depths of night; deep frost was on the panes, and above the brittle winter boughs the quarter of a moon was swinging low; its passionless light fell upon the crystals on the glass, passed through them, and lay across the counterpane like light through a Gothic window whose pictures are too intricate to read—a window without color, in a cathedral of night and frost. It was bitter in the room, an eery, windless hour without a sound, without a single sound to remind one that our winter-wrapt world was not, like the moon, a dead one.

And then the owl called, and I wondered why that sound had ever inspired fear or horror. It was bird song, and I thanked God for it, in the night and the silence and the cold winter's nadir. Bird song in February darkness! A voice, out in the open, like an old crier going about and saying, "All's well, and a fine frosty night!"

FEBRUARY FOURTH

F O R many persons the systematic side of the natural sciences has no interest and suggests only boredom. To other temperaments it has a great fascination.

On this day was born Augustin Pyrame de Candolle, the great Swiss botanist who beat Linnæus at the great Linnæan game, and was the Cuvier of vegetable anatomy and physiology as well. In his *Prodromus* which was forty years going through the presses, De Candolle endeavored with the help of others to describe every flowering plant in the world. But the fundamental importance of De Candolle is not this descriptive work, titanic though it was, but in the fact that, for the first time, he made order out of the hundreds of families and the approximately one hundred thousand species of flowering plants then known. His was unfortunately a system constructed just before the acceptance of the idea of evolution; a new order in botany now prevails, just as it does in zoölogy, an order proceeding from the simplest to the most complex. De Candolle, having a monarchical view of nature, put the lowliest last. The wonder of it is that any man ever entertained in his head so staggering a number of possibilities in the way of relationships, and made system out of them.

Those there are who envy him the opportunity he fell heir to by coming on the scene at the moment when knowledge first permitted such an undertaking to succeed. It was a game that, essentially, could only be played once; the hour was at hand, and the man to play it arrived.

FEBRUARY FIFTH

THE month of February has many fine points, and not the least of them that it is soonest over. Some month had to be distinctly shorter than the others, since twelve does not divide equally into the solar year of three hundred and sixty-five days, five hours, forty-eight minutes and forty-five seconds and fifty-one hundredths of a second. The rectification of the calendar has required not only leap years but an elaborate centenarian system of skipping leap years to split this knotty fraction. The only odd thing is that men should have chosen the second month to bear the irregularities.

The fact is, of course, that February was the last month in the English calendar until 1752, and so it took of the year what was left over. I still think the old calendar was more satisfying. New Year resolutions die notoriously young, because the frayed end of winter wears down our souls. The gods have done what they could for February by putting in Washington's and Lincoln's birthdays, and St. Valentine's day, and so many birthdays of famous naturalists that the maker of this almanac is embarrassed by the wealth of his material, for secretly the sap is rising, hard little buds are forming, and his mind will be coaxed from the past as the days lighten.

For it is in the nature of things that the lowest ebb of the living year is also the most prescient and significant; it is, for the year, the instant of conception, that moment when forces fundamentally abstract determine what it is that shall be born alive when spring is at the full.

FEBRUARY SIXTH

WINTER is a guest that stays beyond its welcome and I am not complaining merely of cold and thaw, thaw and cold. I dislike the loneliness of winter, the flowerlessness of the ground. I miss the birds.

To those who honestly prefer a titmouse or a junco to mockingbirds and mourning doves, I have nothing to answer save that it raises my spirits mightily to remember that somewhere, throbbing on summery air, there are hummingbirds. The gorgeous whistling oriole, the scarlet tanager, the indigo bird, the wood thrush and the bobolink—they are all there in the south and in the tropics, waiting the appointed hour of return or perhaps already taking off.

Before I sleep I close my eyes and try to think of them. I see the map of the continents outspread, in a bird's eye view, snow-wrapt at the north, brown still or faintly greening in the half-sleeping Carolinas, with palm-tipped Florida reaching out into the Gulf. From the West Indies slumbering in the Caribbean, from the jungles of Orinoco and the pampas of Argentine, our own will return to us. It is long and long before their coming; the skies still ache for them. Yet they are astir, upon the move, dauntless, and forgiving us our trespasses against them.

FEBRUARY SEVENTH

EACH year about this time the mail brings to my desk a motley of almanacs, that inform me what will come in the unfolding year. There are few, now, that intersperse all this prophetic wisdom with homilies and maxims by Polonius or Ben Franklin. The more sober tell me the tonnage of the world's fighting navies, and the birthdate of Kepler the astronomer and Edmund Keane the actor. Most of them are but dingy tracts, given away in connection with advertisement of some nostrum, and it confounds the understanding that there are still persons who will accept the astrological voodoo they contain.

Yet there has been a great revival of astrology in our day—ever since, in fact, the world was shaken to its soul by the Great War and its results. Man in his uncertainties asks, as of old, the stars for news. And what is he told? That born beneath a certain sign he is liable to diseases of the legs, is nervous, sarcastic and given to saving his money, and should marry only a woman born beneath a complementary sign, and that his is a lucky month in which to plant onions!

What an astrology there might be, if astrologers were not simply palmists who have dyed their whiskers! It is not inconceivable that the future will develop a science of cosmic radiation and its effect upon living beings. Already man has seized the X-rays, that for all his history had been raining unobserved upon his island home, and turned them to noble purpose.

FEBRUARY EIGHTH

As if it might have been created by God solely for the purposes of heredity research, there is a parasitic fruit fly, Drosophila, whose generations flicker past so swiftly that in a few weeks it may be ancestress to millions of descendants. All unconscious that an army of peering, thoughtful men watch every spot on its wings, every fleck of new color in its normally red and ugly little eyes, it goes on, year in and year out, rushing to sexual maturity in a few hours from the egg, and continuing its monstrous spawning. It is on this perfect laboratory pet that the American biologists have specialized, and to one of them it finally occurred to bombard Drosophila with X-rays.

Nothing visible happened to the animals that he exposed, but the effects of X-rays are notoriously recessive. In the next generation he obtained flies with white eyes, flies with small wings, flies with forked bristles instead of straight, and, in short, variations on an old theme *ad lib*.

It had been Lamarck's supposition that the environment could mold the inheritance; it was Weismann who maintained, and to a great extent he proved, that if that could be done at all it could not be done by any form of impression made upon the ordinary body cells. The external world would have to find a way of plunging its influence right into the sex cells themselves, and of all cells they are the most deeply buried, the most obstinately conservative. Develop or deform your own body as you like, you pass on your heredity to your children as if it were a locked box to which you yourself had no key. Granting this, how then account for the original variations from which species develop?

FEBRUARY NINTH

As MATTER is made up of the atom, so the ultimate unit that transmits heredity lies in the chromosome, a viscid fleck of protoplasm within the nucleus of the sex cell itself. Under the microscope chromosomes appear rather like pollen grains or tiny rods. Each species of plant and animal has its own characteristic number of them. Each chromosome has its own shape, and position in a definite pattern, and at the moment of conception, when male and female nuclei are fused, their corresponding chromosomes, and parts of chromosomes, pair off. It is the selection and arrangement of this pairing that ordains the offspring's character.

The fruit fly, Drosophila, has but six chromosomes to a nucleus, but each one is the bearer of destiny, of thousands of messages and commands for the future. In the great Morgan laboratories Drosophila has been bred over a million times and record kept of all these matings and their multiplex and indelible results. The eye at the microscope has so probed the vagaries of Drosophila that it has deciphered some of the sealed orders to futurity. Experiment has juggled with the fate of its posterity for all time to come.

Here indeed is revealed the very machinery of heredity, into which Professor Muller of Texas plunged the X-ray and found that in a violent and random way he could alter the course of life. The mind leaps swiftly at the possibility that perhaps mutation, perhaps the greater part of creative evolution, may be due to the bombardment of the earth by that form of cosmic radiation that, when we collect it in a special tube, we call the X-ray.

FEBRUARY TENTH

T H E idea that cosmic radiation in part controls evolution is as new as it is exciting. And other influences are being observed at their strange work. There is that case of melanism—of normally pale moths that have become increasingly dark around the great industrial cities of Europe and America—which suggests that the very air around us may breathe the forces of inevitable change. The moths are not merely smoke-coated, like the lungs of a city worker. The internal pigmentation itself has been altered. And, what is more, this taint is hereditary. Something is happening to the chromosomes of these moths in the "black countries." And the experimenter soon guessed the cause— that fumes from factory chimneys contain chemicals that left some mark upon the protoplasm subjected to them. He fed pale moths on doses of salts that contain these chemicals, and true to his secret convictions, the moths' descendants darkened, and transmitted the newly acquired taint to their offspring in the most orthodox Mendelian way. There are as yet only a few other examples in the same vein, such as the induced and inheritable susceptibility to certain diseases amongst rats. But we dare to hope for better things than this! In a century or two we may be inducing inheritable immunity to human ills.

FEBRUARY ELEVENTH

If the X-ray and certain chemicals are able to penetrate the woof of the flesh that hides the sex cells, there may be forces, any number of them, equally potent. These forces, that may, some of them, be among the commonplaces of existence, could then induce what we might call "acquired" characteristics and stamp them on posterity.

Those blind beetles of mine last summer may have gone blind because they became shut off from solar radiation while living in darkness, and not from continued disuse of their eyes. I am even willing to think that caves might exert some positive influence of their own, since they affect so many animals similarly. However that may be, there is a revival of Lamarckism, rejecting his shaky theory of use and disuse but accepting as possible the inheritance of acquired characteristics. Not only is the theory abstractly needed, to explain the origins of instinct, for instance, but laboratory experiment conduces to the belief that environment may lay hands on the sealed orders of heredity and change the writing in them.

Darwin assumed that organisms chanced to be previously adapted to some environment and then survived in it, intensifying their tendencies, by the close breeding natural selection imposes, into marked differences from their relatives. According to him my beetles went blind in sunlight and then found a cave to survive in. It may be so, it may be so, but what a limping leg for the grand march of evolution! To its critics natural selection has never seemed creative. It does not propel, rather it subtracts. There is such a volume of evidence for the case of a response on the part of life to need when need occurs that we must grant that it is one of the properties of living matter to arise to the occasion.

FEBRUARY TWELFTH

IT OCCURS to me that I often set down an objection to the great conceptions of Charles Darwin, and never do justice to his truths and successes. As his is the theory of evolution which is best known and receives the readiest acceptance on the prestige of his mere name, it is unnecessary to explain his ideas in detail, and the whole of his life work rests supreme, above even the praise of common men like myself. But on this his birthday it is a pleasure to pause and pay a tribute to the man himself, whose generous and upright life not even his most violent enemies could calumniate.

All the world knows that in 1831 Darwin accepted the unsalaried post of naturalist on board the *Beagle,* which was to circumnavigate the world in a five-year cartographical journey. He suffered tortures from seasickness and when he returned to England, his head teeming with suggestions induced by the fateful Galapagos Islands, his health was forever impaired. Every day for Darwin was a day of suffering; his work was oft-times confined to a few moments of concentrated thinking. But, in compensation, he was endowed with a sweet spiritual poise. He was free from passion, hate, envy and ambition; he never permitted himself to be drawn into the polemical maelstrom that raged around him. But when well tempered scientific criticism of his theories was offered, he replied with dignity. Few scientists who ever lived so deserved the great personal esteem in which he was held, and when he died in 1882 he was buried in Westminster Abbey not far from Newton.

FEBRUARY THIRTEENTH

F o r twenty years after the *Beagle* expedition, Darwin continued to mature his theory and, unlike a man who would hasten himself into fame, he kept the whole tremendous notion under his hat, because he was never satisfied that he had enough evidence. No saying how long this might have gone on; but then arrived that great corroboration from Wallace in the tropics. Darwin was delighted; at the same time his hand was forced; he published the *Origin of Species* and amongst philosophers and naturalists his name was set in glory. But indignant clergy and outraged Victorian decency would never have barked at his heels for that. He might have escaped public notice as Lamarck did, but for the appearance of *The Descent of Man*.

Then indeed the fat was in the fire. The aging naturalist Owen, an excellent scientist fallen on his dotage, coached his former student, Bishop Wilberforce, for the famed attack. Darwin himself might scarce have replied to the challenge. But in Thomas Henry Huxley Darwinism had a champion in invincible armor. For sheer glitter his mind has seldom had an equal in any land or age and he laid waste about him with the weapon of truth. "The cradle of every science," he chuckled, "is surrounded by dead theologians as that of Hercules was with strangled serpents."

FEBRUARY FOURTEENTH

F e w people now living can imagine the mental and moral tension of the great evolutionary controversy that began in England and swept the world. When Gosse, for instance, repudiated Darwinism after a terrible struggle, it was with the inner conviction that Darwin was right, but the world for its own good had best never know it. The conflict reached the stage of high comedy when the transcendentalist Margaret Fuller could at last bring herself to say, "I accept the Universe," and Carlyle, on hearing of it, exclaimed, "Gad, she'd better!"

With Huxley, Lyell and Hooker in England, Gray in America and Haeckel in Germany to speed the work, Darwinism swept finally to its triumph, not only as a scientific proposition but as a social theory. The times were ripe for that. A phrase like the "survival of the fittest" was just the slogan for the great industrial robber barons of the day. National imperialism could use it. At the same time, the nineteenth century liberalism was delighted with the democratizing effects of the new picture of man's origin; the damage done to Judaic mythology by Huxley filled thousands with glee.

Darwin himself was more or less indifferent to all this. His mind, as it aged, busied itself ever more with theories. He could not help, he admits, forming a theory about the why and wherefore of each phenomenon, however minute —antipodal to Galileo who was proud to say, "I never make hypotheses." Thus employed, Darwin paid a penalty in his old age which would seem to me a heavy one. He lost his youthful pleasure in listening to music and poetry, and though he enjoyed having novels read to him, he demanded little more than that they should end happily.

FEBRUARY FIFTEENTH

WHILE the triumph of Darwinism from outside the ranks of biology looks complete enough, it is not so in reality. What the Darwinians forced the world mind to accept was the fact of evolution. In the meantime Darwinism, strictly speaking, has endured the most probing examination and criticism from minds as active as Darwin's own, as conscientious as the brilliant Huxley's.

The charges against Darwin's ideas came down (if we dismiss objections on religion and moral grounds) to these cardinal points: that Darwinism does not free itself from the teleology which it professes to abhor; that while abjuring Lamarck it really cannot get on without the inheritance of acquired characters; that it cannot explain whence come the variations within the species out of which natural selection evolves the new species; that the struggle for existence cannot create life forms; that there is no struggle for existence; that the breeder who selects varieties pleasing to him (Darwin leaned strongly on breeding work) created nothing new thereby but only took, of what he found, that which was good; that sexual selection—as of the female choosing the handsomest or most tuneful or muscular mate —is a sentimental Victorian illusion; that one can conceive many other ways in which evolution may have taken place, and that, finally, Darwinism is romantic natural philosophy, not demonstrated fact. So at least runs the bill of accusation.

The criticism of Darwin by his peers was marred by none of those bad manners, none of that resort to sarcasm and personal allusions indulged in by persons fancying themselves his betters.

A theory is worth little until all possible objection is brought against it. An idea is unfinished until other ideas have eroded away all that is loose about it, leaving only the perdurable core.

FEBRUARY SIXTEENTH

ON THIS day in Potsdam in 1834 was born Ernst Heinrich Haeckel, of whom I have perhaps spoken on other days as the Prussian of mechanism, thereby misrepresenting his temperament and his real endeavors. Of all Darwin's supporters he lived longest and fought most ferociously, opposing his government when it forbade the teaching of Darwinism in the schools. More than any other man in his generation he affected the course of the study of structure in the laboratory, and at the same time he was the greatest popularizer of biology. He has been called "the astonished microscopist"; when he told what he saw as he gazed in a crystal or into the symmetries of a lovely Medusa from under the sea, he was master of the wonders-of-nature style. *The Riddle of the Universe* sold in England and Germany by the hundred thousand, circulated most widely among the working classes, and is said to have been used in Japan as a text book. The modern verdict is that it is one of the most muddled borrowings of a little of this and that from everybody, that was ever written, but a popular league was formed to support it, not so much by those enchanted with phrases like "the memory of atoms" as by those who relished its boisterous attacks upon state, church, and economic order.

The tragedy and comedy of Haeckel's life is that he was at heart a romantic whose hands were busied with mechanism; the resultant confusion in his head was indescribable. As a young medical student he was already set apart from his fellows as one who would neither duel nor wench but spent his time botanizing or reading Homer and Aristotle whom he admired boundlessly. In his old age, we find him bewildered to despair by the World War, unable to believe that the fellow countrymen of Darwin would treacherously assault the fatherland of the laboratory.

FEBRUARY SEVENTEENTH

O N T H I S day in 1600 at Rome was burned alive for his beliefs Giordano Bruno, "the first in all the world," as has
been said, "who died for truth without the expectation of
reward." The fate of Bruno is a blot on the cause of inten-
tional ignorance which nothing will wash away. Like
Galileo, Bruno was the implacable enemy of Aristotelian-
ism as the Schoolmen preached it, and this he dared in an
age when at Oxford, where he visited and taught, there
were notices posted up that "Masters and Bachelors who
do not follow Aristotle faithfully are liable to a fine of five
shillings for every point of divergence and for every fault
committed against the logic of the *Organon*."

Poet, dramatist, cosmologist, he fled the Dominican
monastery without taking the precaution of putting himself definitely out of the order; he took refuge under the
scepters of Protestant princes without in the least profess-
ing anything that would have enlisted them to protect him
in a crisis; he enraged the professors of Padua, Paris, Oxford, Wittenberg and Prague, lampooned monarchical society and, in short, took no care for his skin in that
treacherous age. His final blunder was to accept the invitation of a young Venetian aristocrat. This false young man
professed a desire to study philosophy and logic, but in
reality he wanted Bruno under his roof, believing he had
the profitable secret of the alchemists. When the philosopher was found without the Stone, his faithless host rendered him up to the Inquisition.

FEBRUARY EIGHTEENTH

BRUNO was not a naturalist in the lighter sense of the word; of wind and weather, bird and flower, he took as little note as the inward-gazing monks with whom he quarreled. His Nature was the universe; stars wheeled perpetually in his head; the atoms danced before his eyes; for him soul strove in tree and earth as in the breast of man.

The marvel of Bruno is not what he knew; indeed, he actually knew very little. It is what he guessed intuitively. His prediction of the resemblance between atomic structure and astronomical law and order was a flash of genius; he is close to hitting on evolution when he asserts that all matter is in a state of fleet. He guesses at the pull of the stars on each other, and predicts that other planets will be found coursing outside the orbit of Saturn. He is close to Newton as he denies Aristotle's idea that there are any absolutely heavy or light bodies; all are heavy only in relation to the attraction of a larger body. He talks as if he had heard of relativity when he proclaims that place, time, and motion are dimensions relative only to the position of the observer.

Two hundred and eighty-nine years after his death, the enlightened world met in the Campo dei Fiori, the Flower Market of Rome where Bruno was burned, and erected a monument to him. A monument is a fine thing for succeeding generations to admire. But if Bruno could know about it, he would not be especially moved, I think. Nothing moved him greatly; eight years of imprisonment and repeated torture could not move him. The truth, he knew, does not change because the majority will not believe it.

PISCES

FEBRUARY 19 — MARCH 20

FEBRUARY NINETEENTH

Now is that strange hushed time of year when Nature seems to pause. The winds of winter are wearied. The weeds, once ranked high in the fields, are low and subject. The weathered leaves begin to fall from the oaks that have clutched them fiercely, as the old clutch at little comforts.

The moment is like a pause in a symphony, when the great composer brings the fury of his music to a stop, a rest so fateful and significant that in the silence the listener counts his own loud heartbeats as though they were his last—hoping for and almost dreading the beginning of the new theme in the next measures.

And what will it be, that melody, but the beginning of spring? The talk of thaw in many runnels, the sounds of birds finding again their voices, of tree toads trilling in chill twilights, of a spade that strikes a stone.

FEBRUARY TWENTIETH

PISCES follows Aquarius and between them they constitute what the astrologers call the watery signs. And now
indeed the world brims over with "old February fill-dyke."
The ancients knew it as "the time of rain and want." The
snows have melted and the Tigris rises; the Nile and the
Potomac fill as of old they did. Footing is treacherous; the
winds are cold, and dampness hangs in all the airs; there
is a feeling of wetness wiped upon the cheek and hands,
and of small icy fingers laid upon the throat.

Before there can be spring there must be water, and
water and more water; flowers appear when the rains are
over and the floods gone down. But before flowering there
must be growth, uprising of sap. Without water there can
be no life; water is its very matrix; it is the medium in
which the vital molecule exists, the fluid in which the colloid of protoplasm is suspended.

FEBRUARY TWENTY-FIRST

WATER is the one imaginable medium in which the ship of life could have been launched and expected to float.

All of the most vital processes take place in this great solvent. The absorption of nourishment is impossible either by a root in the soil, or in the body of man, save as the nutrient elements come dissolved in water. Only through a watery surface may the animal excrete its poisons— through the wall of the lungs, the kidneys and the sweat glands. So water is the seat of all our metabolism, constructive and destructive. The fires of life burn only in water.

Running, flowing, falling though we see it, it is in essence greatly conservative. You cannot easily cool it below the freezing point; so used is woman to the teakettle she does not think how, chemically, it is a hard task to boil water. This is because of its latent heat, and but for that a man's metabolism, the mere business of bodily living, would soon bring on a temperature that would set fire to the carbon in his bones.

Water everywhere, in the soil, in the air, in the seas and ponds, acts as the world's great thermostat, preventing excessive upward march of temperatures or great cold. Between the arctic ice fields and the tropic seas a vast equalizing convection perpetually turns.

TOLERANT, capacious, water conveys and distributes the working material of the world. It is the incomparable solvent. It will hold intact the salts dissolved in it, and at the same time constantly breaking them down into their elements, constantly recombine those elements with others. So for hungry protoplasm it performs a miracle; out of three salts it can make nine. Undisturbed, it handles a great coming and going of molecular traffic.

Water is abundant, willing, and quiet. It is not easily parted into its two component elements, nor changed in temperature. There is always the same unfailing amount of it in the world. It dissolves without altering or being itself altered. Infinitely versatile, it is tranquilly stable. It does not, like helium, desert us for outer spaces, nor, like oxygen, rush to combine with metal and so be lost to use.

FEBRUARY TWENTY-THIRD

I T I S the wetness of water with which a man has to deal these days; wet feet, wet garden soil so heavy that the spade can scarcely turn it, damp seeping into the depleted wood pile. When we say that water is wet we mean that it climbs up things, against gravity, invades, softens, dissolves or alters wherever it creeps. That creep the scientist calls capillarity, and but for the capillarity of water how difficult it were to do our business! We could not blot a page or wipe a surface dry or wash dirt out of clothes. Water falling upon the earth would never rise again; the garden would be thirsty a few moments after you had given it to drink.

But owing to capillarity it climbs, from grain of soil to grain, till it reaches the needy root, or flows out in springs. No other liquid will rise even half as high as water. And not only will it rise directly, but it spreads in every direction; without this, no irrigation would be possible.

The physics and mathematics of capillarity are complex beyond the understanding of such intellects as mine, but fundamentally it all rests upon a property of water more unique than all the rest, more vital to life, its strange surface tension.

FEBRUARY TWENTY-FOURTH

Down by the brook, in one of its quiet bays, the water striders are already out, skating over the calm pool as if it were ice, because the surface tension of the water just suffices to hold them up. If I push one of them through the surface, lo, they are not aquatic insects at all. They drown, like people who cannot swim and have fallen through the ice. Other insects there are in earliest spring that cling just under the surface, like balloons bumping the ceiling.

But this is merely the way in which a few living creatures may be said to have fun with the surface tension of water. This strangest of water's properties penetrates to the very structure of life itself. It goes straight to the colloidal nature of protoplasm, for nothing conceivable will present as much surface as a colloid or permanent suspension of particles in a liquid medium, and to that surface will adhere by surface tension the chemicals brought to the cell. Thus is explained the capacity of living matter to take up dyes; the chemistry of pigmentation hangs upon surface tension.

So water not only dissolves the rocks and by sheer plowing carries the soil down to make the valleys fertile; it is the basis of the beauty of the butterfly's wing, the colors in the crocus petal.

FEBRUARY TWENTY-FIFTH

THERE is visible now a fresh flush of color in the willow and osier twigs, reds and greens and yellows, depending on the species; the sassafras is limber again; the spice bush has a quick look cheering to see.

This work of the sap began long before this mild, pale day with the song-sparrows taking heart and the loam breathing sweetly. It began in the dead of winter, in the darkness of the roots far under ground. The sugar maples of the north are tapped in February or March, while the snow still lingers, for it is then that the sap upsurges in a mighty rush. This is due to root pressure, and often in ice-bound weather I have seen where the gush of sap in a cherry was so sudden and fierce that it burst the tree's internal plumbing and poured out like golden blood from a wound, to freeze there, a sort of modern and momentary amber.

Sap may have to mount to the top of a tree fifty feet in height, every inch of the way dead against gravity. And here, no doubt, the great force of capillarity steps in, the upward seep, inch by inch, through the hair-fine tubes of the living wood. It must pass from one cell to another, through the double walls of thick cellulose, and how this may be is still half a mystery. Osmosis is at work here, a sort of suction across the cell membranes, each cell a little pumping house. And once the leaves are out upon the tree one may add to reasons for the sap's rising the siphoning effect of loss of water from the leaf surface, that provides a continual drag or traction on the great water reservoir of the roots.

But that is weeks away; as I look back across the grim weeks for spring's beginning, I find nothing earlier than the great upsurging of the plants' life blood.

FEBRUARY TWENTY-SIXTH

S H O R T weeks ago I was listening to the icy tinkle of the tree sparrows' winter conversation; now already they sing their spring mating songs, and no longer in droves; each little gray swain withdraws to a bush twig of his own and twirls his song alone, in the sunlight. God knows it is sweet to hear them, and the chuckling of the wrens; it gives the sense of some great forgiveness at the heart of Nature.

In the bitterness of the winter that is gone, I remember how I hate death, hate it for all things' sake, and how each year of my life from childhood I have attained to spring like the spent survivor of a wreck, glad enough to be washed up on the hard shingle of March, to hear the land birds sing.

FEBRUARY TWENTY-SEVENTH

A MAN can scarcely point to anything like irrefutable evidence for the beginnings of spring. He knows that the sun arises a little earlier, and that the floods are going down. That the noons are mild, and that in the last pockets, under the hemlocks in the steep shaded glens, the snow lingers, or a paper of ice on the trout pools. There is an air of certain success to be detected in each day, as the warm yellow mists rise up and become soft patches of sunlit cloud in the sky; this geniality may last but an hour or two and give way, in the afternoon, to pale gray-blue skies and air with a keen edge to it.

Pussy willows are "out" in the popularly accepted meaning; that is, the black scales have fallen from them and the dense soft silk peeps through. But pussy willows are not yet flowers, but only buds; the flowers are a full three weeks from blooming. Yet buds are beautiful in themselves, and on the old wood of last season all the precocious trees and shrubs are swelling now in that profile that Botticelli took to be spring's own, the prescient and plethoric curve—not a mathematical perfection, but stamped with life's subtle oval that both bud and embryo employ.

FEBRUARY TWENTY-EIGHTH

ON THIS day in 1683 was born at La Rochelle, Réné de Réaumur, known in his day as the rival in natural history of Buffon. That age, primarily interested in personalities, remarked with amusement the differences between the two men—the one resplendent, courtly, prolific, admirably publicized, an adept at intrigue, the other modest, retired, preoccupied with such trivia as bees and ants. The times of Louis XV had other notions of worth than ours. It seemed plain then that Buffon was infinitely the bigger man, and his party, under the wing of the Pompadour, actually prevented the publication of Réaumur's great work on ants. Forgotten, unknown to the Hubers, it was only brought to light in 1926 by Wheeler of Harvard.

Swammerdam had gone before Réaumur as a careful student of insect anatomy. But Réaumur it was who first investigated insect society and behavior in the spirit of truthful science. Many a man scrupulously honest with small change could not—cannot today—observe an ant heap without reporting a fine pack of fairy tales. Réaumur, descending one day from his berlin for a stroll along the levee near Tours, first observed and truly reported the marriage flight of the ants; it was the first, in fact, that any one had ever known of the castes of ants, or understood that their winged royalty are the only sexual forms. His brilliant observations on bees and aphids and many other insects led, at every turn, to discoveries equally important. But the age was impressed only by folio editions and sheer bulk, and preferred a book which a courtier might pick up in the certainty that no heavy demands should be made upon his intellect.

376

MARCH FIRST

N o w is that sweet unwritten moment when all things are possible, are just begun. The little tree has not quite leafed. The mate is not yet chosen. To the rambler in the woods all that he can find in heavy books will be of less worth than what he learns by sitting on a log and listening to the first quiver of sound from the marshes, or by prodding with a stick at the soil and turning out the sluggish beetles. It is good enough just to sit still and hold your palm out to the sunlight, like a leaf, and turn it over slowly, wondering: What is light? What is flesh? What is it to be alive?

MARCH SECOND

HERE at the bottom of our sea of air a few creatures of frail flight are just emerged upon the spring. Like somber thoughts left over from the night, like lingering bits of winged sleep, the dark mourning cloaks flutter languidly in the sunlight, or cling on the twigs of the pussy willow, resembling last year's leaves. The midges swirl upon the air, not in the wild autumnal dance of their kind, but dreamily and without apparent purpose over the wood-brown pools of rain among the old leaves; they climb invisible spiral ladders tentatively toward the sun.

In the sky is a lightening, a heightening, after the close gray cap of winter. I notice the vulture there again, now that the winter hawks have gone; it reminds us of summer indolence and makes the day seem warmer than it is. Several airplanes too are out, and I take this for a sign of spring as valid as the first flight of the kildeer over the soppy, fire-browned river meadows. A youngster is stunting, perilously low, and another in his ebullience writes his name in smoke upon the heavens, and I shall be astonished if this is not part of a vernal male strut before a watching woman. I hear the drone of the planes released or suddenly cut off, and from the great hive across the river one after another takes the air in a proud conscious beauty.

MARCH THIRD

T H E waters still are all but lifeless, and as is the way in spring, colder than the air. The air is chill enough; my hands, I know, are grateful for the gloves they wear. It is the earth, so quick to turn a cold and deathly clod in autumn, that in the spring is swiftest to warm up. In my dark winter clothes, when I walk under the leafless boughs of the hardwood groves in the hills, my body feels the sunlight's warmth almost oppressively; it wants to lie down in a leaf-filled gully and vegetate a while. Like the dark cloth, the black wood loam is absorbing from the early sunlight every ray. It is quite naturally the habitat of all the first spring wildflowers, those little geophilous plants—earth-huggers, lovers, as I am, of the soil.

I strip the gloves off from my hands, and see them emerge blanched and smelling a little of soap. Quickly I plunge them down into this mother-stuff called earth. I lift the loam in my palm to smell it, toss it happily in my hand, fritter it away in my fingers just to feel again that marvelous intimate mixture of soil particles with centuries of leaf and flower decay.

There is not a flower yet, to be sure; only small shoots and basal rosettes are pushing up—delicate fronds of Dutchman's breeches, curling fingers of cinquefoil runners and the pale mottled spears of adder's tongue. But when I dig deeper just to feel the cool watery fleshy-pink rootstocks of the wild ginger, I discover the buds below the ground, swelling precociously and ready for the resurrection.

MARCH FOURTH

T H E Y should have been listening for the rustle of a fox's footsteps or watching for the shadow of a hawk, those two. Yet I was walking through the woods in a careless **way**; they must have seen me before I saw them, through the leafless thickets that held no privacy.

At such a moment all animals look somehow pathetic to me, yes, even these two squirrels. They are so rash to trust to life, and there is indeed no other moment in their existences, save in sleep, when they forget death so completely and even in the presence of a foe will remain motionless, unwilling to quit their deep preoccupation, showing neither fight nor flight, but only patience with their spy, a polite attendance upon the better side of his nature.

I turned and walked back as I had come. There is a sweet high whistling of the south wind around my ears. It is not that the wind is yet warm, but only that it blows at last from the right quarter, and presses upon the world with gentle persuasive force. All things this day mean spring— the whitening of the tops of the poplar groves seen over the roll and dip of the naked meadows, the noon flight of the morning's rime, the play of small mammals and the spent arrival of the first redwings, fluttering down with their sharp call notes upon the empty marshes.

MARCH FIFTH

I LIKE the skunk cabbage emerging now in the woods, for other reasons than those that endear to me innocent pretties like hepaticas and trout lilies. It has the fascination of a particularly crafty and devious old man, wrapped in a cape, and puttering about down in the leafless copses for some dubious purpose. It is an unlikely customer to see in these parts, since aroids are a race chiefly of the tropics. With its lingering smell it defies you to touch it, and so, ingeniously protected from our vernal lust for wildflower gathering, this curious old vegetable lives on from year to year, outwitting us all, increasing, as it goes its subterranean way.

N o w are all animals come to the season of the great hunger, beside which winter, with its still remaining store of nuts and berries, is a *mardi gras*. Thin and bewildered, waking from their long sleep, the hibernating mammals emerge from their burrows, their caves and their old hollow stumps. The first small gold bee shoots questingly through a still flowerless air. The shelves are bare for frogs and salamanders, bats and all the pathetic and ungainly creatures that could suffer and die for all men cared.

But it is one of the great compensations of the higher life—biologically speaking—that a creature who cannot find the fare he prefers will not in consequence of that lie down and starve, like an insect or a parasite. It will, under such harsh conditions, adapt itself with a high philosophy to realities and take things as they come. I had a cat once that would have preferred to eat nothing but caviar, but if I had turned him loose he would in an extremity have eaten slugs and caterpillars.

So now the blackbirds, that will fatten on wild rice in September, whistle grace for the first grouse locusts just emerging, the dragon fly larvæ and the back-swimmers. Rabbits, lacking carrots and parsley, nibble at the base of the little saplings, girdling and killing them, and every day a squirrel outside my window comes and runs up and down each branch, biting the leaf buds off, to the tree's great prejudice.

MARCH SEVENTH

O N   T H I S day in 1747 at Versailles was born André
Michaux, a man incomparably superior in body, brain and
soul to the fat monarch who ruled there that day, a man
who came to the American wilderness with a song on his
lips, who robbed it of nothing but the seeds of azalea and
rhododendron, tulip tree and locust, and in exchange gave
to the southern states he loved the chinaberry, the Albizzia
with pink flowers that in the Carolinas they call mimosa, the
tallow tree, and the camellia and the tea plant. He swayed
no destinies, I know; he was not a great figure in botany;
in biology he has not even a place. But I love him for the
gentleman explorer that he was, the chevalier under the
live-oaks and the Spanish moss, the plantsman who would
lift a plant from the ground as if it had been a child. No
mere collector of specimens, he loved the living plant; he
sought the useful or the beautiful, and dreamed only how
he could make it cosmopolitan.

Almost unknown today, Michaux was a great figure of
the old frontier, a Crockett without a rifle. Jefferson and
Clark listened to his plans for a great exploration in the
Louisiana territory; Washington records in his diary that
a Monsieur Michaux dined one night at Mount Vernon, presented him with some very fine cherry stocks, and departed
again to Philadelphia. John Bartram, farmer, madman,
Quaker, botanist to the king, collected with him on the
Blue Ridge, and greatly the two antipodal men amused
each other.

MARCH EIGHTH

IT IS fifteen years ago now that I set off with another boy in the first rapture of an Appalachian spring, to look for the flower called Shortia, the flower that Michaux discovered in some high glen of the Blue Ridge, and that was lost again for a century. One winter dusk it was, in 1788, when Michaux with his silent Indian guides was hastening back to a camp upon a nameless roaring mountain river, that he stopped a moment to pluck a single plant, a little leaf like galax, bearing still a fruit pod. He took it up, and left it in his herbarium in Paris, unidentified. But he never returned to study it, for he was destined to die far from his beloved Blue Ridge, under the killing suns of Madagascar.

And there in France, decades later, it was found by Asa Gray—a plant that no one could name, an American flower that no American had ever seen. The specimen tormented Gray; the hope of finding the plant green and growing went always with him thereafter, on expeditions through the Blue Ridge, to Mt. Mitchell, Grandfather, Roan, the Great Smokies—everywhere his friends and students sought it too. In an old book of Japanese flower prints Gray discovered its counterpart, and understood then that it belonged to one of those strange genera exclusive to the mountains of Japan and to our southern Appalachians. Still it remained elusive, until one evening just ninety-nine years after Michaux had stopped in the dusk to cull it, Charles Sargent (the grand old man of trees) chanced upon it in a dark ravine below Highlands, North Carolina.

There too I found it, in the wild, sad glen dominated by the roar of an angry river, its white foamy bells tumbling down the bank under the perpetual gloom of the laurel's shade.

MARCH NINTH

THERE is no explaining, to those who cannot feel it, the call, the fascination, the feeling in the bones like a tropism, to go plant hunting in the renewing year. I can never forget the bubbling excitement of my first botanical trip, when I too set out to look for Shortia—rediscovered now innumerable times, but what of that? Is it any less exciting when you first see land after a stormy ocean voyage, because a thousand others too have seen Finisterre rising out of the blue, a trembling mirage, a hope, a deception, a fact, a continent! Linnæus on his way to Lapland was not happier than the youngster starting off across the mountains, lost to railroads, inns, beds, houses, and even, at times, to food, to look not only for Shortia but for all the Blue Ridge held that spring of trillium, deliciously fragrant, of long-spurred violet, mountain saxifrage and gentian-colored bluets.

I feel the calling still in bones grown older, and not less poignantly because I have no longer the time nor liberty nor quite the light-heartedness to yield to it, and on this blue and green day step off the edge of the known and vanish into some wilderness without telling where I go. But alas, there is no wilderness left for me. It is not that fifteen years ago the Blue Ridge was truly any wilder, but only that the world was younger, and I expected more of its rewards.

MARCH TENTH

ON THIS day did the cardinal open the morning with a great cry down in the valley below my house, "Three Cheers! Three Cheers!" The wrens are chuckling about private business of their own. Even the starlings have put on a black sheen of the courting plumage, and in the broken voices of street boys call out on the flesh and the devil, with their spring song of "Sweet Beelzebub!"

The elms are backward, and the crocuses look bullied by the wind; the oaks are still asleep. It is the hour, though, when creatures have the same aching restlessness that we call spring fever. Grackles spatter through the woods. I caught a sway-backed old white horse in the act of taking two gamboling steps in the pasture. There is a fine tumult from distant poultry that means that the hens' Grand Turk has lifted the curtain of their apartment. The salamanders have crept out to mate, in that detached, cool-blooded way of theirs, and by tomorrow their eggs may be in the pools.

MARCH ELEVENTH

I HAVE said that much of life and perhaps the best of it is not quite "nice." The business of early spring is not; it takes place in nakedness and candor, under high empty skies. Almost all the first buds to break their bonds send forth not leaves but frank catkins, or in the maple sheer pistil and stamen, devoid of the frilled trimmings of petals. The cedar sows the wind with its pollen now, because it is a relict of an age before bees, and it blooms in a month essentially barren of winged pollinators. The wood frogs, warmed like the spring flowers by the swift-heating earth, return to the primordial element of water for their spawning, and up from the oozy bottoms rise the pond frogs, to make of the half-world of the marges one breeding ground.

It is a fact that the philosopher afoot must not forget, that the astonishing embrace of the frog-kind, all in the eery green chill of earliest March, may be the attitude into which the tender passion throws these batrachians, but it is a world away from warm-blooded mating. It is a phlegmatic and persisting clasping, nothing more. It appears to be merely a reminder to the female that death brings up the rear of life's procession. When after patient hours he quits her, the female goes to the water to pour out her still unfertilized eggs. Only then are they baptized with the fecundating complement of the mate.

It is a startling bit of intelligence for the moralists, but the fact seems to be that sex is a force not necessarily concerned with reproduction; back in the primitive one-celled animals there are individuals that fuse without reproducing in consequence; the reproduction in those lowly states is but a simple fission of the cell, a self-division. It seems then that reproduction has, as it were, fastened itself on quite another force in the world; it has stolen a ride upon sex, which is a principle in its own right.

MARCH TWELFTH

TODAY winter has returned in a tantrum. The ponds, turned bitter gray, look as if ice would gather on them again, and in the high leafless hardwood groves the wind flings about and stamps on the trembling shoots of wild-flowers; it takes the wood in a fury, setting up a great roaring upon a single tone, high overhead, as if it had found the keynote of the trees and were vibrating them to the root. So, house-bound and angry for it, I add a few words less pleasing, perhaps, to the moralists than what has gone before.

A long survey of the ascent of sex has shown all who ever made it that the purpose of this awe-inspiring impulsion is nothing more, nor less, than the enrichment of life. Reproduction purely considered gets on a great deal better without anything so chancy as mating. What sex contributes to it is the precious gift of variation, as a result of commingling. And as variety is the spice of life, it has come to be—thanks to the invitation of sex which creatures accept with such eagerness—one of life's chief characteristics. Thus sex is what the lover has always wished to believe, a worthy end in itself. It is to be revered for its own sake, and the very batrachians know it.

IT IS a complaint of the poets that men of science concern themselves not at all with beauty. But the scientists mind their own business, and they know that all men mean something different by beauty. Rodin preferred men with broken noses, old hags of the street; Romney liked handsome highborn children. To speak broadly, the variety of life is its beauty; you may choose out of that as you will.

In the age of piety, it was supposed that the purpose of living beauty was to be useful. No less a man than Darwin proposed the idea of sexual selection. The breast of a grosbeak was colored to win a mate, the catbird sang in competition with his fellows to win the little female away from them, and thus the whole duty of birds—to be fruitful and multiply—was advanced. You may pretend so if you like, but it is not demonstrable. It is even to be doubted that the color of the flowers serves any such righteous purpose as attracting the bee; many flower-haunting insects seem blind to color. The beauty of a butterfly's wing, the beauty of all things, is not a slave to purpose, a drudge sold to futurity. It is excrescence, superabundance, random ebullience, and sheer delightful waste to be enjoyed in its own high right.

MARCH FOURTEENTH

I SET forth on this high-promising day for the hills, but the slope of the land drew me downward; the brook, running toward the river, led me on, and I walked as a man who knows that the day has something in store for him, something it would disclose. Before very long I was at the lowest level in this neighborhood, on the springy turf, full of green spears of coarse grass, of the river meadows. The sunlight hung in the misty willows. *Pee-yeep...pee-yeep* came the sweet metallic clink of the spring peepers, but when I tried to stalk them, ever so quietly, I was forestalled, surrounded by silence, a man alone on the wild useless bottom land, under the remote candor of the skies that arched the marsh and me. *Pee-yeep*—like the horizon, the sweet melancholy sound receded or closed up behind me.

Among a penciling of last year's reeds, upon the very marge, I stood and saw the frog's eggs in the water. Laid only today, perhaps, the dark velvety globules in their sphere of silver jelly shine softly up at me, reminding me that a year ago I was seeing them in this same pond, and proposing to have their secret. Well, the Ides of March are here, they say. Can I recite the ritual of their ancient freemasonry?

MARCH FIFTEENTH

I LIFT from the chill and cloudy waters of the woodland marsh a bit of frog's egg jelly, and the very feel of it on my fingers is dubious and suggestive. I accept without even cortical repulsion the sensation of their mucous envelope, for I have grown used by now to the gelatinous feel that conveys the very nature of protoplasm. This plasmic feel, traveling up from my nerve ends, asks questions now of my brain.

Suppose that these eggs are so fresh-laid that they are still unfecundated; are they yet come to life? At what instant does individual life begin? Usually, we deem, from the moment that sperm meets egg. Before that happens are the ova half alive? Or do they not simply represent pure potentiality, such as Aristotle meant when he called the rock in the quarry, awaiting the sculptor's chisel, potentiality?

It is just here that the mechanistic biologists have sought to drive in their wedge. They removed the frog's eggs before they were fecundated, and essayed to stimulate them "into life" without benefit of fatherhood. And they discovered that chemicals, or even a mere pinprick in the nucleus, would start the unfertilized egg cell to dividing and developing. In a few brief weeks the half-orphan tadpoles were grown to clamorous, croaking frogs!

MARCH SIXTEENTH

A L M O S T it seems as if the great mechanist, Jacques Loeb, and the clever laboratory man, Bataillon, had found the break in the charmed circle of life.

But the vitalists are ready, with the well taken reply that because a chemical or a mechanical irritation will stimulate the unfertilized frog eggs to develop parthenogenetically—that is, by immaculate conception—it does not follow that conception is but a physico-chemical process as Loeb has boldly stated. For in their preoccupations with acids and needle pricks, the mechanists have forgotten to examine the most remarkable feature of all—the nature of the egg itself. All that the needle and the reagent did was to release the forces of cleavage, development and metabolism that were already stored within the egg. The closed, charmed circle of life remains intact, was never broken.

Behold Driesch grinding the eggs of Loeb's favorite sea urchin up between plates of glass, pounding and breaking and deforming them in every way. And when he ceased from thus abusing them, they proceeded with their orderly and normal development. Is any machine conceivable, Driesch asks, which could thus be torn down into parts and have each part continue to act like a whole machine? Could any machine have its parts all disarranged and transposed, and still have them act normally? One cannot imagine it. But of the living egg, fertilized or not, we can say that there lie latent within it all the potentialities presumed by Aristotle, and all of the sculptor's dream of form, yes, and the very power in the sculptor's arm.

MARCH SEVENTEENTH

So AT the end of it all we come to a truce between the old wrestlings of a mechanistic with a vitalistic view of life. We grant, and gladly, with a sense of kinship to the great elements and forces, that life is built of the same star-stuff as the rest of the universe. It obeys physical and chemical laws. But I am of those who believe that it is a law in itself.

A thing is either alive or it isn't; there is nothing that is almost alive. There is but the remotest possibility of the origin of life by spontaneous generation, and every likelihood that Arrhenius is right when he dares to claim that life is a cosmic phenomenon, something that drifts between the spheres, like light, and like light transiently descends upon those fit to receive it. Life is a phenomenon, *sui generis,* a primal fact in its own right, like energy. Cut flesh or wood how you like, hack at them in a baffled fury —you cannot find life itself, you can only see what it built out of the lifeless dust. Can you see energy in a cresting wave, a shaft of spring sunlight? No, energy is but a name for something absolutely primal which we cannot analyze or comprehend but only measure in science and depict in art. Life, too, is an ineffable, like thought. It is the glory on the earth.

MARCH EIGHTEENTH

Now all life renews, in its hopes and in its threats, in its strict needs and in all that superabundance that we call by the name of beauty. In the same place where last I found them, the pale watery shoots of Equisetum rise; buds of flowers open, all crumpled like babies' hands; the phœbes have returned to the nests at the mouth of the cave, where before they bred and where poignant accidents befell them. With a touching hopefulness all things renew themselves, not undismayed, perhaps, by the terror and chanciness of fate, but because, God help them, they can do no other.

For life is a green cataract; it is an inundation, a march against the slings of death that counts no costs. Still it advances, waving its inquisitive antennæ, flaunting green banners. Life is adventure in experience, and when you are no longer greedy for the last drop of it, it means no more than that you have set your face, whether you know it or not, to the day when you shall depart without a backward look. Those who look backward longingly to the end die young, at whatever age.

MARCH NINETEENTH

I GO TO the cellar for the last logs in my woodpile, and disclose a family of mice who have trustingly taken up residence there. Their tiny young, all ears and belly, mere little sacks of milk in a furless skin, lie there blind and helpless, five little tangible, irrepressible evidences of some moment, not so many nights ago, when in between the walls of my house there took place an act to which I am not so egotistic as to deny the name of love.

But it is not this which moves me, but the look in the mother's eyes as she stares up at me, her tail to the wall, all power of decision fled from her. There I read, in her agonized glance, how precious is life even to her. She entreats me not to take it from her. She does not know of pity in the world, so has no hope of it. But life—no matter how one suffers in it, hungers, flees, and fights—life is her religion.

How can we ever hope, then, to commensurate this thing which we too share, when it is its own cause, its own reason for being, when, as soon as we are challenged to stand and deliver it, we tremble and beg, like the trapped mouse?

MARCH TWENTIETH

To the terror that faces mice and men, a man at least can find an answer. This will be his religion.

Now how may a man base all his faith on Nature when in Nature there is no certain end awaiting the ambition of his race? When all is flux and fleet, the great flood tides of spring that are like to drown him, and the final neap tide of decease? How take comfort from the brave new greening of the grass, when grass must wither, or in the first eery whistle of the meadow larks, saying that life is "sweet-to-you, so sweet to you"? For life is not sweet to all men. It brings some blind into this world and of others requires blood and tears. The sun toward which man turns his face is a brief candle in the universe. His woman and his children are mortal as the flowers.

But it is not life's generosity, so capricious, that makes one man happy. It is rather the extent of his gratitude to life.

I say that it touches a man that his tears are only salt, and that the tides of youth rise, and, having fallen, rise again. Now he has lived to see another spring and to walk again beneath the faintly greening trees. So, having an ear for the uprising of sap, for the running of blood, having an eye for all things done most hiddenly, and a hand in the making of those small dear lives that are not built with hands, he lives at peace with great events.

AFTERWORD

M A L E songbirds are able to sing because they possess, in the left side of their brains, a solid cluster of nerve cells for mediating and regulating this function. Females, songless, do not have such centers; we must assume that they have other specialized receptor cells for listening to the song, but we don't know where these are. It is an interesting observation, frequently cited these days in the vast literature of neurobiology as the first piece of evidence for lateralization of brain function in animals other than ourselves, analogous to the localization of speech centers in the left hemisphere of right-handed humans.

The calls of songbirds have been analyzed by acoustic physiologists for their information content; an immense literature has evolved just in the last decade or so, reducing birdsong to its essential, species-specific content of signals.

A female firefly attracts, from distant trees in the dead of night, males of her own species for the purpose of mating. She does this by emitting sets of flashes in code—repetitions of two tightly coupled flares, for example. Not long ago it was reported in *Nature* that the females of one species regularly switched signals after successful mating, attracting thus a flurry of males of another species, which they then ate.

Bees are able to navigate with accuracy the route between the hive and sugar sources because of lenses for sensing polarized light from the sun. Pigeons find their way home on cloudy days by the use of tiny magnets just beneath their skulls. Certain strains of marine bacteria are also equipped with magnetite, enabling them to orient themselves in deep waters containing nutrient.

The Skylab satellite lost its predicted altitude and fell to earth because of sunspots; the planet's atmosphere expanded just enough to lightly brush against the vehicle, trapping it with friction.

News items like these turn up in almost every week's cascade of scientific journals, and there is no doubt that something like a revolution in science has been going on for five decades or more, with the speed of entry of new bits of information increasing each year. It is not only known that DNA is the essential stuff of reproduction; this material can be handled in the laboratory as easily as tape, spliced, edited, inserted into other strips of DNA and so forth. Bacteria can be induced to make insulin; fused cells can be invented to produce absolutely pure antibodies. Science moves, it seems, from strength to strength.

You'd think that fifty years of such progress would have provided all of us with so rich a library of reductionist detail that a book like Donald Culross Peattie's AN ALMANAC FOR MODERNS would have long since gone out of date, retaining only quaintness in the charm of its prose. Surely, by this time, the larger questions raised by Peattie either have been settled once and for all, or have lost their relevance.

It is not so. Peattie deals with the great puzzles in nature, and we are nowhere near solving them. If there is a difference between his time of writing and today, it is that there are more things to wonder about, and more reasons to be astonished by the world we live in. To be sure, it is useful and satisfying, even stimulating, to know that birdsong can be generated like grammar out of clusters of neurones on one side of a songbird's brain, or that creatures carry bits of iron in their tissues for sensing the earth's magnetic field. Items like these increase our respect for the ingenuity and perfection of nature, but they take away none of the puzzlement about the whole arrangement.

Nor do they help us to explain away the greatest of all the mysteries, the response in our own brains to the world at hand. We have receptors for wonderment and awe, perhaps situated in specialized clusters of nerve cells somewhere, maybe in our right hemispheres, but even if we knew where the clusters were and how they work in receiving the information and firing it off to other parts of the cortex for awareness, we would be no further along than Peattie fifty years ago.

Peattie plays his hunches with what information he finds at hand. On April seventh, writing of man's ultimate fate, he says, "He will do well to have a heed of the nature of life, for of life there is but one kind." On May twentieth, he writes, "The first night life of the year has begun for my brother animals," and then he writes of fireflies, night moths, and night hawks. On another day he notes the symbiotic connection between bacteria, fungi, and the roots of plants. He writes from a central, obsessive hunch: that there is a connectedness among all living things, that the human brain's sensing of wholeness and harmony in nature has its origin in this sense of connectedness.

He would have been enchanted by the new science of molecular biology, with its power to explain, in small part, the delicate genetic mechanisms which determine the property of cells to differentiate into special cell types, and to become the specialized tissues of this kind of creature or that. But the news that would have given him the greatest pleasure, I am sure, would have been the new story about mitochondria, tiny organelles inside all animal and plant cells which provide all the oxidative energy for the functions of the cells, and the similar story about chloroplasts, the green photosynthetic organelles inside plant cells which tap the sun for its energy flow. It now appears that these are essentially foreign beings, symbionts, the linear descendants of bacteria which incorporated themselves inside all nucleated cells long ago and have remained there ever since, replicating on their own, carrying their own private molecules of DNA, foreign settlers. Between them, looked at from the right distance, these microbial creatures can be viewed as the dominant, central forms of life on our planet, snatching energy from the sun, creating oxygen for the atmosphere and carbohydrates for food and then using the oxygen to burn the food for the power and continuance of life. The tadpoles in Peattie's pond, the grasses along his path, the warbler in his tree, the tree itself, and Peattie himself are, if not blood-relatives, protoplasm-relatives, close family connections, because of sharing the same lodgers in their cells, or, better, being shared by them. He would have delighted in the knowledge of this common presence, just as he was enraptured by the luminous bacteria that live as symbionts, lighting the way for their hosts.

Someone sent me for a Christmas card years ago a fold of x-ray film with the skeletal structure of a whorled seashell on one fold and a quotation from Donald Culross Peattie on the other: "I say that it touches a man that his blood is sea-water and his tears are salt, that the seed of his loins is scarcely different from the same cells in a seaweed, and that of stuff like his bones are coral made." This is part of his note for April first, telling you openly the feeling that will come, in and between the lines, throughout the book's year. It is a level of emotion now out of date, out of fashion anyway, along with that peculiar lot of meditative, insatiably curious observers who used to be known as naturalists. We have them no more, or recognize them as authoritative people no more. The people who study nature now, and report on it first-hand, are necessarily specialized in such narrow zones of inquiry that there is no room to step back for a larger view. The only biologists entitled to look at whole sections of nature are the ecologists, but even in this group the liveliest questions today concern the ways of mathematically predicting the course of events in various niches. The need to quantify, by exact measuring devices, all matters in life is fundamental to biological science and there will be no changing this, nor should there be; science needs precision for answering any of its questions, and reproducibility in the measurements.

The question about human feeling is another matter, not yet set aside for any scientific speciality, perhaps never to be approached by any version of scientific method. The quickly indrawn breath at the sight of the earliest spring flower is not a problem, nor is the poet's account of that moment. What *would* be a problem, beyond solving, is the failure of that indrawn breath in a generation of humans removed from any direct involvement in nature. There is, I think, some danger of this lack of response in the years ahead, science or no science, and I wish Peattie were here again, writing as he wrote fifty years ago, to remind us who we are and where we live.

— LEWIS THOMAS, M.D.